Here's What *Others* Are Saying about This Book!

"Just as he has faithfully done so many times as my friend and teacher, Scotty speaks with transparent honesty and contagious passion as he explores the profound depths and demands of the grace of God. May this book take all who reads this 'further up and further in' to God's great heart of love for them."

Steven Curtis Chapman—Author; Songwriter; Recording Artist

"Scotty's take in his chapter on stewardship and ownership is not only biblically sound, but ingenious. Helping the reader see stewardship as a love affair culminating in marriage without a prenuptial agreement is a real insight. Fabulous reading!"

Dave Ramsey—*New York Times* Best-Selling Author, *Financial Peace* and *More Than Enough*

"An examined life always reveals a need for grace. Pastor Scotty Smith has written about the kind of grace that transforms, frees, and provokes us to dig deeper into our lives with the truth of the gospel as both scalpel and stitch."

Dan Haseltine—Songwriter; Lead Singer, Jars of Clay

"Scotty Smith walks where angels fear to tread. Most mere mortals hunker down on God's love or rant about the demands of obedience.

Scotty submits his heart to both good news and a compelling call; and in a way I've never read, sings of obedience with a heart of ravished gratitude."

DR. DAN ALLENDER—President, Mars Hill Graduate School

"*The Reign of Grace* is a perfect meal for the hungry heart. If Scotty's first solo book, *Objects of His Affection,* was the appetizer, then this new book is the feast. Give thanks and fill yourself with words that satisfy."

CHARLIE PEACOCK—Record Producer; Author, *The aWAKE Project: Uniting Against the African AIDS Crisis*

"Scotty has reached my heart and captured my believing imagination in this book as he has done so effectively in his sermons for fifteen years. *The Reign of Grace* has the lyrical ring of a Spurgeon with the weight of an Edwards, the accessibility of a Lewis, and it is all adorned in the sound theology of a Henry Van Til. This one will go in my read-every-year bookshelf."

WES KING—Songwriter; Recording Artist

"I've heard the word *grace* used over and over, yet sometimes the word seems a little ambiguous. *The Reign of Grace* has helped me see what grace really looks like and has caused me to examine my heart to see how willing I am to let God's grace change me."

DENISE JONES—Recording Artist, Point of Grace

"I have been distressed many times by the charge that 'Sonship' teaching is antinomian and encourages an uncommitted Christian life, that the constant focus on God's love in Christ for us his orphans gives believers a license to sin. It is my prayer that such critics will be silenced by this book, for Scotty shows with passion and clarity that security in

Christ's love is the source of obedience, discipleship, service, and self-sacrifice. Read it! Give it! Read it again!"

JERRAM BARRS—Director of the Francis Schaeffer Institute at Covenant Theological Seminary; Author; Professor, Covenant Theological Seminary

"With rare and splendid pastoral vulnerability, Scotty Smith explores the intimate recesses of his heart to discover the power and peace that motivate all hearts where God's true grace reigns."

DR. BRYAN CHAPELL—President, Covenant Theological Seminary

"This book may make you uncomfortable. It confronts us with our idolatries and reminds us of the lavish reign of God's grace. Scotty is honest in uncovering his personal idols, as he shares God's reign of grace in him."

ROSE MARIE MILLER—World Harvest Mission; Missionary; Bible Teacher; Author, *From Fear to Freedom*

"Scotty holds nothing back as he demonstrates, even through his own story, how God loves us as a 'frumpy' Bride. As a member of Scotty's congregation and having seen his vision and passion for the Church, I'm encouraged by his vulnerability and boldness in this important word to our culture."

DEREK WEBB—Singer; Songwriter

"What difference do the Reformation doctrines of grace make—in our lives, in our families, and in our churches? According to Scotty Smith, they should make all the difference in the world. In *The Reign of Grace,* he gives us a glimpse of that extraordinary difference, and he leaves us all the richer for it."

GEORGE GRANT—King's Meadow Study Center

"Brace yourself. Reading *The Reign of Grace* is a wild, gritty unfolding of the human heart laid bare under God's sacred gaze. Scotty's searingly honest search for the implications of grace invites us to enter the land of God's romance. Scotty moves us 'further up and further in' to a discovery of grace as a life-changing, soul-stirring, passionate treasure."

BONNIE KEEN—Singer; Songwriter; Author, *God Loves Messy People*

"Scotty can't help but gush about God's grace to us. It's deep in his heart, and it's everywhere in this book. But he adds a critical question: *Now* what? God's grace changes us. It mobilizes us. Be prepared to love others more deeply."

DR. ED WELCH—Author; Counselor; Theological Instructor, Westminster Seminary and C.C.E.F. (Christian Counseling and Education Foundation)

"In this book, Scotty Smith encourages us to make 'unhurried eye contact' with our loving Father and to move beyond mere visitation to real participation in His glorious reign of grace. With uncommon honesty and vulnerability, Scotty shows us the Lord's hand in the intricate tapestry of his own life story."

CHRISTINE DENTE—*Out of the Grey*, Rocketown Records

The Reign of GRACE

Scotty Smith

The Reign of GRACE

The Delights and Demands of God's Love

HOWARD PUBLISHING CO.

Our purpose at Howard Publishing is to:

- *Increase faith* in the hearts of growing Christians
- *Inspire holiness* in the lives of believers
- *Instill hope* in the hearts of struggling people everywhere

Because He's coming again!

Published by Howard Publishing Co., Inc.
3117 North 7th Street, West Monroe, Louisiana 71291-2227

03 04 05 06 07 08 09 10 11 12   10 9 8 7 6 5 4 3 2 1

Edited by Philis Boultinghouse
Interior design by John Luke
Cover design by Kirk DouPonce, UDG|DesignWorks

Library of Congress Cataloging-in-Publication Data

Smith, Scotty, 1950-
The reign of grace : the delights and demands of God's love / Scotty Smith
p. cm.
Includes bibliographical references (p.).
ISBN: 1-58229-286-8
1. Christian life—Meditations. I. Title.

BV4501.3.S656 2003
248.4—dc21

2003041654

Italics in scripture were added by the author for emphasis.

Dedication

Grant Evan Cunningham

June 12, 1965–July 7, 2002

It is with great sadness but with even greater joy that I dedicate *The Reign of Grace* to the memory of a friend, fellow elder, and passionate lover of the Lord Jesus, Grant Cunningham. My sadness is born from the grief that necessitated my preaching his funeral—a funeral I never imagined I would preach. A likelier outcome would have been for him to lead worship at mine. Indeed, "God's ways are not our ways"—but just as indeed, "He does all things well."

Grant went to be with Jesus on July 7, 2002, after suffering a head injury incurred while playing his beloved sport of soccer. I was well into writing this book at the time of the accident, but the profound impact of Grant's death on thousands of people convinced me that his story must be written into *The Reign of Grace.* That conviction proved to be right but not in the way I expected.

The seventy-page chronicle I wrote—which details the moments and movements of the Holy Spirit from the hour I got the numbing phone call about Grant's accident to the minute we released helium balloons into the blue skies above the spot where we planted this precious man's body—remains safe in my computer and the hearts of many of us.

But Grant's story, his imprint, his presence *permeates* this book—even as the reign of God's grace permeated everything he did. At his funeral I commented that Grant was the most invisible, visible

Christian I ever knew. He impacted his family, friends, company, culture, and church with the glory and grace of Jesus in ways I have seldom, if ever, seen in any other life—*but we didn't fully realize it until his death*. Thus, Grant was a living affirmation of this great truth: *There is no limit to what God can do through the man or woman who does not care who gets the credit.*

In the chapters ahead you will come upon two titles that I came up with simply from knowing and observing Grant's life: "lead worshiper" and "Jesus' best man." Grant was an amazing singer, songwriter, and elder-participant in the worship ministries of Christ Community Church. He was vice president of Sparrow Records-EMI and had more than 130 songs published. But his heart was so captured by the gospel of God's grace that Grant became much more than a gifted worship leader; he became an infectious lead worshiper in the doxological celebration and lifestyle of the reign of grace.

In the weeks leading up to Grant's death, our church family had been meditating on our calling to live as the cherished Bride of Jesus—a theme that winds its way through this book. Of all the metaphors and images that emerge in the Scriptures, giving meaning and life to the sacred romance, there is one which Grant profoundly epitomized and incarnated—that of John the Baptist. John the Baptist came onto the scene as one who found great delight in decreasing that Jesus would increase. He referred to himself as "the friend" of the groom (John 3:29–30). In Hebrew culture, this is the equivalent of what we call the "best man"—the attendant who finds great joy in serving the interests and pleasure of the groom, thrilled with the privilege of uniting the groom to his bride.

Grant knew no greater joy—in life and in death—than serving as Jesus' best man—fulfilling the purposes of the Day when Jesus will receive his Bride and romance her forever.

Grant gave his wife, Kristin, much more than a taste of this sacred romance. She buried her husband with the testimony of having been a well-loved woman—by her husband and by her Husband. And three special young sons—Will, Evan, and Blake—were given more love, affection, and attention in the brief time they had their dad than many sons experience in a lifetime.

Six months prior to Grant's death, God showed his amazing providence and provision as Grant began to envision a new ministry. Grant had dreamed of finding a way to reach and mentor the hearts of boys and girls growing up without a father figure. He and his wife, Kristin, purchased some land in the country, which they named Blue Skies, as an investment and play place for their three boys. Grant dreamed of using this land to help serve fatherless children. Little did Grant and Kristin realize that this gospel-driven vision would include their own three boys.

The vision lives on and has given rise to the Blue Skies Foundation. Blue Skies exists to come alongside fatherless children, helping them discover their God-given gifts and their heavenly Father's greatest gift—Jesus Christ. Through the arts, sports, and discipleship programs, Blue Skies endeavors to show the love of God in the hope that this love will inspire these children to thrive, to pursue excellence, and to ultimately offer their skills and hearts to the glory of God. Please be encouraged to write to BlueSkiesFoundation@hotmail.com for information on how you can participate in helping Grant's last vision come to fruition.

May God increase Grant Cunningham's tribe!—a true servant in the reign of grace.

CONTENTS

Acknowledgments

Though there are dozens of people to whom I owe a huge debt of love for their contributions to this project, I want to single out only one. It is with the greatest joy and sincerity that I thank you, Darlene—my wife, lover, partner in the gospel, friend, and hero of thirty-one years.

I love you.

Introduction

Sprint's TV commercials rock! The premise is so clever: "Use *our* cell phone service to reduce the static on your line so you don't mishear what a loved one is trying to say. The consequences can be devastating." Several hilarious scenes are created to show what can happen when the wrong message gets heard.

For instance: The setting is a professional football team practice. The camera pans onto the field where the players are standing around trying to figure out why a pop music group from the past is performing in the middle of the practice field. One exasperated coach comments to another, "I said, 'Get a back-up for O'Neil' not, 'Get the Captain and Tennille!'"

Here's another: The setting is a home in middle America. A startled mom is staring at her two very white-faced children. Glaring incredulously at the babysitter, she cries out, "I said, 'Put the kids down in an hour' not, 'Cover the kids with flour!'"

The newest edition: At a huge working ranch in the western United States, the owner stares in unbelief as a herd of small German dogs with very short legs runs wild across his property. Two are pinned to the ground under the weight of a large wooden yoke. He remarks to his Sprint representative, "I ordered two dozen oxen, not two hundred dachshunds!"

OK, one last example: The setting is any city in America. A Christian is working feverishly in his backyard, with piles and piles of lumber stacked neatly beside two of his three barns. God shows up and simply comments, "I said, 'Bow to the reign of my grace!' not, 'Add to the size of your place!'" Sprint is right. The consequences can be devastating when we mishear what a loved one is trying to tell us—especially *this* Loved One.

But let's be honest—there is a big difference between mishearing and hearing only what we want to hear, right? We, the people of God, seem to have chronic "itching ears," and we can usually find somebody to scratch till we say "Aaahh" (2 Tim. 4:3). Given the option, we will usually choose bigger barns to serve ourselves over bigger hearts to serve others (Luke 12:13–21). Isn't it obvious that Jesus has come not just to heal those with hearing loss but also those with listening loss?

Ever since Adam and Eve turned God's vintage wine of grace into the lukewarm waters of selfishness, everything has been upside down. We've lived as though grace is a gentle *rain* of private blessing when in fact it is a transforming *reign* of cosmic righteousness—a rolling river of redeeming love, "a never-failing stream" of infinite mercy (Amos 5:24)—changing the landscape of history and the worship of our hearts.

The Reign of Grace chronicles both the placid and unnerving places this river has been taking me since the completion of *Objects of His Affection.* But more importantly, it is a book extending God's generous invitation to *you*—and perhaps to a few of the people with whom you walk most closely. This is a book to be read individually, but it will be processed and applied most effectively in community. For though the Christian life is personal, it is not to be lived in isolation from your brothers and sisters in Christ.

The format is a little unique, so allow me to explain. The first four chapters are a testimony to God's unrelenting commitment not just to bless but to grow his children in grace—to arrange circumstances and providences of his choosing to make us more and more like Jesus. The remainder of the book is a study of the implications of God's grace for many of the significant issues we face. Chapters 5–11 are followed by additional sections titled "Further Up and Further In." This material supplements and expands the topic under consideration.

Since I am writing for a broad audience—including laymen and leaders, young believers and mature believers—I don't want any of you to get bogged down if a particular discussion seems irrelevant. But don't sell yourself short or be cowardly either! I challenge you to go "further up and further in" to what the Scriptures have to say about these crucial matters of the heart. Read and study as one preparing to care for others, not just yourself—for, indeed, this is where the reign of grace will take all of us. In the back of the book you will find reflection and discussion questions for personal and small group use.

It is my prayer that this humble and quite incomplete attempt at conveying the rich delights and radical demands of God's love will honor Jesus and help those of us who are preparing to live as his beloved Wife forever.

Be IMITATORS of God,

therefore, as dearly loved

children and *Live* a life of love,

just as Christ loved us

and gave himself up for us

as a *fragrant* offering

and sacrifice to God.

—Ephesians 5:1–2

Were the whole REALM of nature mine,

that were a present far too small;

Love so *amazing,* so divine,

demands my soul, my life, my all.

Isaac Watts

What are YOU doing

for no other reason than because *you love* Jesus?

AND what have you ceased doing

for no other reason than *his love* for you?

Jack Miller

O to grace how great a DEBTOR daily

I'm constrained to be!

Let Thy *goodness,* like a fetter,

bind my wandering heart to Thee.

Robert Robinson

Nothing could sum up better the BLESSINGS of being in Christ

than the expression *"the reign of grace."*...When we are convinced

that "grace reigns," we will REMEMBER

that God's throne is a *"throne of grace,"* and will come to it boldly

to receive mercy and to find grace for every need.

John Stott

CHAPTER ONE

The Implications of GRACE

"I love you too." He was eighty-two and I was fifty-one, but it was the first time in my life I'd heard my dad speak those words. Though they comprised a "mere" sentence, they carried the freight of heartfelt expectations and bore the weight of long-term implications. Life and conversation have taught me that a great percentage of us die without ever hearing our dads utter this tiny, but titanic, phrase.

Dismissing it as a generational thing, I never expected my dad to verbalize what I knew to be in his heart. In fact, I'd done a pretty good job of convincing myself it really wasn't that big of a deal. They were just words, right? If it had taken *me* half a century to hug my dad and tell him I loved him, who was I to expect the same from a southern octogenarian plus?

It was right after Thanksgiving. As Dad and I were finishing a phone visit between my office in Tennessee and his den in North Carolina, I ended our conversation with the benediction that still feels new to me: "I love you, Dad." However, before I could put the receiver down, Dad made a huge deposit in the treasury of my heart. Without missing a beat, he responded, "I love you too."

With that unprecedented and spontaneous return volley, he simply hung up. Stunned, I replayed each word like a hungry man savoring every morsel of a long-dreamt-about feast. Then I hung up the phone and thrust my arms up in the air like I had just won the New York City Marathon and yelled, "Yes!" loud enough to startle even myself. "My dad loves me!"

I never knew how much the absence of actually hearing my dad express his affection for me had affected my heart until that phone call in December 2001.

With those simple words, "I love you too," I was overcome with emotion. I felt the surprise and joy of a little boy on Christmas morning opening the gift he'd made hints about but didn't think his parents could afford. I felt somewhat awkward and shy, like right after the first time I kissed the beautiful, young woman who would become my wife. I also felt the same freedom and happiness I remember coursing through my whole being when, at last, I *really* had a reason to stand up during the singing of the "Hallelujah Chorus" in December, 1968.

The Implications of Being Loved

Most of my life I've felt like an orphan in my own house—always on the run, never able to sit still very long, uncertain of my place in the family portrait. But when my dad told me that he loved me, something clicked, congealed, converged—deep in my heart. Our relationship, already significantly healed, began to take on a whole new direction. The wonderful status of finally having a *real* dad (not the impersonal "Pop" I'd always called him) segued slowly into the dynamic of my living as a son. Making the emotional transition from being a "boarder" in my family system to being a welcomed son hasn't been easy. It's required a lot of me; it's especially required unhurried reflection and new degrees of vulnerability.

Since the day he spoke that blessing into my soul, I find myself lingering in the *implications* of feeling loved by Dad. I'm aware of being a steward of something very precious. How does a fifty-two-year-old son respond to the heart movement of an eighty-three-year-old dad? It would have been one thing for Dad to have given me a gift of money, but at a far greater cost to him, Dad has given me his heart. What does good stewardship of *this* kind of gift involve?

As I continue to ponder this mystery and movement in my own heart, I see my relationship with Dad as a powerful parable, a mighty metaphor for my relationship with God. To hear Dad say "I love you too" has proven to be the current megaphone by which Abba, Father, is speaking his own "I have loved you" deep into my DNA—not just into my theological hard drive. I find myself reflecting a whole lot more about the dynamic, and not just the status, of being loved of God, about the radical *implications* of his grace, and about good *stewardship* of the most costly of all gifts—the "indescribable gift" (2 Cor. 9:15) of Jesus.

Regarding *my* story, it's the difference between studying and communicating the theology of grace and sitting down (and still) and having face-to-face, transforming communion with the God of all grace—making unhurried eye contact with him. It's the difference between knowing propositions and being known by a Person—between theological vocabulary and the vocation of knowing Jesus.

Further Up and Further In

For those of you who've read my last book, *Objects of His Affection,* you know that in it I tell the story of the death of my mother and the stifling effect it had on my emotional and spiritual growth and my relationship with my father. The automobile accident that took her life left my dad and me emotionally and relationally paralyzed. We simply had no clue how to deal with the devastating loss of the wonderful woman who was my mom and his wife. I was only eleven at the time, and for the next thirty-nine years, Dad and I were held hostage by our undealt-with grief and doomed-to-fail coping mechanisms. No words of love ever passed between my dad and me or my brother. Mom's name—Martha Amanda—was not mentioned even once between us for all those years. None of us shed one tear over her in the presence of the other. We simply couldn't "go there." She was never forgotten—even for one day—but she was never remembered out loud or together.

But shortly before my fiftieth birthday and while in the process of writing *Objects,* the relationship between my father and I began to thaw. During the same time, I finally made my first visit to the tiny piece of real estate in Burlington, North Carolina, that had held mammoth sway over my heart for so long. Standing over Mom's grave for the first time since we'd buried her, a process of resurrection was initiated in my heart that continues to this day. Though rusted shut by years of uncried tears, the prison doors of my soul were ripped off their immobile hinges by that visit in February 2000, and my soul found new meaning and depth in the compelling love of God. It is this new awareness that I explored in *Objects of His Affection* and will continue to explore in this, *The Reign of Grace.*

How, then, would I describe the relationship between these two books? Movement from admiring an intriguing doorway to taking a few steps through the portal into the realm of new-creation living. It is my hope that *The Reign of Grace* is an extension of the call Aslan the Lion (the Christ figure in C. S. Lewis's Chronicles of Narnia) gave to the children and creatures in the shadowlands (life as it is lived in *this* world) to come "further up and further in" into Narnia—Lewis's literary tool for describing life lived in the transforming presence of Aslan. Narnia has now become for me a powerful symbol of the expanding and consuming reign of the Lion of the tribe of Judah, Jesus—the reign of redeeming grace.

In *The Last Battle,* the seventh and last in the series of the Chronicles of Narnia, a conversation between Lucy and her oldest Narnian friend, Faun Tumnus, captures this ongoing journey into Narnia.

"I see," she said at last, thoughtfully. "I see now. The garden is like the stable. It is far bigger inside that it was outside."

"Of course, Daughter of Eve," said the Faun. "The further up and the further in you go, the bigger everything gets. The inside is larger than the outside."

"I see," she said. "This is still Narnia, and more real and more beautiful than the Narnia down below, just as it was more real and more beautiful than the Narnia outside the stable door! I see...world within world, Narnia within Narnia...."

"Yes," said Mr. Tumnus, "like an onion: except that as you continue to go in and in, each circle is larger than the last."[1]

As we go "further up and further in" into the reign of grace, we discover larger and larger implications. We live as participants under its transforming dominion rather than as visitors who casually tour Buckingham Palace—checking out its treasures. We experience grace to be as consuming as it is consoling—for we find ourselves thrust directly into the presence of Jesus. Face-to-face with our Lion-King, we learn how to respond to his beauty, love, and majesty—not merely how grace can help us live a more full and enjoyable Christian life.

Emeth, a latecomer to Narnia, experienced Aslan (Jesus) in this way. Coming into Narnia, he observed:

I looked about me and saw the sky and the wide lands and smelled the sweetness....I began to journey into the strange country and to seek him [Aslan]....So I went over much grass and many flowers and among all kinds of wholesome and delectable trees till lo! In a narrow place between two rocks there came to meet me a great Lion. The speed of him was like the ostrich, and his size was an elephant's; his hair was like pure gold and the brightness of his eyes like gold that is liquid in the furnace. He was more terrible than the Flaming Mountain of Lagour, and in beauty he surpassed all that is in the world even as the rose in bloom surpasses the dust of the desert. Then I fell at his feet and thought, surely this is the

> hour of death, for the Lion [who is worthy of all honor] will know that I have served Tash [the counterfeit Christ—the devil] all my days and not him....
>
> But the Glorious One bent down his golden head and touched my forehead with his tongue and said, "Son, thou art welcome."...Then he breathed upon me and took away the trembling from my limbs and caused me to stand upon my feet. And after that, he said not much but that we should meet again, and I must go further up and further in....And since then, O Kings and ladies, I have been wandering to find him and my happiness is so great that it even weakens me like a wound. And this is the marvel of marvels, that he called me Beloved, me who am but as a dog.[2]

Marvel, indeed! Oh that we will find Jesus to be more terrible and more beautiful, more welcoming and more wounding with the joy he gives! No, the contribution of this book isn't found in newness and novelty, but in the broadening, deepening, and clarifying of the same vision that drove me to write *Objects.* We don't need more than the gospel, just more of the same gospel. Let us go further up and further in.

Misappropriating Grace?

In the winter of 2001 when the edited manuscript of *Objects* went speedily off to print, a subtle temptation crept slowly into my heart, leading me to think, *Now that I've experienced this tremendous healing, I must be a pretty healthy guy! It feels so good to be* me *right now. I can't wait to tell my story, and what a great story it is! I can see it now:*

"Grave Day Becomes Grace Day"
"Father and Son Unite after Four Debilitating Decades of Deadly Denial"
"Frozen Pastor Begins to Thaw Out in His Jubilee Year."

Looking back, I cringe with more than a little embarrassment at such thoughts. But that's one of the occupational hazards that come with writing a book. It's easy to think that with the completion of the last chapter, the story is over. You're now on the other side of something—an "expert," poised to give interviews, sign autographs, speak at conferences, and help others who are struggling where you used to struggle.

What a dangerous and deceiving myth! Publishing a book on grace is not the same as being radically transformed by grace. Significant moments of God's love breaking into one's story is not the same as a significant movement of his love redirecting your story.

But more important than telling my own personal story, *Objects of His Affection* told the story of God's freely given, unconditional, awe-inspiring *grace.* Its message was fueled and flamed by years of interacting with believers who suffer the destructive consequences of bad theology, a grace-less gospel, and toxic faith-experiences generated by legalism and performance-based spirituality. It was for those I wrote the book.

It was from those same people that I received encouraging letters and e-mails that made it easy to feel pretty good about...how else can I say it?...well, about myself and the message of grace proclaimed in *Objects.* Here's a sampling of some of the feedback I've received:

- "At last I have broken free from the paralyzing guilt I've carried like a disease for the past fifty-five years of my life. My joy is great!"

- "I knew I would go to heaven when I died because of Jesus, but I lived with an abiding sense of being a disappointment to God. Now I am beginning to believe he actually likes me."

- "I'm a granddad, and I wept as I read your book. I gathered my family this Christmas and asked them to forgive me for being too busy too much of my life. And they did. It was so healing."

- "I've been a pastor for longer than I care to say, but at last—I've heard God sing."

- "I feel like I now have permission to relax and rest in God's presence. Hopefully, I'm through with trying to be my own savior."

Amen, amen, and amen! Isn't this good news? Absolutely yes! To hear God sing, to rest in his love, to experience his delight, to be enjoyed of God, to finally have the peace that the gospel of God's grace alone can give is essential and awesome! I have dedicated my life and ministry to helping people discover and experience this glorious reality secured for us by the life and death of Jesus. I should have been thrilled at these letters! And I was....

But is this the *whole* of the good news? Is the movie over? Are the credits supposed to start rolling now? Have we completely fulfilled our reason for being when we are truly able to say, "I am saved by grace alone, through faith alone?" Is the chief end of man just to come alive to the delights of God's love? Is the whole point of the gospel simply to free me from the guilt, shame, and fear of bad religion, no religion, civil religion, cultural religion, or religion itself?

I don't think many of us would offer a resounding "Yes!" to this line of questions. And yet we seem to be confused about "the rest of the story," as Paul Harvey would say. Where does grace take us? Where does God's love lead?

Choose Your Gifts Wisely

In time, God used those letters to cause me to think deeply on the implications of his grace and to reexamine my own response to that grace. And I began to consider how I have been interpreting the life of grace for so many others.

As I reread those thank-you notes, I began to wonder, "Did I really give the right gift?" And I started feeling kind of like a department-store Santa Claus—as if I'd played a role that wasn't really mine to play, as if I'd given small gifts to people I didn't actually know and made promises

I couldn't really keep. I had to ask myself: Did I include all the needed explanations and instructions with my gift? Did I present the correct balance?

It wasn't what the letters *affirmed* that bothered me—I praise God for the peace the writers gained from coming to know the grace of God more fully! Rather, it was what they *didn't* say that caused me a great deal of concern.

Though it's usually a great joy to open your mailbox in January and find thank-you notes, there are a few exceptions:

- From a fourteen-year-old nephew who has had a rough transition into teenage years: "Dear Aunt Sally, Thanks for the snowboard! Me and a gang of my buddies are heading off for Colorado in a couple of weeks to learn how to jump off snow covered cliffs—like they do on ESPN's extreme sports shows. We can hardly wait! I love you so much, Billy. PS—Mom didn't have to make me write this thank-you note!"

- From a daughter who just completed her first semester of her sophomore year in college: "Dear Daddy, Thanks sooo very much for the two thousand dollar check! I understand completely that you didn't have much time to shop. But guess what! As you have been so kind in expressing your hopes and prayers that I will get over my sophomore slumps, you are the answer to your own prayer! I've decided not to go back to school this semester. I'm going to take your generous gift and 'hostel' my way around Europe for a couple of months. Thanks Daddy. I already feel better. Love, Lynn."

Oh, blessed ambivalence! These kinds of thank-you notes make you feel joyful and fearful at the same time! Joyful for the expression of gratitude, but fearful for the use of the gift! That's sort of how I've felt in response to feedback from *Objects*—warmed with the appreciation, but warned by the applications!

The Ultimate Gift

Any gift we give or receive in life can be dis-used, well-used, mis-used, or even a-bused. As with Christmas presents, so with an inheritance: Gifts can be underappreciated, cherished, worshiped as an idol, forgotten, invested, or squandered (as in the case of the prodigal son in Luke 15).

God's grace, like any other gift—no, like *no other gift*—can be distorted, even perverted. Jude, the half brother of Jesus, spoke of just such a situation in the first-century church. "Certain men whose condemnation was written about long ago have secretly slipped in among you. They are godless men, who change the grace of our God into a license for immorality and deny Jesus Christ our only Sovereign and Lord" (Jude 4).

Indeed, it is quite possible to pervert that which is precious and priceless. Jude teaches us that to distort grace is to misrepresent and deny Jesus. Grace is not just a theological proposition to be debated; it is a living Person to be honored and loved. To be wrong about grace is to be wrong about Jesus. To be wrong about Jesus is to be wrong about grace.

In his classic volume *The Cost of Discipleship,* German pastor and martyr Dietrich Bonhoeffer wrote about "cheap grace." What is cheap grace? It is a Christ-less, faithless, tearless, joyless, and loveless misrepresentation of the grace of God.

Cheap grace is a gospel with no call to repentance; it is discipleship with an aversion to suffering; it is a church with no sense of mission, a community of believers clinging more to their ideal than to Jesus' cross as a definition of true fellowship. In essence, cheap grace is grace emptied of Jesus. Therefore, it is *un-grace or a-grace.*

Unlike any other gift giver, God takes no nervous risks when he gives gifts—for risk presupposes the possibility of failure, and his plans never fail. God has never had to second-guess giving a fast snowboard to an irresponsible teenager, a large sum of money to an immature coed, or an incomplete book to an impressionable public. And there was certainly no risk, nor was there any hint of second-guessing, when God gave the ultimate gift, sine qua non, of his only begotten Son for ill-deserving sinners. There is no other way we could have become the permanent objects of his affection and delight. There is always wisdom, joy, passion, and intentionality to God's generosity.

We are the ones who are at risk! What we do with God's indescribable gift matters more than anything in life—for it is our response to Jesus himself. Indeed, what we think about God's grace—how we explain, illustrate, extend, and apply this peerless gift to ourselves and others—is essentially our way of saying, "This is who Jesus is. This is why you need to take him seriously and love him above all. This is what it means to know and follow him."

The Reign of Grace

God's grace is given freely and undeservedly, but not without intent and implications. We dare not try to privatize or domesticate the significance of God's grace. We have been called into a dynamic love affair—one that gives more than we could have ever hoped and demands more than we would freely give. To receive God's grace in Christ is to be brought into a revolutionary reign, not ushered into a quiet rest home! God's love is as disruptive as it is delightful, as demanding as it is delicious! God loves us exactly as we are today, but he loves us too much to leave us as we are and where we are.

Grace is free, but not frail! The Scriptures attest over and over to the potent and life-giving effect that grace is to have in our lives as it reigns supreme in our hearts.

- We are to "grow in the grace and knowledge of our Lord and Savior, Jesus Christ." (2 Pet. 3:18)
- We must be careful not to "receive God's grace in vain" (2 Cor. 6:1) by having disregard for Jesus, his cross, and his kingdom.
- We must not "set aside the grace of God" (Gal. 2:21) by reverting to self-righteousness.
- The grace of God is not to be "without effect" (1 Cor. 15:10) in our lives, a mere cosmetic window treatment.
- To revert to salvation by obedience is to have "fallen away from grace." (Gal. 5:4)
- We are to submit to the pedagogy of grace, for it "teaches us to say 'No' to ungodliness and worldly passions, and to live self-controlled, upright and godly lives in this present age." (Titus 2:12)
- Grace doesn't eliminate or leapfrog us over our weaknesses and limitations; on the contrary, "grace is sufficient" to bring God's power into the very things we despise, like insults, hardships, persecutions, and difficulties. (2 Cor. 12:8–10)
- Grace doesn't make us guiltless couch potatoes in the kingdom, rather, "to each one of us grace has been given" so we can do our part to "fill the whole universe" with the glory of Jesus. (Eph. 4:7–16)
- When we choose to live disobedient lives—indifferent to the glory of God, we aren't insulated by grace, we insult "the Spirit of grace." (Heb. 10:28–31)
- Indeed, God hasn't lavished grace upon us to release us from concerns about holiness but so that "grace might reign through righteousness." (Rom. 5:20–21)

If grace is to have its transforming way in our lives, we must submit to it as loyal, devoted servants submit unquestionably to a king. We who have been made objects of God's tender affection have also been made subjects in his transforming kingdom, servants of the era of "new creation," participants in the reign of grace.

How Shall We Respond?

How, then, shall we respond? What does a life lived in response to God's grace look like? Overreaction usually leads to overcorrection—a lesson I am continually learning, especially in spiritual matters. Therefore, I have found it helpful to visualize the process of growth in Christ by creating continuums representing the issues with which I am wrestling at any given time in life.

For me, a continuum represents two dimensions of the same truth—both of which are vital to the whole. Because we don't do balanced living very well, our temptation is to major on one side of a continuum, almost to the elimination of the other. Here are some of the continuums that I am currently wrestling with in my journey and therefore in this book.

I invite you to ponder with me how each side of these continuums is dynamically related to its counterpart. Also, try to project the consequences of choosing to focus on only one dimension of these continuums to the exception of the other.

By the way, do any of your remember Judy Collins?

Both Sides Now

My Personal Story .... God's New Creation Story
Healing As an Event .... Healthy Living As the Goal
The Delights of God's Love .... The Demands of God's Love
Enjoying God's Generosity .... Becoming a Cheerful Giver

Becoming a Whole Person . . . . Becoming a Holy Servant
My Rights As Abba's Child . . . . . . My Responsibilities As Jesus' Bride
Recovery from My Addictions . . . . Repentance from My Sin
My Therapeutic Journey . . . . God's Healing of the Nations
Congruency of Heart . . . . Consecration of Life
Freedom from Past Hurts . . . . Freedom for Present Obedience
Loving the Grace of Jesus . . . . Living for the Glory of Jesus
A Secure Heart . . . . A Surrendered Heart
Jesus, My Merciful High Priest . . . Jesus, My Majestic Enthroned King
Me As a Victim of Others' Sin . . . . Others As Victims of My Sin
My Personal Boundaries . . . . God's Wide Open Territory
Medicinal Living . . . . Missional Living
The Riches of Grace . . . . The Reign of Grace

What's to Come

In the remaining chapters of this book, we'll be looking at what it means to live under the *reign of grace.* We'll examine some of the main arenas of life in which we must learn to love God well. We'll ask and seek answers to questions like: What does it mean to be a good steward of God's grace? Is God more concerned about my happiness or my holiness? When God brings freedom, healing, peace, or some deliverance to my heart by the riches of his grace, what's supposed to happen next? Is there a reason—not why, but wherefore—that God is so generous with us? If God's love is so compelling, what does it compel me to believe, do, and become? We will see that the unsearchable riches of his grace commend and command an exacting response.

We'll also look at how terribly *meddlin'* God is as he loves his children. The God of all grace is anything but tame as he relates to us. Perhaps some of us will discover some stereotypes and sentimentality about grace from which we need to be rescued!

Using the Old Testament book of Malachi as our inspiration and focal point, we'll also draw from the riches of many other passages in the Old and New Testament alike.

My hope is that all of us will be able to see the current enthronement of grace and that we'll surrender to its eternal implications in the dailiness of our own lives. I invite you to walk with me through the pages of this book as together we begin to grasp the connection between God's wildly passionate love and his radical commitment to make foolish children into obedient lovers. As objects of God's affection, we are called to live as subjects in his kingdom—under the reign of his glorious grace. Jesus is calling us further up and further in. Let's go through the portal together. Welcome to the kingdom of grace.

My *heart* melts at the love of Jesus.
He is mine and I am his,
GIVEN to me as well as for me.
I am never so much mine
as when I am *his,* or so much lost to
myself until lost in him.

Arthur BENNETT

I HAVE LOVED YOU WITH
AN *everlasting* LOVE;
I HAVE DRAWN YOU
WITH LOVING-KINDNESS.

—JEREMIAH 31:3

LET THE BELOVED OF THE LORD REST SECURE IN HIM,
FOR HE *shields* HIM ALL DAY LONG, AND THE ONE THE LORD
LOVES RESTS BETWEEN HIS SHOULDERS.

—DEUTERONOMY 33:12

We are NEVER nearer Christ
than when we *find* ourselves
lost in a holy AMAZEMENT
at his unspeakable love.

John OWEN

Jesus, LOVER of my soul,
let me to thy bosom *fly,*
Plenteous *grace* with
THEE is found…

Charles WESLEY

CHAPTER TWO

How Have *You* Loved Me?

Trying to get comfortable in a new counselor's office is like asking me to eat a plate full of canned asparagus—both result in a lot of squirming, stalling, and repositioning. I like being in control of what I eat, and I am convinced that canned asparagus is the clearest culinary indication of the reality of sin. I also like being in control over who gets a peek into my heart—for there are sufficient indicators that I, too, am a testimony to the reality of sin.

It didn't take long to notice that my new counselor was committed to spending a whole lot more time taking notes than smiling approvingly at me. I was hoping for pity; she listened instead. I wanted agreement with my assessment; she resisted my manipulative pull. I wanted theological insight; she gave me an art assignment!

"Scotty, I want you to take this sheet of paper and draw a picture of yourself as a six- or seven-year-old. Be as detailed as you can. And take this box of crayons with you and use whatever colors seem right."

A little perturbed, I thought to myself, *Draw a picture? What's with this? These are pretty expensive art lessons.* That evening I would begin to find out why the drawing wasn't such a corny idea after all.

I did OK with pen and pad until it came time to draw a face on the little guy. Try as I might, all I could come up with was an empty circle. For the life of me, I could not even envision an expression to attempt. It wasn't embarrassment over not being able to draw well—just a blank. Though somewhat taken aback, I soon passed it off as no big deal.

Faceless Orphan

A week later, I walked into her office less apprehensive and defensive than at our first visit. I figured anybody who dispensed drawing pads and crayons couldn't be all that intimidating.

"Well, how'd it go? Are you a budding Michelangelo?" A little sheepishly, I handed her my masterpiece. Though using professional restraint, she took one look and offered a noticeable "Oh, my goodness."

With genuine empathy, she asked me to talk about the "faceless orphan."

"I don't know what to tell you. I drew myself skipping, as you can tell...well, if you can't, that's what my feet are doing up in the air a little! But I just couldn't come up with a face."

After a little more chitchat about the picture, my counselor leaned in toward me, took off her glasses, and offered this observation.

"Scotty, I'm happy you and your dad have had a great breakthrough, and certainly many other good things have taken place in the past year. But my sense is that you're in a dangerous place. I'd be sad if all of this simply ended up as a good story, but with no real change in your heart. Don't be offended, but you seem a little slick to me—more than a little evasive and disconnected on the inside."

She picked up my picture and turned it toward me. "You've got to find this little guy's face—your face as a child—so you can grow as an adult. He's there. You've just got to look."

Though I was too proud to admit that I really didn't understand what she meant by "finding my face," the earnestness and hope with which she spoke grabbed my heart and wouldn't let go.

She continued, "By your own admission, you've got a track record of talking too much about big moments in your life before you take the time to process these things quietly on your own."

Looking me dead in the eye, she continued. "Scotty, don't sabotage what God is doing in your life by running to your pulpit. Right now you've got more answers than raw courage, more insight than follow through. I'm concerned for you." She sat back in her chair as though exhausted.

To think I actually paid for that barrage! But she was right. I looked at her clock, happy we were already two minutes past the hour; but she wasn't through.

"I want you to plan your next visit to your mom's grave—not a 'drive-by quickie,' but a lingering visit and chat. That's your homework assignment. And when you go, I want you to allow your heart to feel what it would be like to have your mom hold your hand and walk with you as a six- or seven-year-old.

"Just visualize some familiar scene or place you remember being with her."

She could tell by my body language that I was beginning to freak a little on this one.

"Trust me, Scotty. I'm not going New Age on you or anything. I want you to get a clearer picture of the depth of your loss. You've chosen to live your life in ways that rob you and others of your heart. I know you love God's grace, but you need it more than you realize."

Disconnect Exposed

My love for God's grace was indeed what *Objects of His Affection* was all about. Helping people understand the rich theology of God's sovereign grace is something I'd been passionate about for a long time. But now I was being called to *become* something, something that would require *surrendering* to the reign of a sovereign. Though it took awhile to see the parallels, my response to God's grace resembled the presumption and complacency that filled the hearts of the Israelites whom Malachi addressed in the last book of the Old Testament.

Malachi was the last of Israel's writing prophets from whom God's people would hear until the dawn of the Messianic Age. His name means "God's messenger," and he was commissioned to record and deliver a fiery love letter. In this letter, God speaks to his children in the first-person voice in forty-seven of fifty-five verses—the highest percentage of first-person speech from God himself to be found in any book of the Bible. In the truest sense, God "gets in the last word" as the Old Testament concludes. We usually think of final words as "Sit up and pay attention" words. The Book of Malachi is no exception. Through Malachi, God gets in our face to get at our hearts.

Malachi reminds us that we are God's chosen people—his beloved family—a people with a history, a heritage, and a hope. *Through Malachi, God addresses us as beloved sons and daughters who have forgotten the family history.* Like faceless orphans, God's chosen people, the Israelites, were trying to make a way, a name, and a story for themselves—forgetting God's story to their own ruin.

God's pithy prophet was commissioned to make bored, cynical children wrestle with the radical implications of being the objects of God's affection—a wrestling match in which losing means winning. With redemptive sarcasm and holy parody, Malachi played the court jester as he exposed the huge disconnect between God's faithfulness to his people and their fickleness toward him. Through Malachi, God reminds us that the delights of grace are to lead to the reign of grace.

"I Have Loved You!"

"'I have loved you,' says the Lord" (Mal. 1:2). What an amazing way to begin the very last book of the Old Testament! A bold and unflinching profession of long-term grace by the God of creation, the God of eternity, the God of the Israelites, the God of you and me.

And how did the objects of his affection respond? With either the worst memory lapse of all time or with out-and-out spoiled brat-i-ness! "*How* have you loved us?" they retorted. Let the weight and the tragedy of their response sink in. They said in essence, "We want proof! Give us evidence. When have you loved us? What have you done for us? If you really loved us, you'd treat us differently than you're treating us today. Where is the fulfillment of your promises?"

Do you hear pathetic, whiny voices or perhaps angry defiance in their tone? Maybe some of each. If you have ever doubted the patience and forbearance of God, camp out at this scene for a while and marvel that he does not simply call down the fire of well-deserved judgment, or at the very least throw up his hands and walk away with his heart filled with incredulous disgust.

Childish Ingratitude

As a parent, have you ever had a conversation like this with a six-year-old?

"Daddy loves you, Jimmy."

"No you don't! You're just saying that. If you really loved me, you would give me the box of matches and the butcher knife. You're no fun. I want a different daddy."

Or maybe you've had an encounter with a fourteen-year-old daughter similar to this one. "Charissa, sweetheart, I do love you."

The door slams, *bang!* Then, from within her playpen—I mean bedroom, "The heck you do! You only care about yourself! You don't trust me! All of my friends get to stay out till two in the morning. Their moms love them a lot better than you love me. It's not fair! Maybe I'll just run away and get pregnant. Then you'll be sorry."

The childish reasoning of this six-year-old is somewhat predictable. And the hormone-charged irrationality of this teenager, though not excusable, is at least understandable. But how do we explain the disconnect that occurred in the hearts of God's people? "How have you loved us?" they asked God.

Where did their hearts go? Where do ours go? What caused believers in Jeremiah's day, who once loved God with the passion and joy of a bride, to be enticed by other lovers? (Jer. 2:1–5). How long did it take for the Ephesian church of "undying love" to need this rebuke from Jesus: "I hold this against you: You have forsaken your first love"? (Eph. 6:24; Rev. 2:4). When did Malachi's contemporaries become so ungrateful, disconnected, and self-absorbed?

Abuzz and a Funk

Life was abuzz in the Mediterranean world at large, but for the Israelite people, things were in a bit of a funk—a grand funk. Upon returning from Babylonian captivity, their eyes had been filled with hope and their heads with dreams of the great day of the coming Messiah. They had rebuilt the temple, and the prophet Zechariah had described visions of spectacular blessings and great hope, fueling their imagination and hearts—at least for a while.

But over time, memories of the manifest presence of the Lord began to fade, and messianic daydreaming gave way to dazed looks of unbelief and disappointment.

The nation was marked by foreign agitation, oppressive poverty, and severe drought. With a meager military and a languishing faith, Israel was vulnerable to attacks on all fronts—especially on the heart. These wearing circumstances became the rich, dark soil in which dying hope and biting cynicism grew like killer kudzu.

Perhaps you can relate to their crisis of faith. Do you ever go through times when you say to yourself as a believer, "Why pray? Why stay vulnerable? I thought I could trust God, but when I look at my life and the world I live in...why bother with pretending any longer? I don't see his promises being fulfilled in my life. I don't see his provision and protection. The things I was led to believe he would do...he hasn't."

Into this context, God declares and affirms his unswerving love—but in a rather surprising way.

Grace for the Un-Graced and Dis-Graced

Indeed, just how had God loved his people? How do you suppose he responded to this arrogant rhetorical question from his dis-grace-full people?

How would you have responded, if you were God? Picking from the whole history of creation and redemption, of all the ways you have (as God) loved your people faithfully and generously, to which ones would you appeal to silence your ungrateful children?

> "I have loved you," says the Lord.
>
> "But you ask, 'How have you loved us?'
>
> "Was not Esau Jacob's brother?" the Lord says. "Yet I have loved Jacob, but Esau I have hated, and I have turned his mountains into a wasteland and left his inheritance to the desert jackals."
>
> Edom may say, "Though we have been crushed, we will rebuild the ruins."
>
> But this is what the Lord Almighty says: "They may build, but I will demolish. They will be called the Wicked Land, a people always under the wrath of the Lord. You will see it with your own eyes and say, 'Great is the Lord—even beyond the borders of Israel!'" (Mal. 1:2–5)

Say what? *Why* in the world did God choose the story of Jacob and Esau as the quintessential, this-will-end-the-conversation validation of his love? And what does Edom have to do with anything relevant to a heated chat questioning God's history of loving well? Let's mark this one down: Though God could have made a long list of particular gifts, he chose to remind his people of the big story of redemption.

The individual riches of God's grace only have meaning as we view them within the overall story of his reign of grace. We are privileged participants, not the focal point, of a larger narrative of redeeming love.

The story of twin brothers, Jacob and Esau—born to Isaac and Rebekah—perpetually reminds us that the relationship we share with God is totally *by* grace and *for* grace. Indeed, we are the objects but not the end of God's unearned affection. His love comes to us and passes through us en route to the nations of the world. The reign of grace does not create a gated community for demanding consumers—but a dynamic movement of other-centered lovers. Malachi's contemporaries were in desperate need of this reminder. So are we.

Nowhere does the Bible teach that Jacob was more loveable than Esau or more deserving of special treatment. Yes, Esau impetuously sold his birthright for the equivalent of a bowl of oatmeal, but it was prompted by the shenanigans of the deceitful Jacob (Gen. 25:29–34). God developed a special relationship with Jacob simply because he is free to do so and because he is gracious to do so. Like Jacob, any of us become the objects of God's affection not because we are *choice* people, but because we are *chosen* people (Deut. 7:6–9; 10:15).

Oh, that our hearts could more fully realize that what matters most, in life and in eternity, is not our desire and effort but God's unrelenting mercy! This is exactly what Malachi's friends and family desperately needed to lay hold of once again.

I Love You More Than You Want

"How have you loved us?" the beleaguered Jews asked. Through the story of Jacob and Esau, God offers this answer. *"I have loved you with an everlasting and undeserved love. Like your forefather Jacob, I have set my affection on you simply because I chose to do so. I have covenanted with you to be your God and to make you my treasured people, forever! Nothing has changed.*

"However, I don't love on your terms, but on mine. If I loved only on your terms, you would have me wait on you hand and foot—like your slave or butler, not like your Lord and Master. You have no claim on my love or corner on my mercies. I am great and gracious well beyond the borders of Israel. I am not your local deity-on-demand; rather, I am the Lord of the nations. My love is better than the life you would settle for and bigger than you want it to be."

Maybe we can begin to see, then, why God chose the *story of his grace* (the big picture) rather than the *stores of his grace* (the many riches) to affirm the perpetual reality of his love to Malachi's audience. We aren't those who call a celestial bellhop to bring Perrier and pretzels into our personal stories. God calls us into the metanarrative of *his* story—the unfolding drama of cosmic redemption through the gospel. The people of God owed their entire experience of his covenant mercy, compassion, provision—even every blessing in life—to God. So do we. How, then, should such a well-loved people live? How are we to respond to the sovereign and soaring love of God?

The Dialogue of Affection

Jesus taught his disciples that the first and greatest commandment is to love the Lord our God with all our heart, soul, mind, and strength. This being so, doesn't it stand to reason that God must have his own love language, ways by which he finds joy and pleasure in our communion with him?

I am very thankful (most of the time) to be married to a woman who hasn't left me guessing about her favorite love language. Darlene has made it very clear to me that she hears me say "I love you" best through the language of time—unrushed, undistracted, involved "watch the sun go all the way down with me" time speaks powerfully to her heart.

My words of affection are believable to Darlene when I do things *with* her, not just *for* her. It's about *connecting,* not collecting brownie points. Darlene wants a lover's dialogue.

If I choose to ignore her dialect for whatever language is convenient or easiest for me, far from feeling loved, she feels ignored and devalued. My heart is no different. I light up when Darlene's love is incarnated into the symbols that shout, "She remembered! She cares! She delights in me!"

Likewise, for us to ignore the specific ways God wants to be loved is to make a mockery of our claims to love him. And this is precisely the theme of the Book of Malachi. The postexilic people of God had become postpassionate to the heart of God and postcommitted in expressing their love for him. Their vibrant journey in the reign of grace derailed at the intersection of forgetfulness and presumption.

But God's story is undeterred. He will have a people who delight in the extravagant excesses of his love and who respond with passion, if not perfection.

The delights of God's love lead compellingly to the demands of his love. For years, many of us have proclaimed this very truth in song: "Love so amazing so divine, demands my soul, my life, my all." Our calling is to do so in life. How? The Book of Malachi (as the rest of Scripture) is generously clear about specific ways we are to live to God's pleasure—about how we can most profoundly express adoration and affection to him. If you took a peek at the table of contents, you got advance notice that God calls us to love him well in worship, relationships, and stewardship—to name a few of his love languages.

But God doesn't start by giving us a list of things to say or do. He starts by giving us his heart. He is constantly pursuing us as his beloved—always precipitating covenant conversation with us. Our relationship with God is a dialogue, a lover's dialogue, a doxological dialogue. He speaks, and we respond. Sometimes he whispers, sometimes he shouts, sometimes he sings—but he is always speaking. Are we listening?

THE LORD BLESS YOU AND KEEP YOU; THE LORD MAKE HIS FACE *shine* UPON YOU AND BE GRACIOUS TO YOU; THE LORD TURN HIS FACE TOWARD YOU AND GIVE YOU PEACE.

—NUMBERS 6:24–26

Zeng Shen said, "I once HEARD the Master say no man *reveals* his true self, except perhaps when he is mourning his parents."

THE ANALECTS, BOOK XIX, NO. 17

How can THEY (the gods) meet with us face to face till *we* have faces?

QUEEN ORUAL, *TILL WE HAVE FACES*

C. S. LEWIS

Our body SPEAKS a language of its own, but no single part of our physical selves communicates as clearly as our faces. Maliciousness, boredom, joy, ecstasy—all those emotions appear in detail on *human* faces. Perhaps that's why the phrase "speaking face-to-face" has the connotations it does. When we look each other in the eye, we expect nothing but the TRUTH. A telephone simply cannot deliver that intimacy....At certain moments in all of our lives we passionately seek face-to-face fellowship. Not until we've met God's eye can we rest. *Only* in that intimacy does the virtual mystery of grace become distinctly and passionately real. Only then dowe see HIS face.

Abraham KYPER

CHAPTER THREE

Finding Face— GAINING HEART

The more copies of *Objects* I autographed, the less joy and contentment I experienced. It's pretty difficult to have written so boldly about a God who serenades his people with great rejoicing and delightfully quiets them with his love and yet feel increasingly cut off from the music and peace. I entered a season in which I felt more alone than ever in my life.

I would later realize that God was singing over me—loudly and lovingly. But I learned that he sings more than one love song. His repertoire includes "I Cherish You More Than You Can Imagine," as well as "You're a Mess, and I Love You too Much to Leave You that Way," along with "Forget the Umbrella, My Son, Here Comes the Reign." Why had I assumed that growth in grace would be less painful than any other kind of growth? Heart surgery is heart surgery, any way you cut it.

God would not let me escape the demands of my counselor's searching words. "I'd be sad if all of this simply ended up as a good story but with no real change in your heart. Scotty, don't sabotage what God is doing in your life. Right now you've got more answers than courage. You've chosen to live your life in ways that rob you and others of your heart. You've got to find your face."

Find your face—the first time she uttered that phrase I couldn't help but think about my college years in the late '60s, when, if you were hip, life consisted of trying to "find yourself." That basically amounted to legitimizing one's irresponsibility, wearing faded jeans and flannel shirts, promoting free love (sex without commitment), and enjoying drugs as a spiritual/philosophical statement. I'm positive my counseling wasn't leading in that direction. And I knew "finding face" meant a lot more than simply spotting my mug in the big group photo of the world. I'm not Waldo.

But who was I, really? The disparity between my public persona of being so alive to the grace of God while feeling so dead on the inside was taking its toll. It got harder and harder to make eye contact with people—even with myself in a mirror. Find my face? I more felt like burying it in a pillow or covering it with a mask or two.

"As water reflects a face, so a man's heart reflects the man" (Prov. 27:19). "A happy heart makes the face cheerful" (Prov. 15:13). The face is the mirror of the heart. To find one's face is to find one's heart—to live in the present moment, knowing and accepting the unadulterated truth about yourself—all props and pretensions aside.

How do we come to this knowledge? By standing naked before the penetrating gaze of God—a redemptive stare that is meant to heal not harm the children of God. "For the eyes of the LORD range throughout the earth to strengthen those whose hearts are fully committed to him" (2 Chron. 16:9). But I wasn't up for being glanced at fully clothed, much less gazed upon in my birthday suit.

Undaunted, God kept arranging circumstances of his own choosing to make eye contact with me. He used many means, including my daughter and an old Greek myth.

Veiled Face

"Dad, I know how much you love C. S. Lewis's stuff. I just finished one of his books I really think you'd enjoy." She was wrong about the "enjoy" part but right about the power of this myth to bring the truth—make that *me*—into the light of *God's* face. Knowing me a quarter of a century, Kristin saw her dad in this book.

Considered by many (including himself) as Lewis's finest writing, *Till We Have Faces* is an updated historical novel of the classical myth *Cupid and Psyche.* It chronicles Queen Orual's slow journey from the ugliness of obsessive love to the beauty of finally "having a face."

It was uncanny to see how much like Orual I am. I started reading this book as though looking through a window; very soon, however, I realized I was looking into a mirror.

Set in the barbaric pre-Christian country of Glome, the story centers on the complex relationship between Orual and her beautiful (inside and out) stepsister, Psyche. Daughter to the king of Glome, Orual suffered a tragic life of great loss, losing to death both her mom and stepmom. The paralyzing fear of losing again determined her every move. (Thus, you can understand my connection with her story.)

Finally, her grief and bitterness drove her to hide under a veil, with which she sought to cover her heart's ugliness. "I now determined that I would always go veiled. I have kept this rule...ever since. It is a sort of treaty made with my ugliness."[1] Crowned queen of Glome after her father's death, Orual became a great reformer, a just ruler, and a renowned warrior throughout the kingdom—but her pained and obsessive heart remained a rebellious and demanding citizen. Haunted by the popular account of her life's story, Orual decided to write her own version.

Eventually, however, the queen experienced a mighty "undeception" (one of C. S. Lewis's great metaphors for conversion). She discovered how her affection for Psyche had been contaminated with the toxins of her own possessiveness. She loved being loved by Psyche more than she actually loved her beautiful stepsister, for *her stepsister's sake.* This revelation became clear as Orual was forced to see the same deadly pattern played out in her other relationships. She consumed people as her bread of life and ended up with her own heart being devoured.

Devastated, Orual decided to take off her veil and commit suicide. What was there left to hide from? What was left to live for? But the voice of a god stopped her from killing herself. It was then, with an unveiled face, that the queen was finally able to come before the gods—dialoguing honestly, no longer needing to make a story (or face) for herself.

In this authentic and naked conversation with the gods, Orual was free to be ugly and real, and she was also free to listen. "To say the very thing you really mean, the whole of it, nothing more or less than what you really mean, that's the whole and joy of words…till that word can be dug out of us, why should they [the gods] hear the babble that we think we mean? How can they meet us face to face till we have faces?"[2]

What became of Orual's unveiled face? After this painful and healing encounter with the gods, the queen went to a pool of water and looked into it. Her reflection was the face of the beautiful Psyche! For the first time ever, Orual experienced beauty as a part of *her* being—beauty was reflected in *her* face.

Unveiled, Orual saw her real ugliness, and unveiled she saw her emerging beauty. The gaze of God was painfully liberating for Orual. She found her face. What will it take for us to find ours?

Facedown

The next stop on my journey to an unveiled face, by assignment of my counselor, was to Mom's grave. Thankfully, I didn't need a map, like last time, to find her grave site. A little less tentative, I walked the twenty yards from my car to that little plot of land with a geography all its own.

Instead of standing, I sat; actually, I lay down on the ground. I don't know how long I was there—looking, feeling, thinking, and trying to remember. I wanted to leave, and I wanted to stay. No particular scenes came to mind—just longings—and some unexpected anger. It took the emotional turmoil of this visit for me to relate to the Book of Malachi in a personal way.

That evening, I took a stack of family photos and picked a handful that captured the two of us at different stages in our brief eleven years together. I did my best to imagine the pictures as a frame of a videotape—on pause. Pushing the Play button, I tried to locate my heart in the brief story of life with my mom.

Trying to remember her touch was particularly painful. These tears were different from the ones I'd cried a year earlier when I made the first visit to Mom's grave. I wept and hurt like the mornings when I would wake up and find that Mom had gone to work before I could tell her good-bye. I hated that feeling. Now at last, I was starting to grieve—not about Mom's death, but for me—for that little boy.

The next morning, I wrote her this letter:

Dear Mom,

It's hard to believe that a year has passed since I first came to see you. I thought after being here last year, the ache would go away—at least a little. I was wrong. Today I miss you more, not less. The more real you've become, the more I just flat out miss you...

Ever since visiting your grave, I've wondered where this journey would take me next. Being one who's used to settling for so little in my relationships, I was prepared to rest satisfied with the milestone of finally coming back to this place—the one place I've dreaded and avoided more than any other in the universe. But "settling" wasn't to be...by the decision of Another.

Last night, Mom, I spent a few hours looking for both of our hearts in some old family pictures. I tried so hard to remember how it felt to walk with you hand in hand as a little fellow. I remembered being with you at Cherry Grove Beach, looking for seashells. I remembered your laugh and watching for dolphins dancing on the shoreline. I remember not being in a hurry.

I started crying like the time I fell on the steps and nearly knocked my front teeth out. Remember that—all the blood? You held me and rocked me. Mom, as I write, there's a pain with searing intensity cutting through my heart. I'm not sure what hurts the most—missing the kindness of your touch or realizing how few memories I actually have of us doing stuff together or feeling the effects of what I've become since you died. It's all of it.

Your death seems to have killed something precious in me—my childhood. Being at your grave yesterday was excruciating, not because I had to admit once more that I'd lost you, but because I had to admit that I'd lost me. In one sense, when they buried you, they buried me. So it's not just you I've not known for decades, but me as well.

This past year brought the great joy of connecting with Dad, but it also generated sadness for all the years he and I weren't connected. Though I've never done anger very well, I am angry. I'm angry at how fragile my inner world is and has been for as long as I can remember. I hate it, Mom. I so wish you were here. Why did you have to die when you did?

One minute, I want to run away—but that's what I've done all my life. The next minute, I want somebody to blame, or I get busy with spiritual gymnastics and explain everything away with "god-speak."

I'm tired, Mom; I'm worn out. It's probably a good thing.

I know that I matter. I know that God is good, but why do I feel so empty? I'm tired of the sad. But I refuse to stay dead on the inside.

I love you. I miss you.

Scotty

Facing Up

How could my counselor possibly have known what that visit would yield? Where were all these painful emotions coming from, and where would they lead?

Dad's words of "I love you too," though healing, had pulled the pin on a time-release grenade placed under my heart's delicate equilibrium. The carefully crafted balancing act I'd maintained for decades between my inner and outer worlds was under the assault of love. I'd always heard that disruptions to the relational rhythms in a dysfunctional family system were hard to accept. Now I get it! Idols topple begrudgingly, even those which have to be propped up constantly.

As God alone could have orchestrated it, the turbulence in my soul coincided with my study of Malachi and several other portions of Scripture wrapped around this fiery prophet's life and times. While soaking in the big picture of the whole book, I was particularly taken by the very last two verses in Malachi—especially in light of recent events with my dad: "See, I will send you the prophet Elijah before that great and dreadful day of the Lord comes. He will turn the hearts of the fathers to their children, and the hearts of the children to their fathers; or else I will come and strike the land with a curse" (Mal. 4:5–6).

How awesome, I thought. *The Old Testament concludes with a promise of turning hearts—dads to their children, children to their dads.* My first impression was to rejoice in this scripture as a reflection of what God was doing between me and my dad—certainly an appropriate application. Dad and I had shared face-to-face and heart-to-heart communion as never before.

However, as I continued to study the contents of Malachi and the larger story surrounding his ministry, I realized that the prophet also had a more fundamental Father-child relationship in mind. Malachi is the account of God pressing his fatherly face into the childish disgrace of his people, beginning with the leaders. It soon became apparent that I wasn't studying Malachi for sermon preparation, but for heart transformation—my own.

Facing the Music

"You have not set your heart to honor me" (Mal. 2:2). God spoke these sobering words to the men charged with being the main conduits of his grace into the community of faith, the healers among God's people. I felt the searching gaze of God expand well beyond a fifth century B.C. group of priests in Jerusalem. His peripheral and timeless vision included me. This is one group picture, unfortunately, I *did* spot myself in.

God's exposing word delivered to the priests through Malachi reminded me of an earlier assessment God made of the priests in Jeremiah's generation: "They dress the wound of my people as though it were not serious. 'Peace, peace,' they say, when there is no peace" (Jer. 6:14).

Have you ever found yourself reading the Scriptures when, quite unexpectedly, a verse, a chapter, or a story wraps itself around your heart in a gripping embrace? At that point, you stop studying the Bible—because it is studying you. That's how I felt meditating on these words. My heart reeled, not with condemnation, but with conviction. *That's it. I'm one of the leaders Jeremiah is talking about! I heal wounds lightly, beginning with my own.*

It hurt to admit that I have a lot in common with ministers of grace who prematurely proclaim "Peace, peace!" when signs of disease and restlessness abound. I could not shake the convicting image of a doctor merely prescribing a couple of aspirin and a Valium for his *own* terminal heart disease. I've often cried "Peace, *peace!*" just to drown out the noisy chaos and fearful uncertainty of my world.

The one word in Jeremiah's rebuke to the priests that stood out like a blinking neon sign was the little pronoun "my," as in, "They dress the wound of *my* people as though it were not serious." It is one thing for me not to take care of myself, but it's quite another to ignore the gaping wounds of sin and death in God's people—or to dress them lightly with an incomplete gospel.

Band-Aids for Heart Disease

What I communicate about the gospel, how I apply the gospel, and how I personally respond to the gospel have great impact on those under my care. These are *God's people,* not mine. That includes those of you reading this book!

What does it means to dress the wounds of God's people lightly? Here are a few examples of which I have been convicted in the past year and a half:

- Extending the free offer of grace without extending an equally clear call for repentance of sin.
- Maximizing warnings against performance-based spirituality while minimizing teaching on grace-empowered obedience.
- Proclaiming the delights of God's love without being just as faithful in proclaiming love's demands.
- Being quicker to apply the balm of the gospel to relieve heart-felt pain than the power of the gospel to overthrow heart-invading idols.
- Confirming the comfort of God's mercy to those with a greater need for the conviction of his Spirit.
- Highlighting the horrors of legalism more than extolling the beauty of holiness.

- Celebrating God's fatherly affection while marginalizing his fatherly discipline.
- Deconstructing merit-based discipleship programs without reconstructing godly alternatives.

Saving Face

Isaiah heralds Jesus as a Jubilee Liberator for the imprisoned, a Comforter for those who mourn, and a Healer of the brokenhearted (Isa. 61:1–3). The freedom that Jesus brought to my heart as I stood by Mom's grave for the first time was just the preview of coming attractions. There are other imprisonments to confront, other chains to break. Jubilee is a movement, not just a moment. It *continues!*

Isaiah proclaims the Jubilee Liberator to be an exacting Arborist, as well. Concerning the ones he sets free, Jesus says, "They will be called oaks of righteousness, a planting of the LORD for the display of his splendor" (Isa. 61:3b). He is not satisfied with merely setting us *free* from the Alcatraz of unforgiveness; he sets us free to *grow* in righteousness and in our growth to display his glory to angels, demons, and the nations alike.

God's grace isn't just an empathetic gathering for hurting hearts; it's no mere pep rally for the glad-to-be-forgiven; it's way more than a support system for recovering legalists. *It is a reign through righteousness unto eternal life* (Rom. 5:20–21). Indeed! God reveals the splendor of his glory and the power of his gospel through oaks of righteousness grown from acorns that were once infested with sin and death.

This is the incredible story of stories. This is the *good* news. But it is also the *demanding* news! How can such magnificent righteousness grow from such pervasive unrighteousness? To grow, *these* oaks need a *reign,* not just the *rain!* Jesus is our trustworthy prophet and our most merciful high priest, but he is also a mighty king! He reigns and rules with grace!

All the turmoil in your heart, all the unsettling feelings of sadness, anger, emptiness, incongruency—they're all a part of the same redemptive drama that fueled Jeremiah's passionate rebukes and great promises. You are *becoming* "oaks of righteousness" to the glory of God. None of us are to live like faceless orphans! We have a story. We matter!

The gospel isn't about "saving face"—protecting ourselves from the risks of embarrassment or shame. It's about *changing* face, *changing our whole beings!* We are made to reflect the glory of God in all that we think, say, and do—but not just as mirrors; we are actually changing and becoming like the glorious One, Jesus!

Unveiled Faces

In some ways as a pastor, I can relate to Moses who, when returning from his meetings with God on Mount Sinai, "would put a veil over his face to keep the Israelites from gazing at it while the radiance was fading away" (2 Cor. 3:13). I mean, who wants to showcase declining glory for the watching world? We pastors often work real hard to keep others from seeing how fast we leak grace.

But in more ways than with Moses, I can relate to Adam and his foolish attempts at veiling himself with fig leaves—or to Orual and her commitment to stay busy, be productive, write her own story, and keep a safe distance from the real God. However, coming face to face with yourself under the gaze of God, in the mirror of his Word, is the only way to ever catch a clear vision of what you were created to become.

How then do we change? How do we move from surface Band-Aids to real health, from pseudo-peace to shalom? "We, who with unveiled faces all reflect [as in reflect upon or contemplate] the Lord's glory, are being *transformed* into his likeness with ever-increasing glory, which comes from the Lord, who is the Spirit" (2 Cor. 3:18).

It is only as the beauty and bounty of Jesus fills our hearts that we become like him. We are invited, no commanded, to make eye contact with the God of all glory and grace—the very thing that previously would have destroyed us. We no longer have to veil our faces or pose our way through life. Rather, we are invited to fix our gaze (meditate, worship, ponder) on God's glory without a veil! Why? "For God, who said, 'Let light shine out of darkness,' made his light shine in our hearts to give us the light of the knowledge of the glory of God in the face of Christ" (2 Cor. 4:6).

Because of what Jesus has accomplished *for us,* we have been given a *face-to-face* relationship with God! The veil of disgrace has been replaced with the garment of Jesus' grace. As the old hymn says, we are "clothed in his righteousness alone, faultless to stand before the throne!" And because of what Jesus is accomplishing *in us,* the glory of God's face will be seen in our faces!

How then are we to live? We are to love God and his glory above everything else! We are to seek the face of Jesus as a wife ravished with the intense love of the only Perfect Husband. We are to live as those who anticipate and welcome the progressive enthronement of the reign of grace in our hearts—knowing that the process isn't always easy or pretty.

May we learn to submit to the disruptions in our lives—to the providential fissures created in our souls, the earthquakes that rattle our foolish foundations, the grenades rolled under our tottering coping mechanisms, to the words of prophets who ask us to unveil our faces and throw down our fig leaves. For our Father purposes a grand crop—oaks of righteousness as a display of his splendor.

Face-to-Face

Coming face to face with me in the mirrors God provides is not *easy*, but it is becoming *good.* I own Paul's great promise with you, "Now we see but a poor reflection as in a mirror; then we shall see face to face. Now I know in part; then I shall know fully, even as I am fully known"

(1 Cor. 13:12). This is a season of the already and the not yet. Our face-to-face relationship with God is not *today* everything it will be *one Day.*

Knowing and being known is an essential part of our growth, only to be completed when Jesus returns. As I make myself vulnerable in the chapters of this book, I invite you to do the same. I have more than one secret that has served to fill my closet with veils and fig leaves of posing and unbelief.

Why make yourself vulnerable to the unveiled face of Jesus? Because as Frederick Buechner says,

> It is important to tell at least from time to time the secret of who we truly and fully are—even if we tell it only to ourselves—because otherwise we run the risk of losing track of who we truly and fully are and little by little come to accept instead the highly edited version which we put forth in hope that the world will find it more acceptable than the real thing.[3]

I'm bored with the highly edited version of me that I try to present to the world, and I am tired of boring others as well. Let's give ourselves with abandon to the reign of grace, for *one* Day—maybe not too long from now—"*They will see his face,* and his name will be on their foreheads. There will be no more night. They will not need the light of a lamp or the light of the sun, for the Lord God will give them light. And they will reign for ever and ever" (Rev. 22:4–5).

And seeing him, "we shall be like him, for we shall see him as he is. Everyone who has this hope in him purifies himself, just as he is pure" (1 John 3:2–3).

Do you know what the most FREQUENT command in the Bible turns out to be? What instruction, what *order* is given, again and again, by God, by angels, by Jesus, by prophets and apostles? What do you think—"Be good"? "BE HOLY, for I am holy"? Or, negatively, "Don't sin"? "Don't be immoral"? No. The most frequent command in the Bible is: "*Don't be afraid.* DON'T BE AFRAID. FEAR NOT. DON'T BE AFRAID."

N. T. WRIGHT

I AM THE LORD, WHO *heals* YOU.

—EXODUS 15:26

THE SON OF *righteousness* WILL RISE WITH HEALING IN ITS WINGS. AND YOU WILL GO OUT AND LEAP LIKE CALVES *released* FROM THE STALL.

—MALACHI 4:2

The healing path does not lead DIRECTLY to healing, but to engagement. First, we are called by God into *relationship* with him. We are also called into service for him. To SERVE God is to bring our story to him and allow our life themes to make God's story *known* to others….A radical life begins with the premise that I exist for God and for his PURPOSES, not my own.

Dan ALLENDER

CHAPTER FOUR

Shalomed by *Grace—the* GOAL OF HEALING

Studying the Book of Malachi was like finding a UPS package at my front door marked "Time Sensitive" and addressed to me. Try to imagine opening such a box, lifting the flaps, and then—much to your surprise—having your den fill up with an ever expanding inflatable balloon in the shape of a huge heart like those in Macy's Christmas parade. If your mind's eye envisions something messier than pretty, you're on track.

The timing of my study proved to be no mere coincidence. It marked the one-year anniversary of my first visit to my mom's grave, my fifteenth anniversary as senior pastor of Christ Community Church, and my twenty-ninth wedding anniversary to Darlene. Throw into that mix a recent back surgery for my ruptured L5-S1 disk.

The intersection (or collision) of the pain and joy, despair and hope of these four memorials provided the arena in which the sweet phrase "growing in grace" took on a whole new bittersweet meaning.

The catharsis that came from my first visit to Mom's grave and the resulting connection with Dad was *huge.* Truly, it was a major grace visitation, a healing event of seismic proportions. But life, marriage, work, and my body were all screaming, "You're a sick man!" The congregation I had led for fifteen years loved the grace of the gospel, yet we were more notorious for *resisting legalism* than for *loving obedience*—largely a consequence of my preaching.

Of all things, it was the journey of rehabbing from back surgery that proved to be one of my most powerful instructors. I learned again that there is no growing in grace without groaning in grace.

"Scotty, do you want to get out of pain, or do you want your back to work properly? I can give you a little more cortisone and Celebrex, and we can see if that works; but my hunch is, and your MRI is very clear, we oughta go ahead and schedule surgery." With those words from my dear friend and "orthopod," Dr. Paul Thomas, a microdisectomy was performed on my ruptured L5-S1 disk in my lower back, within three weeks of that second visit to Mom's grave. That was more than coincidence.

I am so thick and slow to learn that God seems to have to place me in several schools simultaneously for me to get the point he is trying to make! Inner-heart surgery and back surgery have a lot in common. For me, they have both brought huge "healing moments," rigorous rehabilitation, and an ongoing challenge to examine what I want most out of life.

My back surgery went great. With Paul assisting, Mike McNamara, a microsurgery specialist at the Bone and Joint Clinic, did an excellent piece of work. But that was just the beginning of the process.

"Get your rear end in here, Scotty. We've got work to do." Known for his fun, good heart, and skill, the head of my physical therapy program was Hal Henninger, who also happens to be one of our elders at Christ Community.

For the next three months, Hal forced me over and over to think in terms of what I really wanted out of my physical therapy—relief for my pain or the ability to run, lift, play golf, and enjoy so many other things for which a healthy back is required.

There were days when all I could think of was relief—even if it meant never swinging a golf club again. On such days, when I went to see Hal, all I wanted was heat pads, electrical stimulation, and assurance that I was a brave boy. Ha!

I never did get any of those sessions. "Scotty, are you doing your exercises at home? If you don't do what I tell you, you'll regret it later, and I don't want you to come crying to me about how stiff you are. Your surgery went great, but we've got a ton of work to do. What do you want, and how badly do you want it?" Thank you, Mr. Delicate.

Many times my physical therapy hurt worse than the pain I felt *before* surgery. How can the cure be worse than the disease? And the same has proven true as I continue counseling and working on my heart issues.

But I have to ask myself, What do I want in my relationship with God and others, and how badly do I want it? Do I want to be in a recovery group more than I want to recover? Am I on a healing path with no destination in view? Do I want to be told what a brave boy I am, or do I want to grow as a man?

When *healing* experiences become the main theme of the life of faith as opposed to *healthy living,* we begin to think of God more as a cheerleader and recovery group leader than a surgeon and lovingly firm physical therapist.

Though anchored to a peace like I'd never known, the not-so-tame rivers of God's providence were converging, carrying me into uncharted waters of reflection and growth. I found myself thinking, if not praying: *This stinks! Why can't I just savor being reconciled to my dad for a while? Why can't I just enjoy listening to you sing and enjoy your delight? Don't you see how people are getting encouraged as I share what you've done? Why do you have to complicate everything right now, Lord? Just leave me alone to tell my healing story.*

I'm really not that stupid, but I am that self-centered. Though I wasn't surprised at God's agenda, I hated his sense of timing. God made it clear that he was far more interested in developing Christlike character in me than simply giving me a nice cushion of spiritual comfort and a "healing story" to share with others.

From Healing to Healthy Living

What then is involved in the journey of moving from healing to health? First of all, it's important to remember the goal, or end, of all healing. Our hearts have been healed so that we can *love* more freely and fully. Jesus summarized the demands of God's law, revealed in the Old Testament, with two commandments: We are to love the Lord our God with all of our mind, soul, heart, and strength and to love our neighbors as ourselves. In essence, Jesus defined sin as any failure to love God perfectly—by worshiping him, delighting in him, and obeying him in thought, word, deed, and attitude. Sin is also any failure to love others in word, thought, deed, and attitude—as God has demanded. We are diseased to the degree that we fail to love.

Second, health means living in *proper alignment*—in light of God's original design. The healthiest people who ever lived, besides Jesus, were Adam and Eve. They were healthy in the sense that everything about their inner person was righteous—in right order or proper alignment. They were *congruent:* cognition, emotion, and volition all lined up with each other—all were fully engaged with God and his will.

As God's image bearers, each part of their being operated as designed, and each part worked in perfect harmony with all the other parts. The same is true of their physical bodies. They were at peace, or "peace-full," for the concepts of health and peace are virtually identical in the Bible. Peace, or *shalom,* doesn't represent the absence of noise or conflict, but rather, the right ordering of all things—the proper alignment of our entire being.

SIN—THE VANDALISM OF SHALOM

Perfect health, like peace, was forfeited through the introduction of the reign of sin and death. Every aspect of our being, along with everything in the created world, is infected. The shalom of every relationship and the health of the whole world has been violated. Hostility has replaced peace. Therefore, to be in the healing journey requires that we take sin and death very seriously.

Before we go any further, let's reflect a few moments on the very notion of "sin." *If we are wrong about sin, then it will be impossible to be right about grace.* "Sin," like many other important theological concepts, has suffered at the hands of superficial stereotypes, unbiblical caricatures, cultural pundits, and, well…sinners.

The most helpful description of sin I have found comes from author and theologian Cornelius Plantinga Jr., president of Calvin Theological Seminary. He refers to sin as *the vandalism of shalom*—the culpable spoiling of the perfections of God's original creation and the repudiation of his plan of redemption. Thus, sin is always relational (against God) and irrational (corruption of the good, true, and beautiful).

> The webbing together of God, humans, and all creation in justice, fulfillment, and delight is what the Hebrew prophet's call *shalom.* We call it peace, but it means far more than mere peace of mind or a cease-fire between enemies. In the Bible, shalom means *universal flourishing, wholeness, and delight*—a rich state of affairs in which natural needs are satisfied and natural gifts fruitfully employed, a state of affairs that inspires joyful wonder as its Creator and Savior opens doors and welcomes the creatures in whom he delights. Shalom, in other words, is the way things ought to be….
>
> God hates sin not just because it violates his law but, more substantively, because it violates shalom, because it breaks the peace, because it interferes with the way things are supposed to be. God is

> for shalom and therefore against sin. In fact, we may safely describe evil as any spoiling of shalom, whether physically (e.g., by disease), morally, spiritually, or otherwise. In short, sin is culpable shalom-breaking....In sum, shalom is God's design for creation and redemption; sin is blamable human vandalism of these great realities and therefore an affront to their architect and builder.[1]

Sin spoils everything! It breaks the peace of God and in its place brings *perversion, pollution,* and *disintegration.*

Sin *perverts* God's perfect design by twisting it to serve an unworthy end. For example, the appropriate longing for sex is perverted when it is aimed at the wrong object (a child or someone who is not our spouse) or when it is indulged in disproportionately to God's design (leading to addiction).

Sin *pollutes* God's design when it defiles something clean and good by introducing a foreign element. Infidelity pollutes marriage, just as idolatry pollutes worship, and consumerism pollutes stewardship.

Sin *disintegrates* God's original design (shalom) by breaking down what God intended to be whole—a family, a church, the environment, or a heart. Thus, the cry of the psalmist, "Give me an *undivided* heart, that I may fear your name" (Ps. 86:11). "Disintegration is always deterioration, the prelude and postlude to death."[2]

Disease is one of the metaphors used in the Bible to describe the nature and destructive power of sin. The disease of sin is both something we inherited by nature and something we willingly choose to participate in and share with others. We are slaves to sin, and we are voluntary sinners. We are both victims and agents. We are by nature, objects of wrath, and by choice, wrathful subjects.

Though we are made for shalom, we willingly settle for what we usually call *peace.* Generally speaking, we define *peace* as an emotion of contentment based on having enough of certain good things (money, love, a great golf game, an enjoyable job, obedient children, adulation from peers), and being protected from negative things (physical harm, a call from the IRS, life in a nursing home, a diagnosis of cancer, high maintenance family members or employees).

Jesus made a clear distinction between the peace he came to bring and the peace the world offers us. "Peace I leave with you; my peace I give you. I do not give to you as the world gives" (John 14:27a). The peace the world gives is merely a feeling of contentment (control, safety, security) based on having certain things and certain guarantees. It has to do with eliminating or controlling self-centered fears by whatever means possible. The peace Jesus gives is a state of wholeness based on becoming the man or woman God designed me to be. It has to do with living in the fear of God (an affectionate reverence and surrender), by the grace of God, to the glory of God.

Jesus continues to teach us that "peace" is a heart issue and a fear issue: "Do not let your hearts be troubled and do not be afraid" (John 14:27b). This is why, right before revealing the wonderful promise of the coming Prince of Peace and the perpetual increase of his government and peace (shalom) (Isa. 9:6–7), God warned his people: "Do not fear what they fear, and do not dread it. The LORD Almighty is the one you are to regard as holy, he is the one you are to fear…and he will be a sanctuary…a stone…and a rock" (Isa. 8:12–14).

The disease of sin affects every function of what the Bible defines as the *heart:* cognition, emotion, and volition. What's wrong with us? We lack perfect "hygiene" (Greek for *soundness,* i.e., wholeness, health) in our thinking, feeling, and choosing. And we also fear (live in awe of, worship, give power to) the wrong things.

Because our thinking, feeling, and choosing are all contaminated with sin, we are constantly on the outlook for some god(s) to provide us with what we think we must have in order to experience peace. But as we have seen, the biblical concept of peace (shalom), is not a matter of *having*, but of *wholeness*—not an issue of *getting* what our foolish hearts demand, but of *becoming* what our gracious God has designed us to be. There is a HUGE difference between *the quest for having* and *the calling to wholeness.*

In reality, *wholeness* (shalom) quite often leads to the opposite of having; it leads to divesting—to denying self, to generosity, to decreasing so Jesus will increase. The more our mind, emotions, and will are *whole,* the more we will think with the mind of Christ, feel with the heart of Jesus, and make choices primarily centered on the glory of God. In short, we will love as Jesus loves us.

THE RECOVERY OF SHALOM

Our individual healing journey toward the recovery of shalom is a long path whose destination is always Jesus. Progress is not measured in terms of the distance you have traveled, but rather in terms of greater freedom to love God and others. The travel guide consists of several recurring questions with which we must repeatedly wrestle, rather than sequential road markers we can simply check off. We don't move from these questions onto others, just deeper into the same probes.

- How do I define peace? As the contentment of having certain things or the journey of becoming whole?
- Where is the absence of health, or shalom, most pronounced in my life? In what relationships?
- Where does incongruency show up in my life? Where am I most out of alignment? In my thinking? In my feeling? In my choosing?
- What am I most afraid of in life? To whom or what have I given ultimate power over my heart?
- How have I been wounded, and what have I done with the pain?
- Who has wounded me, and what have I done with their failure in love?

- Whom have I wounded, and what have I done with my failure in love?
- What have I done with Jesus, God's provision for sin and death?
- How have I tried to be my own healer and savior? What idols and substances have I chosen for deliverance? What dependencies or addictions have resulted?
- With whom am I walking in healing community? To whom am I accountable for continually asking these questions until Jesus returns?

Isaiah's promise of the coming of the Prince of Peace was dramatically fulfilled with the first coming of Jesus. Paul presents Jesus as "our peace" (Eph. 2:14–18). He is the destroyer of hostility and the maker of shalom. Jesus' three-year healing ministry was a down payment on the eternal healing Jesus will bring at his second coming. Indeed, our wounds are healed by his; his punishment frees us from ours and brings the shalom for which we have been made (Isa. 53:5).

The Progression of Peace

God has lavished his grace upon us not merely to heal diseased sinners and bring them into heaven when they die, but also to bring heaven into the hearts of healthy believers while we yet live!

God's peace—through the triumphant reign of grace—progressively dethrones and dismantles the paralyzing dominion of sin and death! Remember, in speaking of Jesus, Isaiah said, "Of the increase of his government and peace [shalom] there will be no end" (Isa. 9:7). Jesus' peaceful kingdom is increasing incrementally and will be so until the consummation of the fullness of his kingdom. Purpose to be aware of where you are in the journey to perfected shalom. The more clearly you understand the basic movements of *the gospel of peace* (Eph. 6:15), the better.

The reign of grace unto shalom (health, wholeness) begins in our *justification,* with a change in our status: Condemned sinners receive the imputation of Christ's righteousness and are thus declared righteous in God's sight. God is at peace with us, and we are at peace with him.

The reign of grace unto shalom (health, wholeness) continues in our *sanctification,* with a progressive change in our nature: Justified sinners receive the impartation of Christ's righteousness by faith, through the work of the Holy Spirit. The peace of Christ increasingly rules as an umpire in our hearts (Col. 3:15) and grows as an evidence of the Spirit's fruit (Gal. 5:22), while "the God of peace" makes us more and more like Jesus (1 Thess. 5:23).

The reign of grace unto shalom (health, wholeness) will be completed at the second coming of Jesus, in our *glorification:* Justified sinners are instantaneously made to be perfectly righteous, like Jesus. Every violation of shalom will be redeemed. Every desire, even temptation to sin, will be eliminated. We will live forever in perfect relationships, loving and being loved as God designed.

The Road Less Traveled

My journey toward health has taken me places I would never have chosen to go. I understand more than ever what my spiritual dad, Jack Miller, meant when he described the growth under the reign of grace with two "cheer ups." "Cheer up! You're a whole lot worse off than you ever thought! Cheer up! You're much more desired, loved, and cherished than you ever dreamed or hoped." The path to the second cheer up always leads through the first—always. *This,* truly, is the road less traveled. The greater the acknowledgment of our disease, the richer the experience of our Deliverer will become.

So what's the distinction between healing moments and healthy living? It's the difference between enjoying God's singing and actually risking getting onto the dance floor with him. I hope you dance.

What's a BAD marriage? It's a "tick-on-a-dog" relationship—
only with *two* ticks and no dog.

Larry CRABB

HOW BEAUTIFUL YOU ARE, MY DARLING! OH, HOW *beautiful!*

—SONG OF SONGS 4:1

And now, at the end of the story, HE is the bridegroom, the one for whom *we* have longed without knowing it, the one for whom we are made, THE ONE whose love for us is like the sun, and all our *earthly* loves mere reflecting moons.

N. T. WRIGHT

MARRIAGE will either drive you *crazy* or to Christ.

ANONYMOUS

THE MAN SAID, "THE WOMAN YOU PUT HERE WITH ME—SHE *gave* ME SOME FRUIT FROM THE TREE, AND I ATE IT."

—GENESIS 3:13

CHAPTER FIVE

The King *Takes* A BRIDE

In between e-mails, I couldn't help but notice, yet again, *They look so happy, so young, so ready to take on the world...I wonder...* Gracing my home office with magnetic power, a fading eight-by-ten-inch picture of Mom and Dad on their wedding day continues to beg for answers. If Mom were alive, their next anniversary would be their sixtieth. It's been nearly three years now since Dad and I shared coffee, hearts, and tears at the Brentwood McDonald's while looking at another, smaller Kodak chronicle of the first day of their all-too-brief marriage. That day remains one of the most important days of my life.

What did they talk about? What were their dreams? What were they like when all alone? Wanting to "go there," I've been slow to risk more vulnerability without guarantees—sure evidence of a heart pumping with fear rather than faith. After all, one good emotional encounter with your dad in hand is worth two "in the bush," right? Not really, not when the bush is covered with flower buds rather than thorns.

The recovery of shalom in my life is propelling me to study "family photos" and stories in greater detail. The reign of grace no longer allows me to call ignorance an ally or self-protection a friend. Knowing more about my family system and the formative events in the lives of my closest relatives is a high priority. There appears to be a vital connection between entering the stories of one's parents, siblings, spouse, and children and the freedom to love them better. Indeed, to move from piecemeal living to the peace of healing requires the heart to risk the pain and joy that come from knowing and being known.

When Dad's "I love you too" disrupted the equilibrium of my controlled world, it also ignited my appetite to learn more about his relationship with Mom. And the second visit to Mom's grave provided sufficient motivation to press "further up and further in," to begin asking some of the questions for which I knew there were stories and answers—and many were contained in a small, leather world.

Senseless and Insensibility

I cautiously pushed the latches on the handsome little suitcase that had been collecting dust under a drop-leaf table. It contained old family photographs, mostly featuring Mom, but also a ribbon-tied bundle of love letters. The letters are an invaluable collection of Mom and Dad's handwritten correspondence between the years of 1941 and 1946. During this period Dad graduated from the Merchant Marines Academy, near Los Angeles, and began his service as a commissioned officer and navigator of huge tanker ships. The dates place his service during WWII. But that is not all that happened during this tumultuous stretch in world history.

Mom and Dad got married on September 15, 1943. Simple math will tell you, I had in my possession a precious chronicle of the planting, budding, and blooming of my parent's wartime romance and marriage. But here's the irony, no really, the insanity of the situation. Though I treasured *having* these letters, I had avoided *reading* them for so long. How senseless and insensible is that? If you need a good example of the difference between "having" and "wholeness" (à la chapter 4), here it is!

But everything changed when I pulled one end of the little blue bow that neatly held the letters in bundled form. It was as though I opened the cage on a roaring lion! The power of these letters is irrepressible. Smiles gave way to tears as I could see Dad giving more and more of his heart to Mom as his expressions of love moved from tentative hope to settled confidence. Here's a "PG" rated sample of his tender heart for a great lady. I'll keep and treasure the more intimate expressions for myself! Note the dates and the historical development of their relationship.

October 1941

> *Hello Martha. May I renew an old pen-ship acquaintance? Silly of me to think you might still answer my letters, but I hope so anyway.*
>
> *Goo bye,*
> *Thomas A. Smith*

November 1942

> *My Dear Martha. A few lines to show I think of you every minute. Today I'm in one of those depressed moods. Am so anxious to ship, I'm just fidgety. Wish I had some of your company for a while…or for always. Martha—just what do I mean to you? You sign your letters "love," and you call me "darling." You must like me or you wouldn't say these things. I could never hope that you might love me.*
>
> *Lovingly,*
> *Tom*

June 1943

> *Darling Martha. Anything you want to do about our engagement and marriage is OK by me. Read someplace that girls like to do those things up big—besides you're just married once. I hope. Don't worry*

if I'm not back in three months. I have something to come back for and, believe me, I'll swim back if I have to.

Always yours,

Tom

November 1943

My Dearest. Darling, I'd give most anything for another day with you before we go, but of course there are plenty of them in the future. Nothing like the present, though, is there?

I love you now and always,

Tom

December 1944

Dearest Martha. Martha, you are growing to be part of me more and more every day. Without you now, life would be so empty. I never realized you would be such an inspirational helpmate. You are in all my hopes for the future.

All my love,

Tom

April 1945

Dearest Martha. I received your eleventh letter today. What has come over you? Don't you know that letters from you make me love you more, and if I love you more, I'll die. Seriously, I thank you very much.

All my love,

Tom

October 1946

My Dearest Wife. My dear, I wish I could put into words how much I love you and need you. Now that I have you, you are my most prized possession. Providence has really given me the best things in life, a wife who is for me and loves me. Who could ask for more?

Love,

Tom

You can imagine what an emotionally moving and enriching experience it has been for me to study Dad's letters to Mom. I love Dad more than ever and long to see that part of his heart reengaged. I miss Mom more than ever, even as my hope is fueled to see her again one Day.

But the *greatest* benefit I've received from exploring the story of my parents' romance has been to be driven into another Romance—the storied and stormy love affair between God and his Bride. As we find our face in *that* family photo, *that* wedding picture, rehabilitation becomes re-creation, and the greatest Love Story gives meaning to all others!

Reading Mom and Dad's letters in chronological order has reconfirmed the wonder, privilege, and importance of experiencing the Bible as the unfolding of the most glorious wartime romance of all time. God has graciously covenanted to wage war against sin, death, and the devil to secure the hand and heart of a wife to cherish forever. *This* is the Story in which we must find our faces and risk more pain and more joy. Peace, shalom, wholeness can be found no other way!

That which we find so magnetic in great love stories and the intimacy we desperately long for in our own marriages (and a variety of affairs) can be found only in relationship with God.

Indeed, Genesis 1:1 through Revelation 22:21 is an alluring and trustworthy collection of intimate love letters, recorded and kept for us in mint condition. As we read and study the whole "suitcase full" (from cover to cover!) of God's love letters, we find Jesus increasingly revealed as the Bridegroom who has come into the world because of incomparable love for his Bride, the Church. He is the Great Lover who has lived, fought, and died to guarantee his own Wedding Day. Let's use sense and sensibility and untie the bow and let the Lion out.

"Arise, My Darling"

Most biblical scholars believe "the Kingdom of God" to be the prevailing and unifying theme connecting all sixty-six diverse books of the Bible as chapters in one great story—"God's people living in God's place under God's rule." I agree, but this *great* story becomes a *glorious* story when we experience the King of the Kingdom as the Bridegroom of a Bride. *We* have been chosen as the Wife-Queen of Jesus. To live under the dominion of the Kingdom is to live under the reign of grace, and to live under the reign of grace is to live the rest of our lives in anticipation of our Wedding Day!

Hear God's impassioned declarations of marital love as they begin to emerge in the Old Testament: "Your Maker is your husband—the LORD Almighty is his name—the Holy One" (Isa. 54:5). "As a bridegroom rejoices over his bride, so will your God rejoice over you" (Isa. 62:5). "'In that day,' declares the LORD, 'you will call me "my husband"; you will no longer call me "my master"'" (Hos. 2:16). "I gave you my solemn oath and entered into a covenant with you, declares the Sovereign LORD, and you became mine" (Ezek. 16:8).

What an image! Our Holy God has said to the ill-deserving ones, Out of all the people in the whole world, I have chosen you to be a Bride—my Bride! I entered into the covenant of marriage with you. Let these words go deep—"And you became mine!" Our Bridegroom awaits to ravish you and change you. To us, individually and corporately, God says with joy, "Arise, my darling, my beautiful one, and come with me" (Song of Songs 2:10). The intent and intensity of this love affair grow clearer and more compelling as we read through the Bible—just like in my dad's letters to Mom.

Living As Jesus' Wife

Jesus' love for his Bride emerges as the central story in the history of redemption. This being so, the implications for how we view the "institution" of marriage are *huge*—even cosmic and eternal. Marriage was *never* designed to be an end unto itself—rather, it is a living parable, an open-air drama, a magnetic allegory...of the archetype of all marriages—Jesus' relationship with his Wife, the Church. Thus, it is incumbent upon us to reconsider how we customarily understand and apply the various scriptures on marriage found in the Bible.

My generation was often guilty of turning Paul's writings on marriage (for instance, Eph. 5:22–33) into dogmatic assertions about the roles of husbands and wives and endless debates over the nature and limits of a wife's submission. But one of Paul's *main* points in this text, that usually goes unnoticed, is the primary role that *every* Christian has been given—to live as the wife of Jesus. Collectively as the church, we are the Bride of Christ—males and females alike.

Our willing and unquestioned submission to Jesus, beloved Wife to perfect Husband, is to be manifested "in everything" (Eph. 5:24). In fact, this is the best way to understand how the delights of God's love relate to the demands of his love—to ponder the wondrous dimensions of our marriage to Jesus. As a cherished wife, we live for the pleasure of our magnificent Lover.

Human Marriage Symbolizes Christ's Marriage to the Church

Listen to what the apostle Paul is *really* saying in these words:

> Husbands, love your wives, just *as Christ loved the church* and gave himself up for her to make her holy, cleansing her by the washing with water through the word, and *to present her to himself* as a radiant church, without stain or wrinkle or any other blemish, but holy and blameless. In this same way, husbands ought to love

> their wives as their own bodies. He who loves his wife loves himself. After all, no one ever hated his own body, but he feeds and cares for it, just *as Christ does the church*—for we are members of his body. "For this reason a man will leave his father and mother and be united to his wife, and the two will become one flesh." *This is a profound mystery—but I am talking about Christ and the church.* However, each one of you also must love his wife as he loves himself, and the wife must respect her husband. (Eph. 5:25–33)

A passage that is used almost exclusively to convict and motivate Christian men to love their wives (a worthy concern, by the way) has a *far* more profound meaning within the reign of grace. Pastor-professor Ray Ortlund Jr. writes,

> Paul is the one who lifts the hermeneutical capstone into place by revealing openly what our intuitions may have suspected all along, *viz* that *marriage from the beginning was meant to be a tiny social platform on which the love of Christ for his church and the church's responsiveness to him could be put on visible display.* Human marriage is finally divulged to be emblematic of Christ and the church in covenant, destined to live together not as "one flesh" for a lifetime in this world but as "one spirit" for eternity in a new heaven and a new earth. (Italics added by author for emphasis.)[1]

Think about the implications of this for Christian men who desire to become a good husband. *A man is as prepared to be a husband to his wife as he is committed to living as a wife to Jesus.* Think about it!

Why Marriage Is So Sacred

From creation on, each period in the history of redemption has declared this profound mystery and majesty of marriage. Ray Ortlund Jr. continues,

> Theologically, the biblical story explains why Christian doctrine calls for marriage to be "held in honour among all," and the marriage bed

> to be "undefiled" (Heb. 13:4). Among all, men and women, married and single, the institution of marriage is to be honoured and its sexual parameters carefully observed. Why? Because marriage bespeaks a higher reality—the love of Christ for his church, and her joyful deference to him—and is itself enriched by what it bespeaks....This is the real reason why premarital sex is wrong; it toys with the biblical mystery. The moral imperative is concerned with more than the folly of risking a sexually transmitted disease. God offers a theological rationale in Christ. This is why extramarital sex is wrong; it violates the mystery. This is why same-sex marriages are wrong; they pervert the mystery....The gospel tells the story of God's pursuing, faithful, wounded, angry, overruling, transforming, triumphant love. And it calls us to answer him with a love which cleanses our lives of all spiritual whoredom.[2]

Perhaps now we can better understand God's extreme alarm and hurt when he spoke these words though Malachi:

> Judah has broken faith. A detestable thing has been committed in Israel and in Jerusalem: Judah has desecrated the sanctuary the LORD loves, by marrying the daughter of a foreign god. As for the man who does this, whoever he may be, may the LORD cut him off from the tents of Jacob—even though he brings offerings to the LORD Almighty.
>
> Another thing you do: You flood the LORD's altar with tears. You weep and wail because he no longer pays attention to your offerings or accepts them with pleasure from your hands. You ask, "Why?" It is because the LORD is acting as the witness between you and the wife of your youth, because you have broken faith with her, though she is your partner, the wife of your marriage covenant.
>
> Has not the LORD made them one? In flesh and spirit they are his. And why one? Because he was seeking godly offspring. So guard yourself in your spirit, and do not break faith with the wife of your youth.

> "I hate divorce," says the LORD God of Israel, "and I hate a man's covering himself with violence as well as with his garment," says the LORD Almighty.
>
> So guard yourself in your spirit, and do not break faith. (Mal. 2:11–16)

Why was God so upset about the perversion of marriage in Jerusalem? Because it was an utter misrepresentation of his relationship with his people. Marriage is not to be treated lightly nor is divorce to happen easily. Why? *Primarily* because God created marriage to be the clearest representation of the relationship he has freely chosen to have with his covenant people. Marriage is to demonstrate the beauty, wonder, and power of the gospel.

JESUS' BEST MAN

As the last book in the Old Testament, Malachi clearly affirms the whole history of redemption as a story of unspeakable grace—that of a Perfect Lover passionately loving his people while patiently enduring their foolishness. Though the demands of his love required painful seasons in the relationship, God remained faithful to and passionate about his covenant wife.

As Malachi concluded his writing, it would be four hundred years before more news of this great romance would be revealed. But the next time God spoke, he *shouted!* With the coming of the Messiah, prophetic hints of where the relationship was heading would give way to the profuse hope of fulfillment. The shadow of old-covenant symbol would give way to the substance of the new-covenant reality.

However, before the Royal Bridegroom would arrive, Malachi promised that a "messenger" would come first. "'See, I will send my messenger, who will prepare the way before me. Then suddenly the

Lord you are seeking will come to his temple; the messenger of the covenant, whom you desire, will come,' says the LORD Almighty" (Mal. 3:1). As an important statement about continuity within the history of redemption, the forerunner of the new covenant was given an old-covenant identity, "See, I will send you the prophet Elijah before that great and dreadful day of the LORD comes" (Mal. 4:5).

Jesus affirmed that Malachi was speaking of John the Baptist in these promises. Referring to John, Jesus said, "This is the one about whom it is written: 'I will send my messenger ahead of you, who will prepare your way before you.'...And if you are willing to accept it, he is the Elijah who was to come" (Matt. 11:10, 14). This isn't reincarnation but a reaffirmation of God's faithfulness to his covenant. John was born, as promised, and emerged as a rather unique character in the unfolding story of the reign of grace.

We usually envision John eating grasshoppers and pulling Roman soldiers off of horses, while demanding repentance for treason against God's Kingdom. But the real power and joy in John's ministry lay elsewhere. The most telling and tender aspect of John's ministry is usually overlooked. Hear his own words: "You yourselves can testify that I said, 'I am not the Christ but am sent ahead of him.' The bride belongs to the bridegroom. The friend who attends the bridegroom waits and listens for him, and is full of joy when he hears the bridegroom's voice. That joy is mine, and it is now complete. He must become greater; I must become less" (John 3:28–30).

What role did John play in his transitional moment in the reign of grace? He was the friend of the Bridegroom! John saw himself in the story as Jesus' "best man"—the main attendant who gladly does everything in his power to serve the groom's purposes in getting ready for his wedding! John understood that Jesus was coming for a Bride, not merely to create a new political, social, and economic order for Israel.

He realized that this marriage carried implications for the whole world and the entire history of mankind!

John's "great adventure" in life was defined by the sacred romance, the true meaning of history, the greatest story line in the Bible—the reign of grace! Of course, the best man gladly decreased so the fame, renown, and glory of the Bridegroom would increase. John spotted his face and knew his place in the Wedding Story. Do we? Do you?

Now, perhaps, we can begin to appreciate the profound prophetic significance of Jesus' first public miracle—and the well-chosen stage on which it took place. Surely, it was no mere coincidence that Jesus turned water into wine at a wedding as the first deposit on his commitment to "shalom" the universe! (John 2:1–11).

The Bridegroom is here! A wedding is where I belong. It's time to prepare your hearts for a great celebration, for I have come to live and die for my Bride. This wine is the first fruit of my future Wedding Day—but more importantly, it's the symbol of my coming death.

For the next three years of his life, Jesus was, in essence, consumed with wedding preparations. Nothing could distract or dissuade him from his reason for coming into our world—the same is true for him today. The mystery and majesty of Jesus' relationship with the Church will be fulfilled when he returns for his Bride. On that Day every other marriage will cease to exist, except One. Even now our hearts should begin to cry out, Hallelujah! We should begin immediately to consider the implications of the glorious truth.

The Only Marriage Made in Heaven

Surely there is profound significance to the fact that the only marriage that will exist in the new heaven and the new earth is the one between Jesus and his Wife, the Church. Indeed, we must consider how our marriages, and our relationships in the church, can more faithfully showcase the delights and demands of Jesus' love for his covenant wife. Let's join John the Baptist's example and gladly choose this story to be the great adventure that gives meaning to the rest of our days in this world.

In summary: God's reign of grace isn't a free meal ticket to heaven for people who invite Jesus into their hearts. It's the Bridegroom's costly pursuit, dowry, invitation, and proposal to a wedding feast and marriage—*our own!* It's the guarantee that this quintessential romance is not merely a spiritual metaphor but the ultimate transforming reality.

The reign of grace is the developing drama of the *only* marriage made in heaven—revealed in bud form in the Old Testament, brought to blossom in the New Testament, but awaiting full bouquet when Jesus returns for his Bride. God doesn't have an Old Testament "wife of his youth" and a newer, New Testament version. He has *one* Bride—the Church comprised of the old and new covenant communities—chosen from every nation and called from every century. God isn't into polygamy! This is why understanding the covenantal relationship between Israel and the Church is so important.

I treasure each dated letter Dad sent Mom because one story is told in many interrelated parts. Likewise with the Bible—what the divine Husband said in the past to one part of his covenant Bride, he has spoken for the benefit of every part of his one, true love interest. This means that all the steamy love language of the Song of Songs is ours! Along with expressing the intimacy and passion God designed to be shared between a husband and wife, Song of Songs is a profound revelation of the romantic drama between Christ and the Church.

But as the Church, we are also responsible to apply the stinging rebukes spoken by prophets like Hosea, Jeremiah, Ezekiel, and Malachi. When *we* live indifferently or unfaithfully to our Perfect Husband, we are no less guilty than the Church in the Old Testament. *The love of God sings, consoling us; and the love of God stings, convicting us.*

Therefore, let's press on—"further up and further in"—and join the nations in proving, as Isaac Watts put it, "the glories of His righteousness, and wonders of His love." Indeed, Jesus rules the world with grace and truth, and our King has made himself our Husband.

Further Up *and* Further In

Our Big Fat *Wedding* to Jesus

A Study of a Jewish Wedding

Blowing away all prerelease projections, a summer sleeper has now earned the status of living classic. *My Big Fat Greek Wedding* came along like the perfect scratch for an ever present heart itch. Filmed on a tiny five-million-dollar budget, it has now grossed over two hundred and sixty million, making it the highest-grossing independent film of all time and the highest-grossing romantic comedy ever.

What explains this film's power to grab hold of our insides and not let go? Reviews and opinions abound, but after my third viewing (I'm a little slow), I've drawn a few conclusions of my own. The story line presents enough hints and symbols of the gospel to do a lot more than merely entertain us. It invites us, even compels us to acknowledge our longing for love, courtship, and a wedding like that between Ian Miller, a tall, handsome WASP-y vegetarian, and Toula Portokalos, a thirty-year-old Greek woman, who smelled like garlic bread and still worked at her father's restaurant, Dancing Zorba's.

The exciting news is that the beautiful symbols of *My Big Fat Greek Wedding* are experienced in far greater substance through our Big Fat Wedding to Jesus. As revealed in the Bible, the three parts of a traditional Jewish wedding are the betrothal, the interval, and the wedding feast. Before we look at each of these, consider a few hints of the gospel in the way Ian loved Toula.

- The wonder of an unsuspecting, insecure bride being chosen by an ideal groom: Toula is astonished that a man like Ian would desire a woman like her. One of my favorite lines in the movie occurs when Ian recounts the first time he saw Toula at Dancing Zorba's. Toula is mortified, so hoping Ian didn't realize that she was the clumsy, dorky waitress who ineptly served him. Trying to distance herself from embarrassment, she commented, "Oh that was during my frumpy stage." To which Ian responds with stunning tenderness, "Frumpy? I don't remember frumpy." Who doesn't long to be desired, frumpy and all? We can either respond to Ian's words as sentimental claptrap, unrealistic movie fodder, or find in Jesus the only groom who truly desires and accepts us as his Bride, imperfections and all. Great, indeed, should be our astonishment.

- The commitment of a groom to pay any price necessary to have his bride: Ian wanted Toula bad enough to submit to full immersion baptism into the Greek Orthodox Church. Jesus submitted to the full baptism of God's judgment upon the cross in order *to have and to hold* us forever as his Bride.
- The power of committed love to call forth beauty and dignity: As courtship led to engagement and engagement to the wedding, we watched Toula become more and more alive and beautiful in the security of Ian's love. In a much more profound way, Jesus' love calls forth our beauty and makes us alive as nothing else can.

Combine the images of an endearing courtship with our marriage to Jesus and you will be able to understand why the angel said to John the apostle, "Blessed are those who are invited to the wedding supper of the Lamb!" (Rev. 19:9). You will also understand why John fell down in adoring worship when he was given a vision of this astonishing Day (Rev. 19:10).

The threefold pattern of a Jewish wedding reveals the paradigm and rhythm of our marriage to Jesus, as it has been revealed in the Bible.

The Betrothal

The moment you became a Christian, you became the betrothed bride of Jesus. This is similar to what we call "being engaged," but far more binding. In an orthodox Jewish wedding, the betrothal includes a public announcement of the terms of the marriage and the pronouncement of God's blessing upon the relationship. From that day forward, the groom and his bride are legally husband and wife. In fact, a divorce is required to break a betrothal.

Though we wait for our wedding day, we will never be more legally married to Jesus than we are right now. Our assurance—Jesus will never divorce us. Our calling—to live as the legal wife of Jesus.

I will never forget the day I got engaged to Darlene. Everything changed—my schedule, my hopes, my plans, how I spent money, who I still called (no more dating around!). How much more so is this to be the case in our relationship with Jesus! Everything is supposed to change. God has already given you to his Son as his legal wife! Just how definitive of a break with the *single life* did you make when you trusted Jesus to be your Savior and received him as your Husband?

The Interval

This period extends between the betrothal and the wedding feast. For us, it lasts from the first day we met Jesus until he returns. During the interval, the groom pays the dowry to the father of the bride. This happened, once and for all, when Jesus died for us on the cross. What a dowry! "Christ loved the church and gave himself up for her to make her holy" (Eph. 5:25–26). It cost Jesus his life to receive you as a part of his beloved cherished Bride.

During the interval, the couple commits to a life of faithfulness and preparation. Though not engaging in sexual intercourse, it is a season of ever increasing intimacy, fellowship, and communion as the day for the wedding feast draws closer. Understandably, such a delay and waiting period can intensify temptation and compromise. Similarly, in the reign of grace, as we wait for the day of consummation, we must diligently guard our hearts and be wise to the power of temptation.

The apostle Paul had this betrothal period in mind as he wrote to his spiritual sons and daughters in Corinth. Like John the Baptist, Paul found his important role in the great wedding story between Jesus and his Bride. He wrote to the Corinthians with the heart and concern of the father of the Bride. "I am jealous for you with a godly jealousy. I promised you to one husband, to Christ, so that I might present you as a pure virgin to him. But I am afraid that just as Eve was deceived by the serpent's cunning, your minds may somehow be led astray from your sincere and pure devotion to Christ" (2 Cor. 11:2–3).

Based on Paul's model, perhaps we would greatly benefit from reframing discipleship and spiritual formation as premarital counseling and care. To submit to the reign of grace is to live life as one getting ready for the greatest wedding ever! The interval is a time of *anticipation, preparation, temptation, reclamation,* and *procession.*

A Time of Anticipation

Once Darlene and I decided to get married in September of 1972, it got harder and harder to wait. That's why our anniversary is May 5, 1972! We ended up moving our original date forward by four months. How much more should our hearts be filled with desperate longing and painful waiting as we offer up the last prayer recorded in the Bible: "Come, Lord Jesus" (Rev. 22:20). Indeed, this is the cry of the Bride anticipating her wedding day, not a petition from impatient Christians to get "out of this mess."

Martin Luther, the great German Reformer, once commented that there were only two dates marked on his calendar, "This day and that Day," and the life in between was lived as fully as possible to the glory of his Bridegroom.

Our calling is to fill our hearts to overflowing with the beauty and love of our Jesus, as we meditate on our future life with him in the new heaven and new earth. The runaway popularity of the song "I Can Only Imagine," written and recorded by Mercy Me, demonstrates the power of allowing our hearts to become engaged and enthralled with our coming Wedding Day and marriage to the Perfect Lover and Companion. The greatest treasure that comes from pondering the Day, however, is the discovery that Jesus is thinking about and longing to be with us more than we with him. We are betrothed to one who desires us much more than we dare to believe.

A Time of Preparation

Preparing for the greatest Day of our lives involves, above everything else, nurturing a sincere and pure devotion to Christ—the very thing Paul was concerned Satan might rob from the Corinthians. Having performed a wazoo (huge number) and wide diversity of weddings, I know that there are some struggles that are endemic to all of them. But none is more pronounced than the challenge for a couple to stay focused on the relationship during the quagmire of all the decisions and detractions surrounding a wedding. Five years or five minutes from the wedding day, who is going to remember whether you served cashews or Macadamia nuts?

How do we nurture our relationship with Jesus? In a multitude of ways—but never without worship, communion, submission, and obedience to our covenant Husband. We love Jesus because he first loved us, and we obey him because we love him. Though obedience does not merit anything from God, in a most profound sense, obedience is a primary means of experiencing greater intimacy with Jesus.

"Whoever has my commands and obeys them, he is the one who loves me. He who loves me will be loved by my Father, and I too will love him and show myself to him....If anyone loves me, he will obey my teaching. My Father will love him, and we will come to him and make our home with him" (John 14:21, 23). Jesus reveals more of himself and makes himself at home with those who obey him.

In Ephesians, Paul instructed wives to submit to their husbands in all things, *just as the church submits to Christ.* Only grace can empower our obedience with the right motives. Who wouldn't commit to obey a husband who has already died and come back to life for her—one who nourishes, cherishes, and cares for her with such faithfulness and love? What does it mean to submit to Jesus as our perfect Husband in everything? On the front end, it means that we refuse to make any kind of prenuptial contract with Jesus. We hold nothing back—for he has held nothing back from us! To be married to Jesus means that you have become an heir of the whole world! How could we think in terms of loving him with less than a whole heart and mind?

Preparing for eternal intimacy with Christ also means that we become passionate about his passions. What does Jesus love? What is he preoccupied with? Certainly Jesus is where the "least and the lost" are. Certainly Jesus is declaring and demonstrating the gospel to the nations of the world. Certainly Jesus is bringing his righteousness and peace to bear where there is injustice, poverty, racism, inequity, orphans, and widows—the same concerns that Malachi addressed as failures in his own community.

Preparing for our Wedding Day requires that we become increasingly preoccupied with our Lover and with the matters of his heart. Continue to study the Scriptures to know more clearly and fully where your Husband invests his heart.

A Time of Temptation

Paul viewed the interval period in our marriage to Jesus as a season ripe for attacks from our enemy, the serpent. What is Satan's goal? To do anything in his power to rob us of our wholehearted and single-minded relationship to our Bridegroom—overtly and covertly.

To be promised as a virgin to Jesus is both a testimony to the wonder of the gospel and a calling to take very seriously. Let us remember that Paul is writing to converted pagans in Corinth whose lifestyle would be described as anything but virginal. However, by the gift of Christ's righteousness, we are counted as virgins before him. What awesome grace! Nevertheless, we must take Paul's admonition about temptation very seriously. We are still quite capable of manifold infidelity. We must be wise and ruthless with these wandering hearts of ours.

Satan's schemes and strategies abound, but they are all directed at deceiving us and destroying our intimacy with and obedience to our perfect Husband. His ultimate goal, of course, is to rob God of as much of his glory as he can. Our betrothal to the King of Kings presupposes a radical commitment to keep contaminants from our hearts.

Should Darlene walk in on me viewing pornographic material either on the computer or on the TV, what effect do you suppose this would have on our intimacy? The truth is, what would such a failure already communicate about my intimacy with her? We must ruthlessly guard our hearts for Jesus. It's time to throw away your little "black book." All rival love affairs must go: busyness, workaholism, gossip, hobbies, church work—*anything* can become pornographic—an enemy of intimacy.

A Time of Reclamation

As caretakers of our brothers and sisters in Christ, we are called to live as one another's wedding attendants. We are involved in this wedding together! We are each other's bridesmaids and groomsmen. But the bridesmaids don't have to worry about having to wear ugly dresses—(especially like the turquoise ones in *My Big Fat Greek Wedding*!). We are all wearing the righteousness of Jesus, the only true wedding garment.

Corporately, we are the Bride of Jesus; and individually, we are members of that union. Let us invest in the costly lifestyle of loving, wooing, warning, pursuing, laughing, serving, and weeping—together. We do fail. We do have affairs. We are addicts. We must love one another boldly and faithfully—by calling one another to repentance and accountability. We must not ignore or acquiesce to each other's foolishness and sin.

A Time Ending with the Procession

The final act of the interval is the procession—an event of great joy. The expectant Bride has prepared and adorned herself in anticipation of the arrival of the Bridegroom at her home. The groom dons his best attire and is accompanied to the Bride's home by a group of torch-bearing, singing friends. They gather the Bride and return to the Groom's home en masse.

This consummate Day in our marriage to Jesus is spoken (and sung!) about in Revelation 19:6–9. John describes his vision of Jesus coming for his Bride with these sights and sounds:

> Then I heard what sounded like a great multitude, like the roar of rushing waters and like loud peals of thunder, shouting:
>
> "Hallelujah! For our Lord God Almighty reigns. Let us rejoice and be glad and give him glory! For the wedding of the Lamb has come, and his bride has made herself ready. Fine linen, bright and clean, was given her to wear." (Fine linen stands for the righteous acts of the saints.)
>
> Then the angel said to me, "Write: 'Blessed are those who are invited to the wedding supper of the Lamb!'"

John's experience of this vision was so overwhelming that he fell to the ground and began to worship the angel who simply delivered it!

This is the Day to which all of history is heading, the Day for which we, the Bride of Jesus, are to be making ourselves ready.

The Wedding Feast

In a typical Jewish wedding, the wedding feast concludes the interval period. It begins with the wedding supper and then extends for a prolonged period of feasting and celebrating, lasting from seven to fourteen days. The Wedding Supper of the Lamb is the celebration from which all celebrations derive their meaning! It will inaugurate, not a seven- or fourteen-day party, but an eternal celebration as the completed and perfected Bride of Jesus lives with him in the new heaven and the new earth, forever in perfect everything!

My excitement about the Wedding Supper of the Lamb was reignited with great joy when I watched the concluding scene in *My Big Fat Greek Wedding.* All the dancing, the food, the love, the feasting, the music, the acceptance, the reconciliation, the welcome. It's no wonder the Spirit and the Bride cry out, "Maranatha!—Come, Lord Come!"

God our Father—who has chosen, created, called, and adopted us as his children—has graciously given us to his only begotten Son, to be his Bride forever! Who could possibly find a reason to protest such a prearranged marriage? Who would prefer the freedom to "play the field" and to choose for ourselves from among all of the "rivals" to the only perfect Husband?

Further Up *and* Further In

Marriage in the *Four Phases* of Redemptive History

A Progressive Unfolding

As we have seen, the reign of grace is the progressive unfolding of the greatest story conceivable—the redeeming relationship that God has chosen to have with his people. The entire history of redemption is developed through the narrative of Jesus giving himself, in life and in death, for the sake of his Bride, the Church. There is no greater love story. There is no greater love. The end of the world, as we know it, is punctuated with the Wedding Feast of the Lamb.

Thus, marriage has a very unique place in God's overall saving plan. It has been created (like worship and everything else) for our triune God's purposes and glory. The covenant relationship between a husband and a wife bears the weight of existing as a dynamic symbol, a profound hint of the quintessential marriage between Jesus and his Bride, the Church. It behooves us, therefore, to understand, submit to, and rejoice in his design.

There is no clearer evidence of the advancement of the reign of grace than for a husband and wife to accept the consuming calling to live their marriage unto the Lord. This isn't a calling to perform the impossible, but to believe the gospel. Even when only one spouse is willing to make such a commitment, the wonder of the gospel can be demonstrated as he or she submits to the reign of grace—as in the Book of Hosea.

Because all Christians and every church are called to think of themselves and to live as the Wife of Jesus, all of us—married or single—will gain great benefit as we understand four important dimensions of marriage occurring within the history of redemption. This truth, in and of itself, is enough to cause us to fall down and cry out with wonder, love, and praise before the face of our most holy and glorious God.

In the chart on pages 84–85 and explained in the following text, we will see marriage traced through the four phases of redemptive history:

- *Creation*—marriage as created by God and celebrated in the Garden of Eden
- *Fall*—marriage infected and redirected by the reign of sin and death
- *Redemption*—marriage invaded and re-created by the redeeming reign of grace
- *Consummation*—marriage fulfilled in our eternal relationship with Jesus

CREATION

COVENANTAL—*With God and a Spouse*

Marriage was created as a covenant relationship between a man and a woman with God at the center. A covenant relationship creates a dynamic and enduring bond through all seasons and every sphere of life. It is the most intimate and binding of all relationships. It was God's covenant with Adam and Eve that gave meaning, joy, passion, and delight to their covenant marriage. In a most profound sense, therefore, marriage was designed to be a threesome. Adam and Eve lived all of life "before the face of God."

MARRIAGE AS A MEANS—*Glorifying and Enjoying God by Subduing and Filling Up All of Creation to His Glory*

Adam and Eve were created individually as image bearers of God; and yet as a couple, they were called to model his image throughout creation in a way unique to marriage. God designed the first marriage

THE 4 PHASES OF

CREATION	FALL
Covenantal With God and a spouse	**Contractual** With a spouse
Marriage As a Means Glorifying and enjoying God by subduing and filling up all of creation to his glory	**Marriage As an End** Living for personal happiness, fulfillment, and self-glory
Posture Face to face Side by side	**Posture** Back to back
Personal Congruency *Wholeness* Two whole individuals relating unselfishly to each other	**Personal Disintegration** *Brokenness* Two broken and sinful individuals relating selfishly to each other
Perfect Intimacy *Complementarian* Two secure individuals enjoying dynamic interdependence and synergistic oneness	**Pervasive Alienation** *Combative* Two insecure individuals blaming, shaming, and controlling each other while hiding from themselves
Passionate Intentionality *Missional Living* A couple living a called life, partners together in other-centered loving	**Perpetual Agitation** *Medicative Living* A couple living a driven life, existing together in self-protective surviving

REDEEMING MARRIAGE

REDEMPTION

New Covenantal
With Jesus and a spouse

Marriage As a Means
Glorifying and enjoying God as a revelation of the beauty of Jesus and the redeeming power of the Gospel

Posture
Face to face
Side by side
Back to back

Personal Re-Creation
Healing
Two broken and sinful individuals being changed by the Gospel together

Progressive Intimacy
Less Combative and More Complementarian
Two forgiven sinners learning how to conflict redemptively and serve one another in love

Progressive Intentionality
Less Medicative and More Missional
A couple living a called life, partners together in Gospel-transformed living and loving

CONSUMMATION

Covenantal
With Jesus and the whole Bride of Christ

The End of Marriage
Glorifying and enjoying God forever by worship service in the New Heaven and New Earth

Posture
Face to face
Side by side

Personal Glorification
Restoration
Two perfected individuals living and loving as members of the glorified Bride of Christ

Perfect Intimacy
Complementarian
Two completed individuals joining the glorified Bride of Christ for an eternity of perfect relationships

Passionate Intentionality
Missional Living
A couple joining the complete Bride of Christ in an eternity of other-centered living and loving

to bring great glory to himself and deep enjoyment of his presence and presents lavished upon a married couple. There was nothing utilitarian about God's design for marriage. Adam and Eve would never have thought in terms of "What's in it for me?" All of life was lived doxologically—as an act of worship in response to the delights and demands of knowing God.

POSTURE: PHYSICAL, EMOTIONAL, AND SOCIAL—*Face to Face and Side by Side*

Adam and Eve enjoyed face-to-face and side-by-side relationship with God and each other. Their face-to-face relationship was a celebration of utter shamelessness, trust, and security. Their side-by-side relationship consisted of partnering with each other in glorifying God and enjoying him forever. Sex and worship were pure and passionate—beyond imagination.

PERSONAL CONGRUENCY—*Wholeness: Two Whole Individuals Relating Unselfishly to Each Other*

The first marriage consisted of a whole man and a whole woman living with and loving each other well—all the time. Personal congruency allowed Adam and Eve to be dynamically one and yet uniquely individual. Intrigue, enjoyment, appreciation, and respect for the other was their perpetual feast. Communion and communication were perfect all the time.

PERFECT INTIMACY—*Complementarian: Two Secure Individuals Enjoying Dynamic Interdependence and Synergistic Oneness*

Adam and Eve's relationship was a profound expression of the relational world of the Trinity—a celebration of creative synergy and symphonic interdependence. The Father, Son, and Holy Spirit are absolutely equal in being but diverse in their functions as members of the Godhead—so with Adam and Eve. There was equality of being and diversity of responsibility and calling. They were perfectly intimate in every sphere of life. Sex was a passionate celebration of their oneness, not a means of attaining it or recapturing it.

PASSIONATE INTENTIONALITY—*Missional Living: A Couple Living a Called Life, Partners Together in Other-Centered Living*

Adam and Eve were placed in the Garden of Eden to deeply enjoy all things, but also to live as stewards and vice-regents of God's creation. They were called to have dominion, to subdue all of creation under God's design and purposes. As a couple, they were made for the purpose of reigning in life over all things to God's glory. Thus they lived missionally—as servants of God and one another. Nothing was compartmentalized between the sacred and the profane. All of life was worship service—worshiping God by serving him everywhere, all the time.

FALL

Note: This description of the reign of sin and death in marriage conveys what happens when *only* sin is reigning in a marriage. Fortunately, God providentially restrains evil in our hearts and in the world for the purposes of redemption. Every single person is made in the image of God, and we are all quite capable of extraordinary moments of God-likeness, as his image bearers. Remember, the reign of sin and death is pervasive, not perfect. None of us are as bad as we would be if we lived consistently with our sinful nature. But also, none of us are as good, true, and beautiful as we were designed to be. The Fall mucked everything up!

CONTRACTUAL—*With a Spouse*

The reign of sin and death redefined marriage as a contract between two individuals, brokering an agreement. God is totally irrelevant to the relationship. A contract is far more provisional and far less binding than a covenant. The idea of a prenuptial agreement best captures the essence of sin in a marriage—two individuals, consciously or otherwise, putting limits and boundaries on the other, even before they are legally married! Marriage became a fifty-fifty arrangement. "I will bring my 50 percent to this deal, as long as you bring your 50 percent. If you bring only 27 percent or 14 percent, that's what I'll bring too."

Marriage As an End—*Living for Personal Happiness, Fulfillment, and Self-Glory*

The sinful heart of man is always asking, "What's in this for me? What am I going to get out of this arrangement?" With the invasion of sin, marriage is no longer viewed as a means of bringing glory to God and richly enjoying him. Marriage now exists for the primary end, or goal, of "my personal happiness, satisfaction, and fulfillment. I am the point! If you don't satisfy my needs, I will get them met elsewhere."

Posture: Physical, Emotional, and Social—*Back to Back*

When the reign of sin and death permeated the human heart, a new posture was introduced to marriage—back to back. Back-to-back relating can be understood in terms of stubbornness, unforgiveness, withholding, guardedness, and protection of individual rights. This relationship also describes the posture that our sinful hearts take toward God. We turn our backs on him in every way imaginable—the height of arrogance and stupidity.

Personal Disintegration—*Brokenness: Two Broken and Sinful Individuals Relating Selfishly to Each Other*

Ever since the Fall, every marriage consists of two broken and selfish people seeking to live together. The scene of Adam and Eve hiding from God captures this tragic disintegration. A man and woman are different enough by design, but when you throw into the mix the effects of sin and death on two different hearts and two unredeemed lives, you have a recipe for disaster. A marriage under the reign of sin and death is a perpetual game of trying on different fig leaves and blaming each other for all the problems in the world.

PERVASIVE ALIENATION—*Combative: Two Insecure Individuals Blaming, Shaming, and Controlling Each Other While Hiding from Themselves*

The reign of sin and death is an assault on intimacy. Without the life of God permeating the relationship, a husband and wife will foolishly try to find life in each other. Like two premature infants, each will try to plug their umbilical cord into the other, thus demanding, "Be life for me!" Or like two porcupines huddling together on a cold winter night, they will hurt each other and recoil...get cold again, cuddle, hurt each other, and recoil...get cold again, and on and on and on.

PERPETUAL AGITATION—*Medicative Living: A Couple Living a Driven Life, Existing Together in Self-Protective Surviving*

The reign of sin and death turns the heart away from any sense of missional living. Life is all about getting relief from the painful reality of the perpetual agitation of living with another sinner who either refuses to worship me or be God for me. Idols and adulteries abound in this environment.

REDEMPTION

NEW COVENANTAL—*With Jesus and a Spouse*

With the holy subterfuge of the reign of grace, marriage becomes a primary environment of redemption. Two Christians are joined together purposing to cultivate a Christ-centered marriage—that is, a marriage that is defined by and empowered by the New Covenant that Jesus has entered into with his Bride. Jesus' love life with his whole Bride becomes the real drama and delight directing a couple's stewardship of their relationship.

MARRIAGE AS A MEANS—*Glorifying and Enjoying God as a Revelation of the Beauty of Jesus and the Redeeming Power of the Gospel*

Through the reign of grace, marriage once again is received primarily as a means of bringing glory to God. Now, however, thoughts of God's glory are seen expressly in terms of what he has done to reconcile sinners to himself through the person and work of Jesus. Marriage, therefore, becomes a visible symbol of the gospel—a wordless sermon placed everywhere Christians live. A couple becomes more concerned with releasing the drama of Christ in their relationship than merely pursing individual happiness.

POSTURE: PHYSICAL, EMOTIONAL, AND SOCIAL—*Face to Face, Side by Side, and Back to Back*

The reign of grace is an "already and not yet" movement. Though the dominion of sin and death has been broken in our hearts, we are still sinners! There will still be back-to-back relating in a great Christian marriage. However, as a demonstration of the gospel, the hard and heart work of forgiveness, forbearance, repentance, and reconciliation is always going on—thus leading to rich seasons of face-to-face and side-by-side relating.

Sex is reclaimed and redeemed as a celebration of the other-centered loving we have found in Jesus. Sex is honored as a symbolic expression of the intimacy we enjoy with Jesus now but will enjoy more fully when our Bridegroom returns to consummate his relationship with us.

PERSONAL RE-CREATION—*Healing: Two Broken and Sinful Individuals Being Changed by the Gospel Together*

At its best, a marriage lived under the reign of grace will become an environment in which a husband and wife freely enter into the process of becoming more and more like Jesus. Each spouse is committed to getting healthy as well as becoming a means of grace for their spouse's growth. This requires that a couple learn how to be good stewards of each other's weakness, sin, and wounds. It requires an ongoing commitment to learn each other's love language and work hard on communication. As the reign of grace extends its influence, couples have less and less illusions about what it means to live with a sinner saved by grace. Unrealistic, selfish expectations are replaced with the delightful and demanding expectations of Jesus!

PROGRESSIVE INTIMACY—*Less Combative and More Complementarian: Two Forgiven Sinners Learning How to Conflict Redemptively and Serve One Another in Love*

It is important to be under no illusions about Christian marriage. It is hard, but it is good. As surrender to the reign of grace continues in the individual hearts of a Christian couple, much healthier ways of resolving conflicts and communicating emerge. Painful alienation begins to give way to healthy individuating. This means that intimacy is progressively cultivated but not to the exclusion of a healthy and thriving individual identity. Such a journey is very painful and slow but worth all the blood, sweat, tears, and grace required.

When a husband and wife are able to set personal boundaries that function more like a bridge than a high wall, the reign of grace has come near! When a husband and wife live in such a way as to enjoy preparing one another for their Wedding to Jesus—well, look up! This is a sign that the second coming is very near!

PROGRESSIVE INTENTIONALITY—*Less Medicative and More Missional: A Couple Living a Called Life, Partners Together in Gospel-Transformed Living and Loving*

As the reign of grace permeates a marriage, a couple will be more given to missional, or servant living, and less preoccupied with avoiding or relieving personal pain. Knowing that they will not be married to each other in eternity, life becomes the first fruits of the new heaven and the new earth. Such a couple enjoys partnering with their Bridegroom Jesus in his passions and purposes. They rebound fairly quickly when they slip into the old ways of temporary insanity—knowing that ultimate life is found only in Jesus.

The great commission and the progressive advancement of the reign of grace throughout culture, community, and the universe become their food, joy, dreams, and delight. Such a couple laughs louder, cries more often, rests more deeply, and stays more passionate than any others. They become wiser in their investments of time, money, and God's grace.

CONSUMMATION

COVENANTAL—*With Jesus and the Whole Bride of Christ*

At the second coming of Jesus, everything will change—hallelujah! Every member of the betrothed Bride of Jesus, along with the whole of God's creation, will be brought to the fullness of covenant renewal! Our salvation will be completed, and we will be made perfect in love to enjoy the perfections of covenantal life forever! God's covenant faithfulness will be brought to a magnificent fulfillment at the Wedding of the Lamb, and eternity will be a joyful and fruitful expression of this indissoluble bond.

THE END OF MARRIAGE—*Glorifying and Enjoying God Forever by Worship Service in the New Heaven and New Earth*

Marriage will have reached its temporal purpose and fulfillment with the Marriage Supper of the Lamb. The consummation of our marriage with Jesus will bring about the end of marriage as a covenant relationship between a man and woman. We will live corporately as the beloved Wife of Jesus forever—fully experiencing all that "God has prepared for those who love him" (1 Cor. 2:9). We will actually enjoy a better relationship then with the one (or ones!) we were married to in this life than now. Why? Because it will be the first and only time we will experience one another devoid of any influence of sin.

Posture: Physical, Emotional, and Social—*Face to Face and Side by Side*

Fortunately, God has given us some amazing images in the Book of Revelation that help us envision the unimaginable. As glorious as the day was when Adam and Eve were able to stand before God and each other naked and without shame, much more glorious will be the Day when we gather around the throne of grace with the whole Bride of Christ, face to face and side by side, adoring God who sits on the throne and adoring the Lamb who has made himself our Husband! (Rev. 4–5; 7; 19–22).

The visions of that Day are described not just in circular, but in spherical terms. Everything is in perfect symmetry, everything is in proper relationship; in other words, everything is righteous! The reign of grace through righteousness unto eternal life will have reached its end; and therefore, its eternal beginning.

Personal Glorification—*Restoration: Two Perfected Individuals Living and Loving as Members of the Glorified Bride of Christ*

You will be the perfect you. For the first time in your life, everything about you will be devoid of the influence of sin—your thinking, emotions, choices, and body. Everything about you will be as it was designed to be—perfectly sound, healthy, and whole. Try to imagine never having a selfish thought again, always showing the right emotion at the right time, joyfully choosing to love God and others above yourself, and having a body that will never wear out! Now try to imagine living and loving this way with the whole Bride of Christ, gathered from every race, tongue, tribe, and family group from every period in history! Oh, the joy and worship we will enjoy as we see how all of our stories fit together within the one great narrative called the history of redemption. God "will wipe every tear from their eyes. There will be no more death or mourning or crying or pain, for the old order of things has passed away" (Rev. 21:4).

PERFECT INTIMACY—*Complementarian: Two Completed Individuals Joining the Glorified Bride of Christ for an Eternity of Perfect Relationships*

One of the main reasons we will not be married in heaven is that in our glorified state we will be capable of numberless intimate relationships! We will be perfect lovers. We will enjoy the whole Bride of Jesus taken from all nations and all periods of history! The Scriptures call us to think in terms of a new heaven and new earth teeming with life, creativity, passion, feasting, beauty, and perfect society within the New Jerusalem.

We will enjoy an interdependent existence forever with the whole Bride of Jesus. Try to imagine what it will be like to labor, love, and laugh together—each of us a member of the Bride. Everyone will matter and be just as important as the other.

PASSIONATE INTENTIONALITY—*Missional Living: A Couple Joining the Complete Bride of Christ in an Eternity of Other-Centered Living and Loving*

Like Adam and Eve in the Garden of Eden, we will enjoy a dynamic, creative, missional orientation toward everything and everyone in the new heaven and the new earth, forever! Details remain to be revealed, but the promise stands, "No eye has seen, no ear has heard, no mind has conceived what God has prepared for those who love him" (1 Cor. 2:9). As in the old creation, so in the new, we should anticipate ruling and reigning together, living as called and uniquely gifted individuals, one Bride with one Husband, existing for one end—to glorify and enjoy God forever! I hope you weren't counting on sitting on a cloud and playing a harp!

THOSE WHOM I LOVE I REBUKE AND DISCIPLINE.... HERE I AM! I *stand* AT THE DOOR AND KNOCK.

—REVELATION 3:19–20

Discipline is EVIDENCE of God entering our world to rescue us from *spiritual* danger that WE could not or would not handle on our own. Thus, God's *discipline* is not contrary to grace but, in fact, *is* grace.

Bryan CHAPEL

Women who are BROUGHT up in the country are stronger than men who *live* in towns.

CHRYSOSTOM

IT WAS GOOD FOR ME TO BE AFFLICTED SO THAT I MIGHT *learn* YOUR DECREES.

—PSALM 119:71

Christ endured the great shower of WRATH, the black and dismal hours of displeasure for sin. That which falls upon us is as a sunshine *shower,* warmth with wet, wet with the WARMTH of His love to make us fruitful and humble....That which the believer suffers for sin is not penal, arising from vindictive *justice,* but medicinal, arising from a FATHERLY love. It is his medicine, not his punishment; his chastisement, not his sentence; his *correction,* not his condemnation.

Samuel BOLTON

CHAPTER SIX

The Grace of God's DISCIPLINE

> "And now this admonition is for you, O priests. If you do not listen, and if you do not set your heart to honor my name," says the LORD Almighty, "I will send a curse upon you, and I will curse your blessings. Yes, I have already cursed them, because you have not set your heart to honor me.
>
> "Because of you I will rebuke your descendants; I will spread on your faces the offal from your festival sacrifices, and you will be carried off with it." (Mal. 2:1–3)

How would you like to sit under preaching like this every Sunday? Aren't you glad you don't live in the Old Testament days? You know, the age of stone-tablet laws and merit-based blessing, when God got real mad at his people and rebuked them harshly—even *cursed* them. This passage describes a particularly "colorful" form of impending discipline. If certain priests did not repent, God would rub their faces in the dung of the animals used for his worship and then take them off to the dung heap outside the camp of Israel where defiled things belong. Yecch! Talk about old-school, hellfire, Bible-thumping, radio-screaming fundamentalism!

Isn't it great to be living in the age of grace—the New Testament days—the era of a kinder, gentler, more loving God. He will never deal with us according to our sins or reward us according to our iniquity. Because of Jesus, we are loved *unconditionally.* It's all about grace!

Oh, really?

Indeed, it *is* all about grace! But what kind of grace?

- *Royal family grace*—grace without authority or a reign
- *Southern grace*—cultural niceness, more genteel than graceful
- *Graceless grace*—excuses without tears and accountability
- *Greasy grace*—lubrication for nonsense and presumption
- *Quack grace*—wounds wrongly diagnosed and healed lightly
- *Flat-line grace*—theoretical forgiveness for hypothetical sinners
- *Mirage grace*—grace as a private oasis, instead of a missional movement

The God who threatened dung-heap discipline is the same God who said, "I have loved you"—to the *same* people, through the *same* prophet, Malachi! In fact, the whole Book of Malachi reads like a lover's quarrel. It is a record of the only perfect Lover's quarrel with his irresponsible, unresponsive, treasured people. How do God's words of tender affection and promises of severe discipline fit together?

The Journey from Sloppy Agape to Bold Love

"I am a mess. I struggle with materialism, pornography, loving my crabby wife—and I haven't read my Bible in weeks. Why wouldn't God reject me or just strike me down? I believe in Jesus, but come on...God's got to be terribly disappointed with me."

I looked him in the eye, put my hand on his shoulder, and these words flowed out like pure honey. "Because of his grace freely given to us in Christ, God loves you *unconditionally,* and he will *never* be angry with you again for your sins!"

There, take that!—you despondent and heavily weighted heart. God doesn't condemn you; you're just under cruel attack by the accuser of the brethren! Shake off your guilty fears! The enemy is trying to rob you of your joy!

I wish I had a dime for every time over the past fifteen years I've spoken, written, or thought about God's unconditional love for his people and the elimination of his wrath toward us. I couldn't retire, but I would at least be able to buy a nice bamboo fly rod for myself and make a down payment on a sailboat for Darlene.

But do the precious truths I shared with that hurting brother reveal *everything* we need to know about the way God loves his sinner-saint kids? Was my friend's biggest issue despondency or disobedience? Did he need relief from his guilty fears, or did he need a healthy fear of the Lord—one that would lead to a godly sorrow, repentance, healing, and no regret? (2 Cor. 7:8–11).

It's not that I believe these time-honored formulations about God's incomparable love less; it's just that the truth and implications of the gospel keep getting bigger and bigger. The reign of grace just won't fit inside a simple motto or platitude.

Try putting a life-giving river inside of a thimble; try squeezing a picture of all the Swiss Alps into one snapshot; try describing all of the artwork in the Louvre with one sentence; try adequately summarizing the manifestations of God's love and the ramifications of his grace in one breath! If you try, you better be a pearl diver, able to survive three minutes on one breath, because the gospel pearl is way deep!

Does God really love his people unconditionally and all the time? Yes!…and well, it all depends upon what you mean by "love."

Does Jesus' cross guarantee that God will never be angry with his people when they sin? Are we always correct in saying, "God loves the sinner but hates the sin!" Yes!...and well...in a certain sense...not exactly.

How would you respond to the same questions? My tentative answers accurately reveal that I'm in a season of transition. I find myself moving from notions of sloppy agape to bold love.

To see some of your favorite clichés not fully clothed (like the emperor in Aesop's fable) is a little hard to take at first. And yet, as Jesus has taught us, it's the truth that sets us free—even when the truth challenges some of our favorite nuggets and notions about God and his ways. God's grace is always more than we bargained for!

So, just how *does* God relate to his people when we are selfish, petty, disobedient, spiteful, and unloving? How do we connect God's delight *in us* and his discipline *of us?* How does he rejoice over us as his sons and reprove us for our sins at the same time? Is there a difference between the way God loved his Old Testament children and the way he loves his New Testament kids? More importantly, has God changed? Has he gotten sweeter in his old age?

A Personal Story of Greasy Grace

Laying facedown on the well-groomed Bermuda grass, my weary and exhausted frame welcomed the early spring shower that began to fall ever so gently. I received the delicate pitter-patter of this reviving rain as a sign from above, a kiss of grace for God's weary servant.

I had just, as they say, "lost my cookies," after playing ninety-seven holes of golf in a little over five hours—passing out somewhere between the seventeenth green and the eighteenth tee box.

The occasion was a golfing marathon fund-raiser, hosted by one of the many outstanding ministries in the Nashville area. As one of several pastor-participants, my challenge was to secure as much money as I could in per-hole pledges from members of my congregation and then play as many holes of golf as possible within an eight-hour period.

As a friend followed close behind, ferrying my clubs in a golf cart, I sprinted from shot to shot and hole to hole, playing a game that looked more like manic polo than any semblance of real golf.

The transition from late winter to early spring was marked by the brightest sunshine of the year and the highest humidity in six months. Zealous to maintain my rabid pace (all for a good cause, of course), I disregarded any number of well-positioned water-bottle stations. But as the beautiful morning gave way to the early afternoon mugginess, I was forced to accept the fact that when it comes to H_2O, I am a mere man, not a desert camel.

Suddenly a large grove of trees in front of me began spinning. *Maybe this is what the Bible means when it says the trees are going to clap their hands*—a passing thought as I slowly crumpled to the ground, having given up any food left in my stomach. I'm sure I wasn't out more than a few seconds before God "showered me with grace." An early afternoon rain cloud watered my prostrate body, waking me up and providing a little cooling relief.

I managed to get up (all by myself!) and stagger into the clubhouse for about fifteen minutes, before coming back out with stoic and evangelical resolve to play thirty more holes "to support the ministry."

"Scotty, are you OK? You've already raised a bunch of money. Why don't you call it a day?" a couple of concerned friends proffered. I shot back, "Nah, I'm fine. Wasn't that shower awesome? God is so good! He'll give me sufficient grace to meet my goal. I'm gonna finish what I set out to do."

My caddy had already retired for the day, but that didn't matter. I'd press on. It had already been a "day of grace." After finishing one hundred and twenty-seven holes, I was finished in more ways than one. Out of shape and out of electrolytes, I was dehydrated and disoriented, and I had blistered fingers (I played without a golf glove), a swollen knee, and a sunburned face (on a guy with a history of skin-cancer surgery).

To be honest, I was more driven that day by an obsession to play more holes and raise more money than anyone else in the tournament than I was by the cause I was playing for. I relished the idea of beating my fellow pastors—two in particular. But for the next couple of weeks, I felt as sick and miserable as I ever have.

Though I milked a little self-pity and appreciation for "sacrificing my body," I wasn't a ministry martyr, I was a moron! It wasn't God's grace that kept me going, but my presumption and stubbornness.

Love's Pain

Looking back, I believe my posttournament misery was a clear expression of the grace of God. My aches and pains were an appropriate consequence of the choices of a proud and foolish man. The truth is, I could have seriously harmed myself—and, therefore, a lot of other people I am committed to love well. Because God is committed to loving me well, I experienced his discipline (a much neglected and confusing theme for many of us "recovering Pharisees" and lovers of grace).

Not that a tit-for-tat correlation can always be made between our obedience and blessings and our disobedience and troubles. How arrogant we would be to assume that all of our "blessings" spring from our "doing it right." And how paralyzing it would be to think that every pimple, pothole, and pain can be traced to some failure on our part! But if we sow stupidity, we shouldn't be surprised when we reap a bumper crop of woes and whines. God is *never* nonchalant about our destructive choices and unloving attitudes. He's forbearing and forgiving, but never nonchalant.

I needed a lot more than the refreshing rain to wake me up on the golf course that day. A *refreshed* proud and foolish man is still a proud and foolish man. I needed *then* what I continue to need *today:* the reign of grace, the transforming dominion of God's redemptive generosity ruling in my heart—not excusing, but expelling my sinful presumption and immaturity.

What, then, was God's attitude toward me on that day? As God the Righteous Judge, he fully accepted and loved me on the basis of the righteousness of his Son—in full view of my sin. As my heavenly Father, my sin displeased, offended, saddened, and grieved him, because of his committed love for me. He had every right to rebuke and discipline me as his beloved son, just as he had every right to take strong measures with his children under Malachi's ministry.

If this were not so, God would be a different kind of Father: He might be a sugar Daddy—easy to manipulate, or an absentee Daddy—totally uninvolved in my life, or a codependent Daddy—needing my affirmation to survive, or an abusive Daddy—not really caring what happens to me. But God loves his children so much better and more severely than that!

Keep Yourselves in the Love of God

"Keep yourselves in the love of God." Those seven, bold words are a command from Scripture. And they are from the New Testament! Jude implores the congregations to whom he is writing in a time of crisis, "Keep yourselves in the love of God" (Jude 21 NASB). Doesn't the call to obey this admonition presuppose the possibility of not obeying it? And if so, in what sense are Christians ever *not* in the love of God?

Jesus seems to be making the same point with this exhortation: "As the Father has loved me, so have I loved you. Now remain in my love. If you obey my commands, you will remain in my love, just as I have obeyed my Father's commands and remain in his love" (John 15:9–10). Certainly, Jesus never had to earn God's love by his obedience. And we know that anyone who relies on his or her obedience to the law of God for salvation is under a curse! For it is impossible to gain acceptance with God by obedience. Our acceptance comes only through faith (Gal. 3:10–12). How, then, does our obedience enable us to "remain" in God's love? And how does disobedience rob us of this experience?

Conditional Enjoyment— Not Conditional Acceptance

In a most profound way, the Bible teaches that God, indeed, loves his people unconditionally—even *contra* conditionally! Jesus has met *every* condition for us, so that God "legally" loves his own, with an unwavering, undiminished love. In this judicial sense, we can rightfully say, "God will never love his children more than he does today, and he will never love them less."

However, the Judge of all men has made himself a Father to his children. It is in light of this father-child relationship that we can understand how obedience and disobedience affect our experience of the love of God.

God's love *is* conditional—not in terms of our meriting or forfeiting his eternal acceptance, but in terms of the *degree* to which we enjoy his rich affections or incur his fatherly discipline.

D. A. Carson writes, "God's discipline of his children means that he may turn upon us with the divine equivalent of the 'wrath' of a parent on a wayward teenager. Indeed, to cite the cliché 'God's love is unconditional' to a Christian who is drifting toward sin may convey the wrong impression and do a lot of damage."[1]

Unconditional Love or Undeserved Favor?

Perhaps it would be better to reclaim the older definition of grace championed by earlier generations of Bible scholars and lovers of the gospel. Instead of describing grace primarily in terms of *God's unconditional love for his sinful children,* perhaps it's more helpful to refer to grace as *the undeserved favor God's sinful children receive in Christ.* "Undeserved favor" places the proper emphasis on the full and eternal *status* of acceptance we enjoy with God through our union with Christ.

The phrase "unconditional love" places too much emphasis on God's *emotional state* toward his children. It also reveals a rather sentimental understanding of love and a one-sided perspective on anger. For example, the statement "God isn't angry with you; he loves you!" implies that anger and love are mutually exclusive. God is love, and he never gets angry. But this line of reasoning also implies the following:

- Anger is equivalent to rejection, bad moods, disfavor, resentment, irritability, intent to harm, loss of control, abuse, vengeance, etc.
- Love is equivalent to gentleness, never getting upset, always overlooking mistakes, harmlessness, sweetness, predictability, total acceptance, safety, etc.

But such descriptions of love and anger are woefully inadequate, and worse, they are unbiblical misrepresentations of God's love and anger. Apply these definitions to the Book of Malachi, and you are forced to conclude that God was very angry and very unloving to his children—contrary to what *he* claimed!

God does what no one else ever has: He loves perfectly and expresses anger perfectly.

- God's *love* for his children means that he will only express anger appropriately and redemptively. God's anger has no hint of irritation, exasperation, vengeance, or contempt. His hand of discipline will never come as a shaming backhand across one's face or as a demeaning blow to one's dignity.
- God's *anger* toward his children means that his love for them is

> pure, holy, and refining. God's love is not blind, dismissive, or accepting of what should *never* be accepted. His patience is not to be confused with acquiescence or his forbearance with tolerance.

God is committed to maturing us. He is committed to disciplining us in love—gentle love and bold love. Oh, to be more alive to the beauty, security, and hope of this vital and, at times, vexing dimension of our growth in grace.

Further Up *and* Further In

A Harvest *of* Holiness and Peace

Hebrews 12

Practically speaking, how does God's grace-driven discipline play out in our daily lives? Before we can understand the truth on this question, many of us need to recover from two equally faulty views of discipline: (1) God is a temperamental perfectionist waiting to pounce on our every act of disobedience and failure at loving well. (2) God punished and disciplined Jesus in our place; therefore, he will never respond to our disobedience and failures at loving well. He doesn't see our sins; he only sees the righteousness of Jesus with which we are covered.

How do the Scriptures and the gospel address both of these caricatures?

From the wisdom literature of Israel we read, "My son, do not despise the LORD's discipline and do not resent his rebuke, because the LORD disciplines those he loves, as a father the son he delights in" (Prov. 3:11–12). The writer of Hebrews (who gave us what many consider to be the most important chapter [12] on discipline in all of the New Testament) quoted these very words as he offered great wisdom and pastoral insight into the way the God of all grace disciplines his beloved children.

Hebrews was written to a group of believers whose initial joy of knowing Jesus had abated. They had experienced the suffering of persecution, the weariness of life in a fallen world, and the disappointments of unfulfilled expectations. Plus, they were probably getting pretty bored with one another in the church. Does this sound familiar? It's almost a carbon copy of Malachi's day.

These believers needed encouragement and perspective on their hardships. And *how* did the author of Hebrews encourage these weary, disappointed believers? He encouraged them by extolling the majesty, superiority, and sufficiency of Jesus Christ. For ten chapters of his epistle, the writer proclaims that Jesus is the one who perfectly fulfills all the types, promises, and hopes of the Old Testament. Jesus is the Messiah, the only Savior, the final Prophet, the great High Priest, the King of Kings—reigning from a throne of grace.

Jesus is grace incarnate! We only understand God, ourselves, suffering, life—really, all things—by the light of the Son. Focusing on the all-sufficiency of Christ, the writer instructs us in how we are to endure God's discipline.

How Are We to Endure God's Discipline?

1. Gaze upon Jesus as You Run the Race

> Therefore, since we are surrounded by such a great cloud of witnesses, let us throw off everything that hinders and the sin that so easily entangles, and let us run with perseverance the race marked out for us. Let us fix our eyes on Jesus, the author and perfecter of our faith, who for the joy set before him endured the cross, scorning its shame, and sat down at the right hand of the throne of God. Consider him who endured such opposition from sinful men, so that you will not grow weary and lose heart. (Heb. 12:1–3)

The writer of Hebrews chose an intense, athletic image to describe the Christian life and our growth in grace. Why? Because *discipline is primarily God's proactive commitment to mature us, not a reactive response to punish us.*

He places his audience (and us) on the field, not in the stands! We are participants, not spectators. This is a *race* into which God has placed us—a race which involves preparation, results in perspiration, requires perseverance, but ends with paradise!

Knowing Jesus isn't a casual game of tennis played at the club by Buffy and Jody wearing cable-knit sweaters tied around their necks. It's more like a supermarathon run through the rugged terrain of life, in all kinds of weather conditions, with all kinds of opposition and traveling mates.

Throw Off Encumbrances

This race requires that we throw off anything that encumbers our progress—namely, "the sin that so easily entangles." In the reign of grace, sin is not excused; it is excised! Growth in grace will always bring with it a deeper and more specific repentance of sin. Only grace enables us to move from seeing ourselves as "generic sinners who struggle in general" to those who must rid ourselves of specific encumbrances—and grace frees us to get real specific. We are encumbered by such things as gossip, roots of bitterness, a love for the approval of others, a desire for money and the things it can buy, etc. What particular sins presently have entangling power over your heart?

Earthly Models versus the Perfect Savior

The "great cloud of witnesses" surrounding us aren't spectators either. Hebrews 11 is filled with well-chosen examples of those "commended for their faith," godly believers who "pleased God" by their love and obedience—our brothers and sisters who experienced all kinds of discipline in the race as they ran before us. We are to choose our models in the Christian life wisely—and they are not Buffy and Jody! Who are some of yours?

Lest we fuel our performance-based inclinations by simply trying hard to emulate our heroes, the writer of Hebrews directs our gaze where it should always be, on Jesus—"the author and perfecter of our faith." Let us glance at our models, but fix our eyes on Jesus! *Our models show us a life of faith; Jesus gives and perfects the faith we must have!*

To "fix our eyes on Jesus" isn't to look at our favorite artistic rendering of Jesus or to mystically envision him as he walked the streets of Galilee loving children. Rather, it is to trust in his once-and-for-all work on the cross for our justification (Heb. 10:12). It is to ponder his current work at the right hand of the Father, ruling over all things and effecting our sanctification. It is to long for the joy of his second coming and the future wonder of our glorification and the perfections of the new heaven and the new earth.

2. Remember Your Sonship as You Groan in Grace

> In your struggle against sin, you have not yet resisted to the point of shedding your blood. And you have forgotten that word of encouragement that addresses you as sons: "My son, do not make light of the Lord's discipline, and do not lose heart when he rebukes you, because the Lord disciplines those he loves, and he punishes everyone he accepts as a son." (Heb. 12:4–6)

As already mentioned, the recipients of the Hebrew epistle had experienced significant challenges and persecution since coming to know God's grace in Christ (Heb. 10:34–36). They were weary, confused, and losing heart. No doubt much of their discouragement was born out of false expectations. Perhaps they thought, like many in our day, that the abundant life was to be filled with prosperity and blessings. They were right! But God often defines prosperity and blessings differently than we do.

Perhaps they were also tempted to conclude that afflictions and difficulties were an indication of God's indifference, unfaithfulness, or lack of compassion for them. "God, if you really loved us, wouldn't you fix this situation? Why would you let us suffer so much?"

Fatherly Discipline

Before discussing the discipline of God's grace, he reminds them of the grace of their adoption. "You have forgotten that word of encouragement that addresses you as sons" (Heb. 12:5). The pain of hard providence is actually a sign of good parenting.

As God's sons and daughters, we should not be surprised when we experience various forms of hardship—like Malachi's contemporaries. If God did not love us, he would not discipline us. The Greek word for *discipline* basically conveys the idea of training or "bending" a child toward maturity. It's a familial term: A Father is doing the disciplining. The *context* of our maturing in Christ (the family of grace) is just as important as the *process* (the discipline of grace).

When life is hard and we no longer hear God addressing us as beloved sons, the encouragement of *sonship* gives way to absorption in *self:* the arrogance of self-righteousness, the despair of self-contempt, the futility of self-salvation, or the foolishness of self-medication.

When *you* no longer have a sense of God as your loving Father, where do you take your heart in times of pain, weariness, suffering, and groaning?

Growing Pains

The apostle Paul used many images in describing the sometimes painful journey from childishness to maturity. In 1 Corinthians 13:11 he recounts just how comprehensive the curriculum in the school of discipline is. "When I was a child, I talked like a child, I thought like a child, I reasoned like a child. When I became a man, I put childish ways behind me." A good father is more concerned about shaping his children's thinking, reasoning, and speech than merely preparing them to be socially acceptable and culturally relevant.

What a challenge! It's much easier to window dress a child in the uniform of external legalism or the thin garments of laissez-faire grace than to train his or her heart in the ways of godliness. It's an overwhelming calling because "folly is bound up in the heart of a child, but the rod of discipline will drive it far from him" (Prov. 22:15). It's just as painful to discipline well as it is to be disciplined! No doubt, that's why Paul admonished parents with these words, "Fathers, do not exasperate your children; instead, bring them up in the training and instruction of the Lord" (Eph. 6:4). "Fathers, do not embitter your children, or they will become discouraged" (Col. 3:21). God our Father, alone disciplines perfectly, yet not painlessly.

We who are already sons in Christ want to become sons like Christ! The apostle John describes this waiting period with similar longing and passion.

> How great is the love the Father has lavished on us, that we should be called children of God! And that is what we are! The reason the world does not know us is that it did not know him. Dear friends, now we are children of God, and what we will be has not yet been made known. But we know that when he appears, we shall be like him, for we shall see him as he is. Everyone who has this hope in him purifies himself, just as he is pure. (1 John 3:1–3)

It's only as we remember that we are God's beloved children with a magnificent destiny that we will…

3. Welcome the Grace of Discipline As a Family Friend

> Endure hardship as discipline; God is treating you as sons. For what son is not disciplined by his father? If you are not disciplined (and everyone undergoes discipline), then you are illegitimate

> children and not true sons. Moreover, we have all had human fathers who disciplined us and we respected them for it. How much more should we submit to the Father of our spirits and live! Our fathers disciplined us for a little while as they thought best; but God disciplines us for our good, that we may share in his holiness. (Heb. 12:7–10)

What is discipline? God's loving commitment to mold his adopted children into the likeness of his only begotten Son.

What is the grace of discipline? The various means by which the God of all grace administers his transforming discipline.

Grace in Its Less "Gracious" Forms

Though there are many manifestations of the grace of discipline—some that are less than "pleasant"—let's consider three highlighted in the Book of Hebrews.

1. The Hardship of Suffering

Is suffering really a means of grace? Indeed, the apostle Paul is quite specific about the "gift of suffering." In Philippians 1:29, he writes, "For it has been granted to you [literally, "grace gifted to you"] on behalf of Christ not only to believe on him, but also to suffer for him." Those who received the Hebrew epistle experienced the hardship of suffering for Jesus' sake. They needed to be reminded that their suffering was not in vain. It "disciplined" their hearts to be compassionate with other sufferers and to live for "better and lasting possessions."

> Remember those earlier days after you had received the light, when you stood your ground in a great contest in the face of suffering. Sometimes you were publicly exposed to insult and persecution; at other times you stood side by side with those who were so treated. You sympathized with those in prison and joyfully accepted the

> confiscation of your property, because you knew that you yourselves had better and lasting possessions.
>
> So do not throw away your confidence; it will be richly rewarded. (Heb 10:32–35)

There is another variety of suffering we need to receive as an expression of the grace of discipline—affliction generated by our own sin. "If you suffer, it should not be as a murderer or thief or any other kind of criminal, or even as a meddler" (1 Pet. 4:15). How tragic it would be if grace eliminated all painful consequences of our destructive choices.

Discipline born out of sin is certainly a gift of grace. The psalmist sings, "Before I was afflicted I went astray, but now I obey your word.... It was good for me to be afflicted so that I might learn your decrees" (Ps. 119:67, 71).

Do you need other reasons to embrace the "discipliner" nobody wants? Here are a few:

- Suffering produces perseverance. (Rom. 5:3)
- Suffering enables us to identify with our brothers and sisters scattered among the nations of the world. (1 Pet. 5:9; 1 Cor. 12:26)
- Suffering purifies our faith and deepens our love for Jesus. (1 Pet. 1:6–9)

2. The Sting of Rebuke

The statement "Do not lose heart when [the Lord] rebukes you" (Heb. 12:5) presupposes that sometimes the Lord's rebukes are quite strong—perhaps not feeling much like "love."

Jesus said, "Those whom I love I rebuke and discipline. So be earnest, and repent" (Rev. 3:19). Do you remember what follows next in this text? "Here I am! I stand at the door and knock. If anyone hears my voice and opens the door, I will come in and eat with him, and he with me" (Rev. 3:20). Jesus disciplines us with strong rebukes so we will enjoy rich fellowship with him and one another! Only a fool would reject such a "life-giving rebuke" (Prov. 15:31).

3. THE PAIN OF PUNISHMENT

God "punishes [scourges or whips] everyone he accepts as a son" (Heb. 12:6). Of late, I have reexamined my belief that God will never "punish" his children for their sins.

It is gloriously true that our Father will never punish us *retributively*—that is, he will never exact equivalent payment from us for our sins. God has dealt retributively with Jesus on the cross. Hebrews 13:12 tells us that "Jesus...suffered outside the city gate to make the people holy through his own blood." It was there he "endured the cross, scorning its shame" (Heb. 12:2).

Do you remember the passage from Malachi 2 with which we began chapter 6? God promised to punish faithless priests by cursing them, defiling them with animal dung, and then taking them outside of the city gate. In a most profound way, the fullness of that curse, defilement, and shame was poured out on Jesus. He became defiled with our sins. He has born the curse of our law breaking. He has taken our shame—completely. What wondrous love is this?

The reason God will never deal with *us* as our sins deserve is that he has dealt with *Jesus* as our sins deserve! The perfect love of Jesus, given to us through the cross, drives out any fear of eternal punishment (1 John 4:18). Through Jesus, God has "taken away [all retributive] punishment" (Zeph. 3:15) from his children. "The punishment that brought us peace" was given to Jesus (Isa. 53:5).

But God will punish us *reformationally*—that is, he will chastise us out of love, not contempt. God will not deal with us as our sins deserve, but as he deems best in accomplishing his good purposes in our lives. Yes, it can hurt, big time—"He who spares the rod hates his son, but he who loves him is careful to discipline him" (Prov. 13:24)—but his reformational discipline is for our ultimate good and God's glory.

Submit to the Pain of Discipline for a Grace-Full Harvest

> No discipline seems pleasant at the time, but painful. Later on, however, it produces a harvest of righteousness and peace for those who have been trained by it.
>
> Therefore, strengthen your feeble arms and weak knees. "Make level paths for your feet," so that the lame may not be disabled, but rather healed. (Heb. 12:11–13)

The writer of Hebrews is quite honest about the school of discipline. It's not pleasant! In fact, it is painful. Many bail out of the process. Many "don't get it"—like Malachi's audience!

But for those who "submit to the Father of our spirits" and his good purposes in sending the discipline, there is life! To be trained by discipline is to yield, in time, a bumper crop of righteousness and peace. More importantly, the wounds of discipline create hearts and hands of healing. Those who are being healed become a means of healing for the disabled and lame.

Be trained by your hardships. Don't waste your suffering. Listen to the life-giving rebukes of your Father. Submit to his chastening. He loves you thoroughly. He loves you boldly.

Further Up and Further In

The Gift of Desert Thirst

Hosea

God is not just the best Dad ever, forgiving us and taking us to the woodshed to train us up right. He is our faithful husband, pained by our affairs and committed to alluring us through the desert of discipline into his consuming embrace. To be pursued with relentless passion by your covenant Husband and Lover, even into the bedroom of your many adulteries, is to be "graced" with a pain and pleasure like none other.

For many of us, it's only when we begin to see our sin as adultery that we weep with a healing sadness, and worship with a faith-full hope. Let's relive, from Hosea, the story of God and his whorelike wife. Consider the discipline of perfect love.

Hosea ministered during a season of abundance and prosperity in the eighth century B.C. But bad kingship in Israel and poor stewardship of blessings had corrupted the worship of God's wife. She had been "sleeping with" the gods of the Canaanites, especially the fertility god, Baal. Moral and political compromise abounded in the northern kingdom.

Speaking to the whole covenant people, God cried out: "Rebuke your mother, rebuke her, for she is not my wife, and I am not her husband. Let her remove the adulterous look from her face and the unfaithfulness from between her breasts" (Hos. 2:2).

"The reality has gone out of our relationship," God proclaimed. *"You're living as though we aren't even married—worse, you're living like an adulteress—even worse, a prostitute! I will not stand by passively!"*

Responsible for Our Fellows

Notice how God's rebuke was delivered: It was to be given *by* God's son (Hosea), *to* God's other children. Discipline begins with God calling *us* to get involved and stay involved in each other's lives. As the Bride of Christ, we are to live as each other's Wedding attendants—preparing one another for the Wedding Feast of the Lamb. We must learn to "be merciful to those who doubt; snatch others from the fire and save them; to others show mercy, mixed with fear" (Jude 22–23).

To deliver a rebuke is not to play Holy Spirit in one another's lives; it's to offer a lifeline, to extend a hand of warning, welcome, and rescue. If you see a married friend "fooling around" emotionally or physically, you should love him or her enough to "get after" your friend redemptively. Likewise, we need to view any and all unfaithfulness to our perfect Husband, Jesus, as "fooling around." Have you ever seen yourself as an adulterer or adulteress—has sin ever been that hideous to you? That's how God sees it.

So how does a loving covenant Husband respond in the face of unfaithfulness? Jesus has many ways to intensify his disciplining love and transforming grace. The Book of Hosea reveals several forms of discipline Jesus may use with us—his beloved but sometimes adulterous Wife:

Jesus May "Slay Us with Thirst"

> I will strip her naked and make her as bare as on the day she was born; I will make her like a desert, turn her into a parched land, and slay her with thirst. I will not show my love to her children, because they are the children of adultery. Their mother has been unfaithful and has conceived them in disgrace. She said, "I will go after my lovers, who give me my food and my water, my wool and my linen, my oil and my drink." (Hos. 2:3–5)

God promised severe measures if the invitation to come home was left unheeded. Jesus will "slay us with thirst" if we persist in our affairs.

In my heart, I see the prodigal wife (like the prodigal son) sitting in a field eating pig food, with a hunger and thirst transcending the desire for a good meal. Jesus often gives us an insatiable thirst as a means of disciplining us. Can you remember a time in your life when your heart's thirst became incurably "quench-less"—*nothing* could offer relief but Jesus? Perhaps that's what's going on in your heart right now.

God became painfully specific about the horror of his wife's actions. Though she was conceived and married with unimaginable grace, she produced dis-grace-full offspring. Her life became a-grace. Sometimes Jesus has to draw back the curtains on our "mistakes," "human foibles," "weaknesses," and "mess-ups" and reveal them for what they really are—idols and adulteries and prostitutions. It's the only way to reach our deluded hearts.

Consider how God experienced his wife's actions: *"Here's what, in effect, you are saying with your life. 'I am going to run into the market square and jump into bed with whoever can give me what my heart desires.'"* There is always some perceived payoff as we choose something to worship or someone to jump into bed with—beyond or alongside of Jesus.

When she finally wakes up, I can hear the promiscuous wife of Jesus saying in her heart, "Against you and you alone have I sinned, O perfect Bridegroom." But more often than not, coming to our senses is preceded by coming to our knees. Affairs of the mind, heart, and body aren't easily broken. We must learn to see our sins as expressions of who we have become: We are idolaters who cultivate addictions and adulterers who engage in prostitution.

JESUS MAY GIVE US PAINFUL THORNS AND UNASSAILABLE WALLS

> Therefore I will block her path with thornbushes; I will wall her in so that she cannot find her way. She will chase after her lovers but

> not catch them; she will look for them but not find them. Then she will say, "I will go back to my husband as at first, for then I was better off than now." (Hos. 2:6–7)

It's *essential* that we primarily focus on the *purpose* of discipline rather than on the tit-for-tat correlation of every painful event of life. Discipline's purpose is to recapture our hearts. *Divorce is not an option.* What pain and closed doors has God already used in your life, leading you to say, "I will go back to my husband, Jesus, for when I was with him, I was better off than I am now." Are there situations in your life beyond your control that may represent a thorny hedge or a wall too high for you to scale? Maybe you have even asked friends to pray for the removal or change of the very thing God intends to use to recapture your heart: a job change, a health challenge, an economic crisis, a broken engagement, a rebellious child, a season of feeling absolutely alone, the failures of those you have always counted on…

Stop and think for a moment. Remember when you first came to the assurance of your salvation. What words or images describe the joy and peace you experienced? Think about the "better off-ness" of that season in your life compared to what life feels like today. Do you remember a time when your heart was able to say, "Your love, Jesus, is better than life"? Let's come to our senses and return to the enjoyment of his embrace.

Jesus May Withhold Fruit from Our Labors

> She has not acknowledged that I was the one who gave her the grain, the new wine and oil, who lavished on her the silver and gold—which they used for Baal. Therefore I will take away my grain when it ripens, and my new wine when it is ready. I will take back my wool and my linen, intended to cover her nakedness. (Hos. 2:8–9)

God's wife had been saying, *"my food, my water, my wool, my, my, my,"* as though her prostitution entitled her to provision and ownership. But Jesus says to us, "*Whatever you have, it comes from my joyful generosity. Everything that exists belongs to me—even your next breath. I am going to cause your lovers to fail you. This will hurt. It's supposed to.*" Because she did not acknowledge that her blessings came from God, God said he would withhold those blessings—even take back what he'd already given.

I am reminded of proud king Nebuchadnezzar of Babylon who was advised by Daniel: "Renounce your sins by doing what is right, and your wickedness by being kind to the oppressed. It may be that then your prosperity will continue" (Dan. 4:27). But the king ignored the advice and suffered the consequences:

> As the king was walking on the roof of the royal palace of Babylon, he said, "Is not this the great Babylon I have built as the royal residence, by my mighty power and for the glory of my majesty?"
>
> The words were still on his lips when a voice came from heaven,…"Your royal authority has been taken from you." (Dan. 4:28–31)

Because of his pride, God withheld the fruit of his labor. Through painful providence—including eating grass, a baptism of dew, and taking on a "birdlike" appearance (read it for yourself! Dan. 4:33)—the king was brought to repentance and finally said, "At the end of that time, I, Nebuchadnezzar, raised my eyes toward heaven, and my sanity was restored. Then I praised the Most High; I honored and glorified him who lives forever" (v. 34).

What would you *willingly* have Jesus withhold from your life so that you might once again be able to say, "Whom have I in heaven but you? And earth has nothing I desire besides you. My flesh and my heart may fail, but God is the strength of my heart and my portion forever!" (Ps. 73:25–26).

Jesus May Expose Our Idols and Adulteries

> So now I will expose her lewdness before the eyes of her lovers; no one will take her out of my hands. (Hos. 2:10)

When infatuation and intrigue with our idols and affairs begin to fade—if we are fortunate—a healthy shattering is on the way. What is worse than being shattered? Being exposed before our impotent lovers. Jesus loves us enough to expose us through a wide range of "sting" operations. If you have ever been involved in an intervention of a loved one suffering the destructive power of an addiction, then you have an image of what's going on in this passage.

Jesus, our husband, will intervene in our affairs. And sometimes, we will hate him for it. But later we will bless him for caring enough to bring us to our senses.

Jesus May Dull Our Experience of Worship

> "I will stop all her celebrations: her yearly festivals, her New Moons, her Sabbath days—all her appointed feasts. I will ruin her vines and her fig trees, which she said were her pay from her lovers; I will make them a thicket, and wild animals will devour them. I will punish her for the days she burned incense to the Baals; she decked herself with rings and jewelry, and went after her lovers, but me she forgot," declares the LORD. (Hos. 2:11–13)

It's easy to understand that Jesus will quite effectively, in his own time, remove the enjoyment of our affairs from us. After all, we always choose our idols and affairs based on some desired payoff. If the payoff is gone, then why continue the affair?

However, we also need to realize that Jesus may discipline us by

taking from our hearts the normal enjoyment we experience in reading the Bible, worshiping him, and praying—*truly* slaying us with thirst. Doesn't that make sense? Why would he allow our hearts the taste of rich intimacy when we are sleeping around?

Some of us are having affairs with worship, rather than experiencing the other-centered adoration of Jesus, our Husband. In our consumeristic approach, we run from worship leader to worship leader, praise band to praise band, smells and bells to smells and bells, and church to church—a thinly veiled attempt to keep the "spiritual high" going without serious reflection in our hearts.

If you aren't *enjoying* worship right now, perhaps you adore other lovers more than your Husband Jesus. Maybe you aren't really bored; maybe your heart is making love somewhere else. In all of our worship, have we forgotten Jesus?

Jesus Always Takes Us "Away" to Recapture Our Hearts

> Therefore I am now going to allure her; I will lead her into the desert and speak tenderly to her. There I will give her back her vineyards, and will make the Valley of Achor a door of hope. There she will sing as in the days of her youth, as in the day she came up out of Egypt. (Hos. 2:14–15)

In all the different ways Jesus disciplines us as his beloved Bride, *this* is always the end, the goal, the feast, the almost unimaginable purpose. He will fill his embrace with *us* and fill our hearts with the song of the gospel and turn our deep valley of trouble into a wide-open door of hope. What wondrous, painful, persistent love is this?

It is only the angry, sick, evil husband who batters his wife into submission. Jesus, our Husband, *allures us into the desert to speak tenderly to us.* The desert is a place of being cut off or separated from our idols and lovers for the purpose of being recaptured, re-enraptured with Jesus, our Lover. Ray Ortlund Jr. comments on the original context:

> Yahweh will reinvigorate Israel's first love by leading them back into the wilderness. The point is that the opulence of Samaria will never provide the surroundings in which her heart can be won back. But separated from her lovers, deprived of her pleasures through adversity, she will fall in love with Yahweh again. He will manifest his love in winning ways, and she will be his.[1]

Some of you reading this are beginning to see little lights going on somewhere in your hearts. Does "desert" come close to describing what you feel on the inside? Maybe, "wilderness," "barrenness," "vacuum," or "emptiness" describe your inner pain. Don't run on to the next chapter too fast. Is it possible that Jesus has been luring you into a desert of discipline so that you might know the dessert of his delight? Think about it. Can you hear him wooing with words like these, "You have forsaken your first love. Remember the height from which you have fallen!" (Rev. 2:4–5).

Jesus Relates to Us As Husband, Not Master

> "In that day," declares the LORD, "you will call me 'my husband'; you will no longer call me 'my master' [my Baal]. I will remove the names of the Baals from her lips; no longer will their names be invoked. In that day I will make a covenant for them with the beasts of the field and the birds of the air and the creatures that move along the ground. Bow and sword and battle I will abolish from the land, so that all may lie down in safety. I will betroth you to me forever; I will betroth you in righteousness and justice, in love and compassion. I will betroth you in faithfulness, and you will acknowledge the LORD." (Hos. 2:16–20)

Jesus wants us, increasingly, to relate to him as our Husband-Lover, and not merely as a master-god. There is actually an intended play on words in this text. The phrase "my master," in verse 16 means "my Baal" in the Hebrew. To know Jesus better and better as our glorious Bridegroom is to be less and less deceived into looking to other lovers for life or crediting them with what Jesus alone can do.

Jesus' marriage covenant with us, the new covenant, will eventually make everything new—not just our hearts. A new heaven and a new earth will be our marriage chamber forever. The guarantee of such bliss stands with Jesus. Three times in these verses he affirms his betrothal of us, his legal commitment to us as covenant Husband. Jesus will never divorce his Bride, *never!* Righteousness, justice, love, compassion, faithfulness—he brings all of these into our marriage and into the world he is making new.

The result? We will "acknowledge" the Lord. The Hebrew word for this type of knowing is that used of the glorious, pleasure-full, fruit-bearing celebration of sex—the sacred gift and holy dance of covenant partners in marriage. Jesus intends and will enjoy connection with us that is only symbolized in the best of our relationships and the most intimate of moments. Peter Kreeft writes, "This spiritual intercourse with God is the ecstasy hinted at in all earthly intercourse, physical or spiritual. It is the ultimate reason why sexual passion is so strong, so different from other passions, so heavy with suggestions of profound meanings that just elude our grasp."[2]

But let us never, ever forget: It is only because Jesus experienced our divorce and death on the cross that he is able to love us with a transcendent, troubling, and triumphant love. Let's give up our affairs and come home to Jesus. Indeed, he will embrace us in his arms. What are we waiting for? *Oh, blessed alluring desert of tender words and refining grace, do your patient and persistent work in our hearts! Even so, Lord Jesus, the Spirit and your Bride say, "Come!"*

Idolatry is WORSHIPPING anything that ought to be used, or using anything that is *meant* to be worshipped.

AUGUSTINE

Sooner or later one ASKS even of Shakespeare, even of *Beethoven,* "Is that all?"

Aldous HUXLEY

DEAR CHILDREN, KEEP *yourselves* FROM IDOLS.

—1 JOHN 5:21

God made man in HIS own image and man *returned* the compliment.

Blaise PASCHAL

I AM THE LORD YOUR GOD, WHO BROUGHT YOU OUT OF EGYPT, OUT OF THE LAND OF SLAVERY. YOU SHALL HAVE NO OTHER GODS *before* ME. YOU SHALL NOT MAKE FOR YOURSELF AN IDOL IN THE FORM OF ANYTHING....

—EXODUS 20:2–4

CHAPTER SEVEN

Freedom for Idolaters *and* Addicts—Like Me

"Scotty, the phone's for you." I'd just finished the endless job of dusting and straightening the knickknack section. It was late August, right before I began the tenth grade. I'd recently taken my first "store job" at a local drugstore. Though I didn't have a driver's license yet, I could bike there easily enough. Quite unsuspectingly, I picked up the phone. "Hello, this is Scotty. May I help you?"

"Well, that all depends," came the sultry voice. "What are you doing tonight?"

I didn't recognize her voice at first, but she didn't miss a beat. "This is Mary [not her real name]. When I came in today to pick up a prescription, I got to thinking that it might be fun to get together tonight. I've got a bottle of vodka. What do you say? I can pick you up and take you home later."

There I was wearing my white drugstore shirt with chocolate ice cream stains—all of fifteen years old—and I was being pursued by an older woman (she had just turned seventeen). "Well, uuugh, sure. Sounds great! Why don't you come by about seven." My heart started beating faster than Tiger Woods can swing a golf club. Wild images of the evening ahead coursed through my fertile mind.

As we walked through her front door, I spotted the bottle of vodka on the floor. Up until that point, I hadn't experimented with alcohol. She poured both of us a glass, diluted with some orange juice. I so wanted acceptance—hers or anybody's. I sipped a little. It tasted like gasoline! I hated it, but wouldn't let on. It felt so good to be desired, to be wanted, to be pursued.

Pseudo-Healers in My Medicine Bag

Alcohol was not the first substance I'd abused. It was one in a string of pseudo-healers that I'd been collecting in my medicine bag since my mother's death. *Pseudo-healer* is a euphemism for *idol.* An idol is anything we trust in for deliverance in the place of Jesus and his grace.

Coming to grips with the implications of God's grace has required me to rewrite the story of my woundedness as a story of idol worship and substance abuse. I encourage you to think of your own story as you follow this evaluation of mine.

Collision at the Intersection

We primarily choose our pseudo-healers, or idols, at the intersection of our sinful nature and significant wounds (or other formative events of life). For instance, the collision that occurred in my eleven-year-old heart at the intersection of my mom's fatal car wreck and my sinful nature destroyed the only secure foundation I knew.

To be thrust into a world of intense aloneness, social alienation, and emotional chaos was devastating. It's only been since writing *Objects* that I have been able to see and own the degree to which deep insecurity took over my heart. I've worked so hard to deny and dance around the lack of confidence and sense of incompetence that I bring into so many areas of life. Even to this day, when my heart is not feasting on Christ, I can be paralyzed by feelings of shame and insecurity when confronted with tasks and situations that threaten to reveal me as an impotent man.

Feeling very much an orphan, I experienced God as little more than a superstition or cultural add-on until I turned eighteen. So I chose something else to worship—something else to trust in—a "god" (idol) that offered the assurance of blessings I desperately sought and the avoidance of further curses. The idol I chose was *comfort.* My wounded, foolish heart told me: "Your world is filled with chaos, uncertainty, and insecurity—your only hope is *comfort.* Seek its face!"

It's little wonder that four decades later after choosing to worship comfort, my favorite written confession of faith has become the Heidelberg Catechism—a sixteenth-century celebration of the gospel and its implications. Take a moment and reflect on its first question and answer:

> Q. 1. What is your only comfort, in life and in death?
> A. That I belong—body and soul, in life and in death—not to myself but to my faithful Savior, Jesus Christ, who at the cost of his own blood has fully paid for all my sins and has completely freed me from the dominion of the devil; that he protects me so well that without the will of my Father in heaven not a hair can fall from my head; indeed, that everything must fit his purpose for my salvation. Therefore, by his Holy Spirit, he also assures me of eternal life, and makes me wholeheartedly willing and ready from now on to live for him.[1]

But since I was a stranger to Jesus and the comfort of the gospel, I had to find a mediator, or means, of relating to my illusionary idol of comfort—some substance, entity, or person to grant me entrance into the holy place of my god. My first substance of choice became food, especially sweets. After Mom died, desserts and "carbs" became the mediators between my wound and my idol, comfort. I felt very much at peace, at least momentarily, as long as the sugar in my blood was at a certain level.

Collusion Between Co-Conspirators

However, all idolatry eventually brings about a co-conspiracy between your idol and your substance of choice. The two become cobelligerents in destroying your life and bringing further alienation from the one true God. Instead of a consoling substance, your heart begins to experience the control of substance. This is the fertile soil in which addictions are sown and grown. Within two years, I was five feet tall, weighed one-hundred and seventy pounds, and was tagged with the nickname "Meatball." I began to despise my body.

So moving into junior high school, the god of "comfort through food" failed to satisfy the demands of my wounded, sinful heart. Like every preadolescent or early adolescent child, I was feeling the need to connect with my peers. So in addition to comfort, I added two more idols to my pantheon—*significance and acceptance.* I reasoned, "If I can be welcomed by kids my age and known for something cool, then I will feel comfort." I wanted to matter. I wanted freedom from the paralyzing chaos of deep insecurity. I wanted to be noticed without really being known.

Sugar wasn't enough anymore. Desserts could no longer serve as the fuel for my idolatry, so I purged. I spent a summer eating little more than lettuce, and I established a regimen of jogging in my neighborhood, wrapped in plastic wrap under sweat clothes. I lost forty pounds in three months, becoming anemic but noticed. Needing a new substance to usher me into the presence of significance, acceptance, and comfort, I next chose *clothes.*

Clothes became both a means of gaining acceptance and significance and an effective way to stay hidden. I remember flipping through my brother's high-school yearbook the summer before my freshman year. I came to the superlative section—the place where certain seniors are awarded the "best" and "most likely" awards by their graduating class.

I remember distinctively saying to myself. *I will have the "best dressed" superlative as a senior.* The heck with "most likely to succeed" or "most well-rounded" or "best personality." I set my heart to be superlative at wearing fig leaves. The consuming desire to be noticed and wanted plus an inviolate commitment to be neither known nor exposed took over.

The more I felt significant, accepted, and comforted through appearance, the more willing I was to do *anything* to make or steal money to get more clothes. It really didn't matter what the style was, as long as I was the first to be sporting the newest trend with the right labels.

Recently I have noticed (of course glancing, not gazing) young girls wearing jeans and other pants with lower and lower and lower waistlines. I've grieved for myself and for them. If I were an eleven-year-old girl living today with my deep insecurities, I would be the one in my school most likely to be sent home for taking the jeans down that last half-inch too far. Our idols demand as much as we are willing to give, and much more. And based on the degree of alienation we experience from God and ourselves, we will pay almost any price. Israel was even willing, at times, to sacrifice their children to appease their idols (Ezek. 20:31).

Painful, shameful secrets have emerged in my healing journey—including this one: I remembered finding my mom's purse, in a closet among other items stored after her death, and taking the remaining cash simply to feed my drug of choice—more clothes. The payoff of my idolatry—the blessing of significance, acceptance, and comfort—was worth the addiction to my substance, clothes—even to the extent that I stole from my dead mom's purse.

Every idol and substance eventually proves insufficient, for there is only one Savior who can truly meet our desperate need. So in the summer between my junior and senior year of high school, I added a new substance to aid me in my worship of significance, acceptance, and comfort—alcohol. That brings us back to the account of how I abused alcohol and how it abused me…

It was about a year and a half after my encounter with Mary when I got a job playing in a beach-music band. I couldn't believe it: I was the organ player for a ten-piece R & B band playing the music I so loved! It felt awesome to belong! Thrilled, but nervous before my first date with the band, I dug out a bottle of Turpenhydrate cough medicine from the cabinet, remembering that it had made me feel a tad woozy as a child when Mom gave me a teaspoonful. I thought it might ease my nerves a little. I tucked it into my garment bag.

"Hey, anybody want one of these?" Just before we went on for our first set, one of the guys pulled out a six pack of beer, a risky thing to do at the YMCA. Once again, desperate to belong, to have family… "Heck, yeah. Give me one!" So I drank my cough syrup and chased it with a beer. For a few hours I was flying! It felt good to be secure, confident, liked, welcomed. However, when I went home, the fun ended with my hugging the base of the toilet for about an hour, puking up my acceptance and confidence. "Oh God, I will never do that again!"

Try the next weekend and the one after that and the one after that. "What do you guys want me to get from the package store? Have you ever tried grape vodka?" It was the uncle of our bass player, the driver of our van, and "chaperone" for our jobs. My desperate longing for acceptance was beginning to be superseded by a greater longing to feel high all the time. I liked me so much better when I was loaded. Now the vodka actually tasted pretty good.

My weekend drinking began to bleed over into the week. There's a lot riding on that final year as a senior in high school—college and all. But I was "clever" enough to get into UNC without working very hard, so… "Guys, we've been asked to play for a grain-alcohol party, and they're gonna have a stripper!" I didn't know what grain alcohol was, but I did know what a stripper was. It didn't matter, after being introduced to a certain grain-alcohol drink called PJ, I didn't notice the stripper or anything else—but I sure liked me.

It was during that final year of high school that I became a Christian—a pretty dramatic conversion out of a life of indulgence and partying and playing in a band. "Yes, I'm sure," I said, and my uncle prayed with me as I gave my heart to Jesus. Did my idols and substance abuse die right on the spot? How I wish. The summer of 1968 included traveling with a group of other young Christians on my first mission trip—to Mexico. After returning, we formed a musical group called The New Directions, a group I performed with all during my college years.

The Deceitfulness of Christian Riches

In the context of serving in this ministry group as a young Christian and by attending various campus ministries at the University of North Carolina, it became pretty obvious that God had given me a gift I neither sought nor deserved (as though we deserve any of his gifts!). That gift was the ability to grasp and communicate great biblical and theological truths. The anomaly in this is the fact that I had never been a reader or disciplined student up till that point. I'd never read a single book all the way through, until college—though I had won my sixth-grade-class reading award, partially by inventing nonexistent titles of books and names of authors. Idolaters resort to desperate measures.

But when I got my first taste of significance and acceptance through spiritual knowledge, the desperate need for alcohol and clothes receded...a little. I cut a whole week of classes at UNC to underline my New Testament so as to be even more familiar and impressive with my new drug of choice.

Let me summarize the story up to this point. From the wreckage of my sinful heart and the death of my mom, a strong and deep-rooted insecurity settled into my heart—about me and life in general. I chose the idols of comfort, significance, and acceptance to worship and love with all my heart, soul, mind, and strength. To empower or fuel my worship, I chose food, clothes, and alcohol as substances. After becoming a Christian, I became a forgiven idolater, and then added biblical and theological knowledge to my list of substances to abuse.

Then, during my freshman year in college, the girl I dated most often through high school was also killed in a tragic car wreck—another collision at the intersection of my wounded and sinful, but now forgiven, heart. The pain of losing the most intimate relationship I had since Mom's death was too much to sustain—especially since Debbie was ripped from my life in the same way Mom was. What gods would serve me now? It didn't take long to identify and welcome two more idols into the worship center of my heart. I rolled out the red carpet for *painless heart* and *control.*

The great security of knowing I would go to heaven if I died didn't do squat to heal the deep insecurity that still paralyzed my heart. Therefore, I chose to believe a lie. I believed I needed a painless heart and control over my world more than I needed Jesus and what he chose to give me.

So did I consciously reject Jesus? Oh no, no, no—far, far from it! I chose to become an even greater abuser of my new substance—biblical and theological knowledge—especially the theology of God's sovereignty and grace. I became addicted—flat out mainlining, snorting, puffing, inhaling addicted—believing that a painless heart and control over my chaotic world was more beautiful and worthy than Jesus. *I hope you can realize how painful it is to document that last sentence.*

It's amazing what one can do with a wounded and deceitful heart, a stockpile of theological knowledge, and a rather quick mind. It proved to be the most effective and deadly idol structure of any I had created. I succeeded—until recent years—to get comfort, significance, acceptance, a painless heart, and control through *what* I know rather than a shalom that passes all understanding through *whom* I know. The saddest part is, many times I didn't know the difference.

Idols of the Heart

When Malachi came on the Israelite scene—about one hundred years after the end of the Babylonian captivity—God's manifest presence had once again flooded the holy city. The temple had been rebuilt, the sacrificial system reinstated, and the wall around the city completed. But the excitement level was more in line with a backyard sparkler party than a huge fourth-of-July celebration.

Externally the people continued to worship God; but internally they worshiped...not God. Though Malachi inherited a congregation of bored and boring believers, they were far from sedentary. They may have been lethargic in temple worship, but in terms of heart worship, they were lethal!

The more obvious idolatries weren't present—the ones that sent God's people into exile in the first place. No one was tempted to set up an Asherah pole; no hand-crafted altars to the Canaanite deities of Baal were in use; the Egyptian fertility gods weren't being invoked alongside of YAHWEH. And yet the omnipresent idols—the idols that you and I carry around and crank out like the daily news, the idols that Ezekiel spoke about in the early years of the captivity—these idols were subtly and surely taking over once again: idols of the heart.

> Some of the elders of Israel came to me and sat down in front of me. Then the word of the LORD came to me: "Son of man, these men have set up *idols in their hearts* and put wicked stumbling blocks before their faces. Should I let them inquire of me at all? Therefore speak to them and tell them, 'This is what the Sovereign LORD says: When any Israelite sets up *idols in his heart* and puts a wicked stumbling block before his face and then goes to a prophet, I the LORD will answer him myself in keeping with

> his great idolatry. I will do this to recapture the hearts of the people of Israel, who have all deserted me for their idols.'" (Ezek. 14:1–5)

What are idols of the heart? Anything and everything that I desire more than I desire God and his glory. Anything? Anything! Power, sexual pleasure, control over my circumstances, acceptance, prestige, revenge, being worshiped, a certain physical appearance—all can be idols of the heart.

The Hebrew language makes a powerful play on words when comparing the worship of God with the worship of idols. One of the main names by which the Scriptures refer to our great covenant God is *Elohim.* But the Hebrew word for *idol* is very similar, *elolim.* How much difference does one letter make? *Elolim* means "revered nonsense," or "empty nothing." To cling to an idol is to have reverence for an empty nothing.

When Judah was worshiping the foreign gods, the empty nothings of the Canaanites, their external acts of reverence were actually efforts to gain the demands of greater idols—freedom from fear, economic security, and control over their destiny. Even though Malachi's audience was "sleeping through church," their hearts were quite fired up about worship—but they were worshiping gods other than the Lord.

How intense can the desires for things other than God become? Very strong. To the point of lust? That's normal. To the point of obsession? Easily so. To the point of addiction? All the time.

ADDICTION?

Stop and think for a moment. Do you have anyone in your immediate or extended family who is addicted to alcohol or some other controlled substance? Have you personally struggled or do you know anyone who has or is struggling with an eating disorder? Are you aware of any family members, associates, or friends in Christ who have acknowledged a sexual addiction or some other addiction? My wife recently asked this question to a gathering of nearly three hundred ladies. Nearly two-thirds of them raised their hands. The power of addiction is epidemic.

Destructive addictions have left their ugly trail in my family and in my wife's. One of my aunts was addicted to heroine for ten years and lost her family, her health, and much more. My father-in-law suffered from alcoholism and took his life not many months after becoming a Christian. That's just the tip of the iceberg.

Though I have never been chemically dependent on any substance, nevertheless, I have abused alcohol to meet the idolatrous demands of my heart. I have used the ministry to prop up and feed my idols. I have indulged food and visual material (I might as well say it—pornography) as a way of granting me what I sometimes obsessively want and don't think God will give—excitement, pleasure, escape. I'll gladly be quite vulnerable in print if it will encourage more of us to take this whole topic of idolatry and addiction very seriously.

If we are honest about our idols, we position ourselves to experience a tremendous movement of the reign of grace. What are the implications of grace for idolatry and addiction? Very great and very many. Indeed, we are victims and agents of our own destruction.

The Descent of Idolatry into Addiction

The following chart demonstrates how easy it is to get hooked into the downward drift of idolatry leading to addiction. Since I'm personally familiar with the deceitfulness and prevalence of its abuse, I'll use alcohol in this illustration. But plug in your idol(s) and substance(s) of choice, and see if you can trace your own descent into slavery. Many thanks to my friend Dr. Ed Welch for helping me understand the phenomenon of addiction through the lens of a biblical world-view.

An Unguarded and Thirsty Heart

Naive, forgetful, or careless about the power of indwelling sin, you experiment with alcohol, thinking it may give you what you want. For instance, you want acceptance, so you drink a beer that's been offered to you. The idol? I *must* be accepted by my friends. God's love is not better than life. Life is acceptance.

Intrigue and Flirtation

You begin a "relationship" with the substance because it seems to fulfill your deepest longing—acceptance with friends. But now, you actually start to like the taste of beer.

Infatuation and Euphoria

You start to like who you are when you're a little high. You begin a more regular and exciting relationship with alcohol. The heck with just being accepted by the original friends. You're accepted by cool strangers. You graduate from beer to stronger drinks.

Love and Betrayal

Now, however, life isn't one big party. The inevitable pain and disappointments of life are encroaching. You have to be loaded to deal with the pressures and stresses of life. But the more you drink, the more you sneak around, play games, become irresponsible, let people down. You're no longer just using; you're getting used.

Worship and Addiction

Dependence has led to obsession, and obsession to addiction—either chemical or psychological. You're no longer in control. You know it, and you deny it. Your idol of the heart (wanting acceptance more than God and his glory) has been replaced with the worship of alcohol. You have to have it. It is better than life, because it has become life.

Ed Welch's definition of addiction brings the picture into clear focus: "Addiction is bondage to the rule of a substance, activity, or state of mind, which then becomes the center of life, defending itself [the addiction defends itself—personification used here!] from the truth so that even bad consequences don't bring repentance, leading to further estrangement from God."[2]

The Relationship between Idolatry and Addiction

What do you personally make of the whole topic of addiction? How have you been taught, if at all, that addictions are generated and are to be dealt with? Christians vary in their opinions about the relationship between sin and addiction. Cornelius Plantinga wisely comments, "Addiction is a dramatic portrait of some main dynamics of sin, a stage show of warped longings, split wills, encumbered liberties, and perverse attacks on one's own well-being—some of the same dramatic machinery that moves the general tragedy of sin forward. Addiction shows us, once more, the progressive and lethal character of moral evil, the movement of corruption that Patrick McCormick calls 'a conversion unto death.'"[3]

At a time when support groups, recovery groups, and addiction groups are multiplying throughout the culture and in our churches, we have a tremendous opportunity and responsibility to become informed about these matters. Welch offers invaluable insight into this enslaving and destructive journey.

> Did you ever notice how many biblical stories can be summarized with these questions: "Whom will you worship? The Creator or the created thing, God or man, the Divine King or worthless idols?" The basic story line of the Old Testament is about people who find idolatry irresistible. Then God, ultimately through Jesus, comes to rescue his people out of their enslaving practices. Accordingly, all sin is summarized as idolatry (e.g., Deut. 4:23;

> Eph. 5:5)….With this in mind, notice the paternal warning at the end of 1 John: "Dear children, keep yourselves from idols" (5:21).
>
> Idols include anything we worship; the lust for pleasure, respect, love, power, control, or freedom from pain. Furthermore, the problem is not outside of us, located in a liquor store or on the Internet; the problem is within us. Alcohol and drugs are essentially satisfiers of deeper idols. The problem is not the idolatrous substance; it is the false worship of the heart….The desired payoff? The purpose of all idolatry is to manipulate the idol *for our own benefit.* This means that we don't want to be ruled by idols. Instead, we want to *use* them.
>
> We don't want to be ruled by alcohol, drugs, sex, gambling, food, or anything. No, we want these substances or activities to give us what we want: good feelings, a better self-image, a sense of power, or whatever our heart is craving….Idols, however, do not cooperate. Rather than mastering our idols, we become enslaved by them and begin to look like them. As idols are deaf, dumb, blind, utterly senseless, and irrational, so "those who make them will be like them, and so will all who trust in them" (Ps. 115:8).
>
> How can these lifeless idols exert such power? They dominate because of a powerful but quiet presence that hides behind every idol, Satan himself (Eph. 6:12)….Satan wants to overturn God's order and have physical desires rule the person. Instead of food, sex or rest being treated as God-given pleasures, they are exalted to become ruling lusts that enslave.[4]

Examining the biblical theme of idolatry provides an invaluable way to reflect upon the development of many addictions. This is not to dismiss, replace, or minimize the important conversation about genetic or physiological addictions. Rather, it is appropriately to emphasize that the central issue of life is always: "Who do you say the Son of Man is? What have you done with Jesus and the 'comfort' that only he can provide?"

We are made to worship, love, and serve God above all else. Our hearts are always worshiping something or someone. Addictions are not all generated in the same way, but all addictions are invariably related to the worship of one's heart. And inevitably, we idolaters and addicts must deal with our dysfunctional polytheism—ceasing to blame our dysfunctional families for our steady diet of misery. *The reign of grace confronts our false worship. All other forms of grace are simply insufficient to deal with the core issue in life.*

Further Up *and* Further In

One-of-a-Kind *Love* Affair

Ezekiel 16

As God's image bearers, there is romance DNA written into every cell of our being. The craving to be championed and cherished shows up in our art, advertisements, arguments—anywhere you look. Author John Eldredge uncorks the tantalizing aroma of this constitutive longing better than any writer I have discovered since C. S. Lewis. His skill at calling us to risk the wild adventure of coming alive to the echoes of Eden and the first fruits of paradise have confronted a passionless evangelicalism and a generation without an ultimate narrative by which to understand our irrepressible longing for deep connection. He writes, "The Romance has most often come to us in the form of two deep desires: the longing for adventure that *requires* something of us, and the desire for intimacy—to have someone truly know us for ourselves, while at the same time inviting us to *know* them in the naked and discovering way lovers come to know each other on the marriage bed."[1]

However, the more we immerse ourselves in the Story and stories of God's Word, the more we will find ourselves revealed not as *hopeless romantics finally getting asked to the ball,* but as *irresponsible prostitutes becoming the beloved queen of the King of glory, Jesus.* The sacred romance isn't a biblical version of Cinderella. It's actually the reversal of Cinderella. Imagine one of the ugly stepsisters being wanted, wooed, and won by the passionate affections and unimaginable sacrifice of the Great Prince.

The prophet Ezekiel's telling of this one-of-a-kind love affair is surpassed by none. Though I will only be able to present the highlights of Ezekiel 16, I challenge you to read the whole chapter very slowly, savoring each detail and image as though your life depended on it. For in a certain sense, it does.

Above all, look for Jesus in this story, for he is the one of whom Ezekiel wrote about from afar. Become as familiar as possible with the way Jesus' love for his Bride is revealed in this allegory of passion and finds fulfillment in the gospel of grace. For surely, the most powerful way to topple the idols and terminate the affairs of our hearts is to gain a richer understanding and deeper experience of Jesus as our incomparable Bridegroom. Know the sacred Romancer so well that all other deceptive counterfeits and seductive suitors will be mocked sooner, rather than later, by your betrothed and enraptured heart. Seek to know your sin and Jesus' song as well as the Cleveland Symphony knew Mozart's *Magic Flute.*

One evening this great body of musicians was performing before a packed house, when an electrical storm caused the lights to go out in the auditorium. Undaunted by the darkness, the members of the symphony knew the music so well that they finished the concert without missing a beat or note. The audience expressed their appreciation with a rousing standing ovation and thunderous applause.

Not for the praise of men, but for the glory of our Bridegroom and because of a desire to love him more wholeheartedly, know the music of the gospel so well you can live it in the dark places and sing it in the face of raging temptation.

How Deep Is Your Love?

If one word captures the essence of all sin, it is *idolatry*—giving to someone or something the adoration, affection, and allegiance that rightfully belong to God alone.

If one word captures the truly offensive nature of Judah's idolatry, it is *adultery*—idolatry viewed as the violation of God's glorious marriage covenant with us.

And if one word captures the horrid degree to which Judah's adultery had been carried, it is *prostitution*—using the very gifts God gave her to attract any passerby to be her lover.

Ezekiel 16 is a lurid account of God's intense romance with his ill-deserving people. "Hosea's Israel was simply a foolishly promiscuous woman. Ezekiel's Jerusalem is a thoroughly depraved and degraded prostitute."[2] Ezekiel describes the story of idolatry and addiction in terms of a powerful love story. Story has a way of conveying the profound realities of the gospel like nothing else—especially when the stories are true.

The backdrop of this unearthly love affair is the Israelite exile to the powerful Babylonian empire. God's people have been deported. The captives cannot believe that God would treat his covenant people so harshly. The prophet Ezekiel is called upon to speak the heart of God. Just as the prophet Nathan confronted King David's adultery through an allegory, so Ezekiel confronts a whole nation with theirs. In essence, God's people were asking the same question early in the captivity that they asked Malachi over a century and a half later: "How have you loved us?"

God's Compassionate Love for an Undeserving Bride

The first section of this amazing chapter (vv. 1–14) gives an overview of the beginning of this love affair. Israel is depicted as being an unwanted baby, the offspring of pagans, "thrown out into the open field, for on the day you were born you were despised" (v. 5).

But God had compassion when he saw her and said to this infant girl, "Live!" (v. 6). Left for prostitution by her parents, Israel was rescued unto adoption by the perfect Father. God caused her to grow, providing everything necessary for her health and nurture. In time, this little girl showed signs of emerging puberty.

The allegory then shifts into an endearing scene in which God pursued and secured this young woman in the riches of his grace, pledging covenant marriage. "I spread the corner of my garment over you and covered your nakedness. I gave you my solemn oath and entered into a covenant with you, declares the Sovereign LORD, and you became mine" (v. 8). "You became mine"; there is no phrase God can utter which carries more arresting power and charm than this one. The act of covering her with the corner of his garment is a picture of how a Near-Eastern man would publicly express his intent to marry. God betrothed himself to an unsuspecting bride. We love him, only because he first loved us.

Verses 9–14 record the lavish generosity God showered upon his beloved Bride. There are seven uses of the personal pronoun "I" in this paragraph: *I* bathed you; *I* clothed you; *I* dressed you; *I* adorned you; *I* put bracelets on your arm; *I* put a ring on your nose; *I* gave you splendor. An unwanted, left-for-dead, baby girl ends up becoming the beloved, bejeweled, and beautified queen of God. There is only one explanation for this great reversal: God's merciful *reign of grace*—surely a symbol of the unsearchable riches of grace God lavishes upon us, the Bride of Christ.

But the depth of our depravity and the insanity of sin are painfully exposed against these extraordinary affections with which God enriched his Bride. She scorned his gifts and attention and prostituted herself with foreign lovers: "But you trusted in your beauty and used your fame to become a prostitute. You lavished your favors on anyone who passed by and your beauty became his.... You also took the fine jewelry I gave you, the jewelry made of my gold and silver, and you made for yourself male idols and engaged in prostitution with them" (vv. 15, 17).

Christopher Wright comments, "The temptation to make the gifts of God the object of trust instead of trusting in the giver himself is one that has never failed to snare God's people through history. The very things that most prove the grace of God—the gifts he has given us—become the things that we use to replace him."[3]

How deceitful and ugly is sin? Those who are called to be for the praise of God's glory choose to live for the fame of their own story. The graced become a disgrace. The cherished of God become the chattel of Johns.

Adultery unto Prostitution

How does adultery lead to prostitution? In the same way idolatry can lead to addiction. The theme of *adultery unto prostitution* may prove to be an ever more powerful way for us to understand how idolatry develops and how it can lead from compulsion to obsession to various degrees of addiction. Ezekiel's allegory continues, as he reveals the names of the lovers into whose arms Gods people have placed themselves.

Religious Prostitution

> You took some of your garments to make gaudy high places, where you carried on your prostitution. Such things should not happen, nor should they ever occur. You also took the fine jewelry I gave you, the jewelry made of my gold and silver, and you made for yourself male idols and engaged in prostitution with them. And you took your embroidered clothes to put on them, and you offered my oil and incense before them. Also the food I provided for you—the fine flour, olive oil and honey I gave you to eat—you offered as fragrant incense before them. That is what happened, declares the Sovereign LORD. (vv. 16–19)

Throughout the period in which Israel was ruled by kings (the monarchy), "high places" were centers of idolatrous worship of pagan gods—often seducing God's people away from the exclusive worship of God (1 Kings 11:7–8). The mark of a good king was to tear down the high places, but a bad king tolerated this affront to the worship of God. The "high places" were also the elevated couches prostitutes used in pagan temples to offer sacrifices to fertility gods.

The message is clear. God's bride was sleeping around. Worship is to our relationship with God what sexual intimacy is to marriage. To compromise God's worship is to commit spiritual fornication. Unchecked, idolatry and adultery can lead us to engage in the unthinkable. "You took your sons and daughters whom you bore to me and sacrificed them as food to the idols. Was your prostitution not enough? You slaughtered my children and sacrificed them to the idols" (Ezek. 16:20–21).

Whether this reference to child sacrifice is literal or figurative, let's catch the full force of what God is saying here. *"I rescued you from death, as an unwanted infant, possibly from a life of prostitution. And now you have taken the children you have birthed unto me and have sacrificed them as currency for your prostitution."*

"In all your detestable practices and your prostitution you did not remember the days of your youth, when you were naked and bare, kicking about in your blood" (v. 22). Forgetting the unsearchable riches of God's mercy and grace, whether we do so intentionally or otherwise, begins the descent into idolatry. This is why we must sing Jesus' love song (the Gospel) to ourselves, and one another, continually. Such a serenade isn't narcissism, but fidelity.

Political Prostitution

> Woe! Woe to you, declares the Sovereign Lord. In addition to all your other wickedness, you built a mound for yourself and made a lofty shrine in every public square. At the head of every street you built your lofty shrines and degraded your beauty, offering your body with increasing promiscuity to anyone who passed by. You engaged in prostitution with the Egyptians, your lustful neighbors,

> and provoked me to anger with your increasing promiscuity. So I stretched out my hand against you and reduced your territory; I gave you over to the greed of your enemies, the daughters of the Philistines, who were shocked by your lewd conduct. You engaged in prostitution with the Assyrians too, because you were insatiable; and even after that, you still were not satisfied. Then you increased your promiscuity to include Babylonia, a land of merchants, but even with this you were not satisfied. (vv. 23–29)

In the period leading up to the Babylonian captivity, God's people had formed "working alliances" with other nations in a vain attempt to maintain political and economic equilibrium in the region. Rather than trusting in her covenant Husband for protection and provision, God's Bride increasingly "jumped into bed" with one lover after another—with Egypt (v. 26), Assyria (v. 28), and Babylon (v. 29). The very nations to whom she was called to be a light, she now lived among as a blight.

Just how frank is God in describing Jerusalem's unfaithfulness? Not a paraphrase, but a literal translation of the Hebrew text of Ezekiel 16:25 states that she "spread her legs for anyone who passed by." We may blush at such a graphic description of sin, and well we should. Because the period leading up to the Babylonian exile was one in which God lamented about his Bride, "They have no shame at all; they do not even know how to blush" (Jer. 8:12). This love story loses its power the very moment we forget to pray: Though I am made for wonder, I am prone to wander, Lord Jesus. Here's my heart, take and seal it, seal it for your marriage chamber that is to come.

The Covenantal Roots of Idolatry

What is the attraction of idolatry? How can we be so easily seduced? The concept of idolatry has covenantal roots. Look carefully at these instructions God gave his people before they went into the Promised Land.

> My angel will go ahead of you and bring you into the land of the Amorites, Hittites, Perizzites, Canaanites, Hivites and Jebusites, and I will wipe them out. Do not bow down before their gods or worship them or follow their practices. You must demolish them and break their sacred stones to pieces. Worship the LORD your God, and his blessing will be on your food and water. I will take away sickness from among you....Do not make a covenant with them or with their gods. (Exod. 23:23–25, 32)

In these wonderful words of promise, God pledges to bless the nation of Israel in the land of Canaan with good food and water and to take sickness away from his people, as they worship and serve him alone.

But Israel was also strongly warned against making a covenant with a foreign nation or making a covenant with (that is, worshiping) their gods. In the ancient Near East, a covenant document included several important details of the relationship between the covenanters. A prominent aspect of the covenant was a list of blessings to be provided for faithfulness to the covenant and a list of curses to be brought to bear upon covenant breakers.

Piecing these concepts together helps us recognize the covenantal nature of idolatry. *We enter into a covenant with a nation, a god, or an idol based on an intense desire for certain blessings and/or a desperate need to be protected from certain curses.*

For instance, God's Bride "got into bed" with Assyria when King Ahaz of Judah appealed to Assyria for help against the alliance of Syria and the northern kingdom of Israel. Ahaz was counting on a certain blessing: protection against attack. But he was also counting the aversion of a certain curse: the humiliation of possible defeat. Ahaz believed that a covenant with Assyria could bring blessings and avert curses for

Judah in a way that God's covenant with Judah would not. Thus, idolatry ensued.

How does this principle connect with our stories? What covenants have we entered that represent idolatry and spiritual adultery? When we believe there are blessings to be had and curses to be avoided that relationship with Jesus cannot provide, then we begin looking for another "god" that can meet our need. We begin worshiping that "god"—trusting, loving, serving our idol in the belief that blessings will come and curses will be averted.

The intensity level of my desire to be "blessed" and avoid being "cursed" will determine my willingness to "jump into bed" with another lover, or two, or three—thus, committing adultery against Jesus. These affairs most often begin when a normal temptation becomes an inordinate desire to be blessed with a lot of money, great popularity, power over people, a perfect physical shape, a happy marriage, or whatever.

The choice to commit adultery also becomes attractive when a normal concern grows into a huge fear that you may be cursed with a bald head, have a barren womb, get cancer, never own a Lexus, never graduate from seminary, or that you may not be able to fit into a size six dress when you are forty.

What "lovers" might someone be tempted to "jump into bed with" in order to obtain the blessings and avoid the curses listed above? What "blessings and curses" have great alluring power over your heart, even as you read this book? What "lover's" embrace are you tempted to run to right now in order to be blessed or to protect yourself from being cursed?

BEYOND PROSTITUTION

Is there something worse than unbridled prostitution?

> How weak-willed you are, declares the Sovereign LORD, when you do all these things, acting like a brazen prostitute! When you

> built your mounds at the head of every street and made your lofty shrines in every public square, you were unlike a prostitute, because you scorned payment.
>
> You adulterous wife! You prefer strangers to your own husband! Every prostitute receives a fee, but you give gifts to all your lovers, bribing them to come to you from everywhere for your illicit favors. So in your prostitution you are the opposite of others; no one runs after you for your favors. You are the very opposite, for you give payment and none is given to you. (Ezek. 16: 30–34)

Already exposed for her prostitution, now the adulteries of God's Bride are described in even worse terms. She became a nymphomaniac—actually paying her lovers to sleep with her! She used the gifts of God to bribe other lovers to sleep with her. At least a prostitute receives payment for services. Here, God's Wife has become someone who actually pays to be used by others.

In contemporary language, this may be about as good of an example of addiction as we will find in the Scriptures. Dr. Ed Welch writes,

> Can you see how the biblical theme of idolatry fits hand-in-glove with modern addictions? Drugs and sex are the modern golden calves erected by addicts to find meaning, power or pleasure apart from God. Addicts often believe they have found life, but any payoff they experience is short-lived and deceptive. They are blinded to the fact that they are having a banquet in the grave. They are truly out of control, victims of their own lust.[4]

Indeed, addiction is a worship disorder—a descending movement away from glory to darkness. Most addictions pass through idolatry to enslavement. We become enslaved to our addictions because we have become proficient in worshiping our idols.

In one sense, the whole story of the Bible can be seen as a worship war. God, who alone is worthy of our worship, powerfully rescues us, through the gospel, from enslavement to false gods and the destructiveness of idolatry. Though the war has been won by Jesus and the ultimate outcome secured, the battles rage until the Day he returns and perfects us in love.

Nothing has made my history of idolatry more painful than to see it as a history of adultery. But, at the same time, nothing has strengthened my faith, quickened my hope, and assured me of God's love more than to meditate on being a part of Jesus' Bride.

The Scriptures are unambiguous: Jesus knows that he died to make a prostitute his queen. The gospel is *this* wonderful and true. There are no surprises left for Jesus; he is under no illusion about the past of his Bride—or the present, for that matter, or the future. As depraved as we are, he is preparing us to be his utter delight. *This* is the only comfort that will bring health to these foolish and enslaved hearts of ours. God's Bride may have broken God's covenant, but she couldn't destroy it—and God's covenant is full of surprises!

Shocking Grace—Stunning Restorations

"However, I will restore....I will remember the covenant I made with you in the days of your youth, and I will establish an everlasting covenant with you" (vv. 53, 60).

If we were shocked by the account of the Bride's sin, then we should be even more shocked by this account of God's grace! She continually forgot to persistently remember the covenant, but God *never* forgets! God's memory is the foundation for our hope. God remembered the inviolate covenant of grace he established in order to have a people to whom he would rejoice over as a bridegroom rejoices over his bride (Isa. 62:5). He chose to establish this relationship as an "everlasting covenant."

Promised by Jeremiah well before the Babylonian captivity, the new covenant was put into effect through the first coming of Jesus as the revelation and ratification of this everlasting covenant.

> "The time is coming," declares the LORD, "when I will make a new covenant with the house of Israel and with the house of Judah. It will not be like the covenant I made with their forefathers when I took them by the hand to lead them out of Egypt, because they broke my covenant, though I was a husband to them," declares the LORD.
>
> "This is the covenant I will make with the house of Israel after that time," declares the LORD. "I will put my law in their minds and write it on their hearts. I will be their God, and they will be my people. No longer will a man teach his neighbor, or a man his brother, saying, 'Know the LORD,' because they will all know me, from the least of them to the greatest," declares the LORD. "For I will forgive their wickedness and will remember their sins no more." (Jer. 31:31–34)

As the New Testament unfolds, it becomes obvious that the new covenant is Jesus' marriage covenant with his Bride.

How Can Jesus Possibly Desire and Love a Wife like Us?

"So I will establish my covenant with you, and you will know that I am the LORD. Then,…I [will] make atonement for you for all you have done" (Ezek. 16:62–63).

Indeed, how can a whore become the beloved Wife and Queen of Jesus?

God the Father hates sin. He must judge it. Ezekiel graphically describes the consuming intensity of God's wrath that had to be poured out in response to the sin of his people (vv. 35–59). But God loves the sinful Bride he has promised to his Son. How can God possibly present such a Bride to his Son?

There is only one way. Jesus loved the Bride the Father promised him so much that he propitiated God's wrath and made atonement for her sin through his own death. On the cross, Jesus became the stripped and shamed promiscuous nymphomaniac, the blasphemous polytheist, the "arrogant, overfed and unconcerned" Sodomite (v. 49) for us! This is the ultimate dowry, the most expensive and glorious wedding arrangement imaginable. And, hallelujah, it is *ours!*

Sing this song to your heart, in the night and in the day. Sing it as your purest worship to Jesus. Sing it to our neighbors and the nations alike! "The Spirit and the bride say, 'Come!' And let him who hears say, 'Come!' Whoever is thirsty, let him come; and whoever wishes, let him take the free gift of the water of life" (Rev. 22:17).

Further Up *and* Further In

The Gospel Way of *Dismantling* Our Idols

GALATIANS

As a great prince seeking a bride, Jesus has won the war *for* our hearts and has secured our hand (our whole being!) in marriage. He "gave himself for our sins to rescue us from the present evil age" (Gal. 1:4). But the war *in* our hearts will continue until he returns to make us his perfected wife. Life between our justification and glorification is, as one of my friends loves to say, a glorious mess! We are the beloved, and yet, many times we think and act like the bedeviled. We truly love Jesus, *and* we truly love so many *empty nothings.* The wise Bride of Jesus cries out, "Give me an undivided heart…for great is your love toward me" (Ps. 86:11, 13). How does Jesus answer this cry?

In the Book of Galatians, the apostle Paul shows us how the advancing reign of grace is alone powerful enough to dethrone all rivals for Jesus' affection and free us for a life of worshiping God and loving others.

THE REIGN OF GRACE IS A SUBPOENA TO FREEDOM!

What leads to the slavery of idolatry and addiction? An intense craving and demand for counterfeit freedom (that is, autonomy), "I gotta be me!" What do slaves to idolatry and addictions need? *Real* freedom (that is, a life liberated to love and serve Jesus above everything and everyone else.) And that's exactly what Jesus provides: "It is for freedom that Christ has set us free" (Gal. 5:1). "You, my brothers, were called to be free" (Gal. 5:13).

Jesus' love compels those who know him to "no longer live for themselves but for him who died for them and was raised again" (2 Cor. 5:15). Indeed, the gospel of God's grace alone gives us *real* freedom.

Freedom from Slavery to Self-Adoration

Before they became Christians, the people of Galatia "were slaves to those who by nature are not gods" (Gal. 4:8). They were pagans who either chose from the pantheon of prevailing cultural gods or invented their own designer gods in an uncompromising commitment to make life work on their own terms. But in coming to Christ, they found their true center, identity, "sonship," and inheritance (Gal. 3:26–4:7). Now, however, they were reverting again to the slavery of idolatry—this time, by "turning back to those weak and miserable principles" (Gal. 4:9) of performance-based spirituality through a perverted form of Christianity, legalism. This was tantamount to deserting (Gal. 1:6) their great Lover, Jesus.

Every idol promises to free us so that we will finally *feel good about ourselves*—about our *place and performance in life.* The substances we choose to provide the blessing and benediction of our idols—i.e., alcohol, money, spiritual performance, sexuality, knowledge, etc.—suck us into varying degrees of dependence and addiction. Idols promise a life of purpose, peace, control, and affirmation, but they cannot deliver the goods. They only deceive and destroy. Idolatry (in its religious and irreligious forms) is just a destructive mirage full of empty IOUs.

Relationship with Jesus is the end of our struggle to make a name for ourselves. His grace frees us from the tyranny of living for our own glory; we are freed to live for *his* glory. Jesus isn't merely the godly means of finally feeling good about ourselves. He isn't, as a youth musical of the '70s dubbed him, our "natural high."

To know and experience that we are fully and eternally accepted by God in Christ makes the false marketing of idols much less attractive.

FREEDOM TO LOVE AND SERVE ONE ANOTHER

By nature, we are captive to our own self-worship. Only the power of grace can begin to totally reorient the direction of our hearts toward the worship of God and the service of others. As this happens, we begin to look less and less for idols with which to support our own deification. We begin to find more joy in living for the pleasure of Jesus and less for the approval of men. A primary sign of the diminishing rule of idols and addictions is seen in our increased joy in loving and serving others.

Paul reminded the Galatian believers of the time when their lives were marked by great joy, when the beauty of Jesus was so preeminent in their hearts that they cared for the sick and weak as though they were caring for Jesus.

> It was because of an illness that I first preached the gospel to you [apparently an ophthalmological malady]. Even though my illness was a trial to you, you did not treat me with contempt or scorn. Instead, you welcomed me as if I were an angel of God, as if I were Christ Jesus himself. What has happened to all your joy? I can testify that, if you could have done so, you would have torn out your eyes and given them to me. (Gal. 4:13–15)

Now, however, these same believers saw more beauty in performance-based legalism than in the grace and face of Jesus. Even the apostle Peter got sucked into this temporary insanity when the approval of visiting Jewish legalists had more power over his heart than the freedom, beauty, and truth of the gospel. Peter's love for Jesus had freed him to enjoy rich table fellowship with Gentile converts. But this freedom to love "outside of the box" was forfeited to the idol of legalism and an obsession with the approval of men (Gal. 2:11–14). In time, unchecked idolatry, obsession, and addictions can lead whole groups of Christians to bite and devour each other and, in the end, "be destroyed by each other" (Gal. 5:15).

Can you relate? Take a moment to ask yourself, "How am I like Peter? In what settings am I more inclined to live for the approval of men than the pleasure of Jesus? What people have more power over my heart than Jesus does?"

The Reign of Grace Is a Vocation That Must Be Taken Seriously

Yes, we are called to an extraordinary freedom. Freedom is a blessed gift, but Paul warns us that it can be disused, misused, and abused: "Do not use your freedom to indulge the sinful nature; rather, serve one another in love. The entire law is summed up in a single command: 'Love your neighbor as yourself.' If you keep on biting and devouring each other, watch out or you will be destroyed by each other" (Gal. 5:13–15).

As with the exiles returning home from captivity, we must learn to use our freedom wisely. The misrepresentation and poor stewardship of grace lead to being lax about sin and idolatry.

Grace never frees us to take our sin less seriously, just the opposite. No longer condemned for our sin, we can now deal more ruthlessly with our idol structures. There is nothing automatic about wholeheartedly worshiping God and loving others well. If we throw our forgiven hearts into "cruise control," we can quite easily eat each other for lunch. How then can we make progress in the calling to dismantle the idol structures of our hearts? Do we simply let go and let God? How does the reign of grace exalt Jesus in our hearts and free us to live with joy and sacrifice for his pleasure?

The Reign of Grace Is Empowered by the Holy Spirit

The Holy Spirit Wages War against Our Idol Factories!

"So I say, live by the Spirit, and you will not gratify the desires of the sinful nature. For the sinful nature desires what is contrary to the

Spirit, and the Spirit what is contrary to the sinful nature. They are in conflict with each other, so that you do not do what you want. But if you are led by the Spirit, you are not under law" (Gal. 5:16–18).

Though the dominion of the reign of sin and death has been broken once and for all in our hearts, the desires of the sinful nature will continue to live within us until we are glorified at the second coming of Jesus. But God's Spirit, who now also lives within us, is waging a war against our idol factories, a war that he will ultimately win. The reign of grace will prevail! Our calling is to live by the Spirit. What does living by the Spirit entail?

To live by the Spirit is to listen intently to his testimony. We must stay preoccupied with what the Spirit says about God: "He is your Abba, Father"; about Jesus: "He is your righteousness"; and about ourselves: "You matter, you are mine, and you are free!" (Gal. 4:6; 1 Cor. 1:30; Eph. 1:5–7; Heb. 9:15).

To live by the Spirit also includes accepting, with joy, our calling to holiness, for he is the *Holy* Spirit. Lastly, to live by the Spirit means relying on his power to wage war against our idol structures and addictions, for he is the power of resurrection. We must join the Holy Spirit's violent assault on our idol structures. We are not passive observers or mystical yielders but active combatants! God's grace plus our grit does not equal the recipe for legalism but the road map for liberty!

THE HOLY SPIRIT IDENTIFIES SPECIFIC IDOLS AND THEIR DESTRUCTIVE FRUIT

"The acts of the sinful nature are obvious: sexual immorality, impurity and debauchery; idolatry and witchcraft; hatred, discord, jealousy, fits of rage, selfish ambition, dissensions, factions and envy; drunkenness, orgies, and the like. I warn you, as I did before, that those who live like this will not inherit the kingdom of God" (Gal. 5:19–21).

How can we identify our idols? One of the ways is by learning to recognize the fruit of idolatry. The above list of the fruit of idolatry (also known as the "works of the flesh") is not exhaustive, but suggestive. The worship of idols *may* result in addiction, but it *always* results in destruction. Consider this list and seek to identify some of your idols and addictions. For instance, if you resonate with selfish ambition, what idols may be producing this deadly fruit in your life—the idol of *success* or the *approval of man* or perhaps the *fear of failure?*

What potentially addictive substance are you leaning on to obtain what your idol promises to deliver? Your job? Maybe this has led you to workaholism. Or maybe your success idol has to do with physical fitness, and you have become either obsessed with or addicted to working out a certain number of times a week. Allowing the Holy Spirit to identify the idols in your life is the first step in rendering them impotent.

The Reign of Grace Calls Us to Evaluate Our Emotions

Paying careful attention to emotions that grow to near neurotic proportions is one of the most effective ways to identify our specific idols. Whether manifested as spontaneous outbursts or chronic life patterns, these exaggerated emotions can provide an unobstructed view into the cathedral of our idol worship. The main questions to ask ourselves in light of such intense feelings are: *What do I think I have to have in life beyond Jesus and what he chooses to give me? Has something or someone become* too *important to me?*

When *anger* gets out of control, ask yourself: What am I being blocked from having that I believe is a necessity but really isn't? Marriage, children, success, a Ph.D., a record deal? If *fear* threatens to overwhelm you, ask, What is being threatened that I think is essential but really isn't? My 401K, my life, my physical looks, my reputation? If *despondency* consumes you, consider: What have I lost that I believe is critical to have but really isn't? A starting position on the football team, my spouse's approval, my parents, the ability to drive a golf ball three hundred yards, my wrinkleless face? If *shame* debilitates you, ask yourself, What have I failed at/in that I believe is unforgivable but really isn't? Marriage, my job, the ministry, school, sobriety?

The Reign of Grace Advances Violently but Produces Peaceable Fruit

"But the fruit of the Spirit is love, joy, peace, patience, kindness, goodness, faithfulness, gentleness and self-control. Against such things there is no law" (Gal. 5:22–23).

The Holy Spirit applies relentless and unyielding antagonism against our sinful nature so that the beauty and likeness of Jesus will be created within us. The Spirit's fruit is evidence of the advancement of the reign of grace in our heart, but it is also a means by which we are further equipped to wage war against idolatry. Notice that the fruit the Spirit produces is primarily relational strength, not private contentment. We are being freed to love well, not isolate comfortably.

The disciplines of grace are an essential—if not the most essential—means of dismantling our idols. Our relationship with Jesus is free, but it requires costly work on our part! We do not merit Jesus' love by a disciplined life of Bible reading, prayer, meditation, caring for the poor, service, worship, and fellowshipping with other believers. But we do profit *enormously* by faithfully giving ourselves to these disciplines, and we lose *significantly* if we don't! God's Spirit leads us into a doxological lifestyle of centering our lives on Jesus, and the fruit will be just as evident as is the fruit of idolatry.

The Reign of Grace Calls Us to Declare War on Our Idolatries and Addictions

"Those who belong to Christ Jesus have crucified the sinful nature with its passions and desires" (Gal. 5:24).

We must learn to be vigilant and violent with our particular idols and our idol factory (sinful nature). In the Old Testament, God always instructed his people to tear down and destroy their idols. We aren't to pray for strength to tolerate, domesticate, or ignore idols; we repudiate them! Jesus taught us, "If your hand or your foot causes you to sin, cut it off and throw it away" (Matt. 18:8). By that he wasn't teaching mutilation but mortification—the commitment to deal immediately and decisively with the desires of our sinful nature and our idols.

Our sinful nature was crucified when God placed us in union with Christ. His death legally became ours. However, there is an ongoing crucifixion, or putting to death of the sinful nature, that we engage in daily. Paul described this redemptive violence in his letter to believers in Colossae:

> Put to death, therefore, whatever belongs to your earthly nature: sexual immorality, impurity, lust, evil desires and greed, which is idolatry. Because of these, the wrath of God is coming. You used to walk in these ways, in the life you once lived. But now you must rid yourselves of all such things as these: anger, rage, malice, slander, and filthy language from your lips. (Col. 3:5–8)

Crucifying our sinful nature involves identifying the things we desire more than we desire God and his glory (our particular idols), as well as identifying the substances we are depending upon to empower the worship of our idols. Then we must take pitiless and decisive action. For God's grace teaches us to say "No!" to all forms of ungodliness and idolatry and "Yes!" to filling our hearts with the beauty and bounty of Jesus.

I have recently become reacquainted with the critical need to obey the strong admonitions Paul has given us in this passage. Ever since my counselor first talked to me about "finding my face," I have been in turmoil. For sure, she wasn't talking about "saving face." No, she was talking about *finding my face before God.* Living in a face-to-face relationship with God means coming out of hiding—looking God squarely in the face and trusting his gaze to expose me, love me, discipline me, and heal me. All of life is to be lived *coram deo,* before the face of God.

This reacquaintance has led (is leading) to some decisive "putting to deaths." For instance, I have had to acknowledge that I am *still* inclined to worship the gods of comfort, control, acceptance, and significance (among others). I will do just about anything to stay in control. My main drug of choice, as previously confessed, has been spiritual knowledge and verbal skills. By knowing more about God, the Word, and theology than the general populace, I have been able to manipulate my world mentally and verbally. Thus, I'm less likely to lose control to people who might intimidate me or to sticky situations and circumstances that reveal my insecurities.

How is God bringing death to my idol structures? One way is through the aging process. My short-term memory just isn't what it used to be. I am not as able to preach from memory as I once was. I forget where I am in a sermon (and in parking lots) more easily than ever. My strength is becoming weakness. I used to be able to preach five times a Sunday, but no more. I am being humbled. My idols are snickering—but God is loving me so well.

Occasionally (I praise him it's only occasionally thus far), when I revert to trusting more in what I know than in who knows me, God will crank up the reign of grace a few notches and bring me "back home." I recently experienced a "reining in" that I don't want to forget.

Steven Curtis Chapman and I were co-leading a plenary session at a Youth Specialties event in Cincinnati, Ohio. There must have been around seven or eight thousand conferees there, many of whom had to watch us in an overflow auditorium on a huge screen. After Steven shared his tender heart and a few powerful songs, he introduced me with kind and generous words. I sauntered forward ready to launch into the speechless wonders of God's grace, but all of a sudden my mind, and then my heart, went totally blank. I forgot *everything* I was going to say. Stammering and stumbling, desperately trying to salvage the moment and, more importantly, save face, I tried to draw on a few speaker tricks, but things went from bad to worse. It felt as if someone had bound my brain and tongue with barbed wire. I have never been more professionally humiliated in my life.

I was dying—or at least that's what God had in mind for me—dying to self and to self-worship. He let me know in no uncertain terms that the Lord giveth and the Lord taketh away. The calling and talents he has given me are for his glory, not mine. I'm *not* in control, he is.

Such painful gifts still hurt when they are divinely delivered, but I more readily receive them as "friends" as a result of being convinced, more so than ever, that Jesus is more worthy of my heart's worship than anything or anyone else.

The Reign of Grace Calls Us to Deal with Idolatry and Addiction as a Community of Sinner-Saints

> Since we live by the Spirit, let us keep in step with the Spirit. Let us not become conceited, provoking and envying each other. Brothers, if someone is caught in a sin, you who are spiritual should restore him gently. But watch yourself, or you also may be tempted. Carry each other's burdens, and in this way you will fulfill the law of Christ. (Gal. 5:25–6:2)

One of the most important lessons we can learn from the recovery group movement is the absolute necessity of walking in community with other idolaters and addicts. The reign of grace, though personal, is a corporate movement. To "keep in step with the Spirit," we must resist the normal tendencies of our sinful nature to be critical. Rather than being judgmental, we are to move toward each other when we see the entanglements of their idolatries and addictions taking over. Gentle restoration is to be our goal, even as we commit to love one another boldly.

How I thank God for the brothers and sisters who have come alongside me in seasons when my heart has been involved in its greatest foolishness and warfare. With whom are you walking in such a fashion? To what church family are you committed as an essential expression of your love for Jesus and resolve to wage war against your idol structures?

Ed Welch challenges us to consider some amazing scenarios that would make your church and mine leaders in caring for idolaters and addicts—just like us. Imagine this…

- When addicts look for help, the word on the street would be that the local church really loves people.
- When addicts look for help, the word on the street would be that addicts who have gone to the local church have changed.
- Every church would have enough members who have struggled with addictions to have weekly prayer and accountability meetings.
- Churches would pray that they would attract men and women who have struggled with addictions because their strengths could bless the entire congregation, for they tend to be practical, quick to help others who struggle, and able to speak the truth in love.
- Every church member would see the idolatrous bent to his or her own heart. As a result, we would all see addicts as no different from ourselves.[1]

Catching a clear glimpse *together* of the sacred romance we celebrate in the gospel will move idolatry from the abstract realm of pagan religion to the everyday world of infidelity. Only against the backdrop of such privilege, beauty, and goodness do we begin to taste the sinfulness of sin. Only *then* will idolatry be seen for what it really is—*adultery against the perfect Lover.* Addiction then becomes the equivalent of prostitution and is exposed in all its ugliness, power, and tragedy.

Then, grace becomes much more than an appreciated hug. It becomes a rescue mission of irrepressible love—a dominion of all-conquering tenderness, a powerful reign of restorative passion!

Therefore, I URGE you, brothers, in view of God's mercy,
to offer your bodies as living *sacrifices*, holy and pleasing
to God—THIS is your spiritual act of worship.

—Romans 12:1

Why do people in CHURCHES seem like cheerful, brainless tourists on a packaged tour of the Absolute?...Worship is *dangerous*.... Does anyone have the foggiest idea of what sort of power we so blithely invoke? Or, as I SUSPECT, does no one believe a word of it?

Annie Dillard

I can't stand your RELIGIOUS meetings.
I'm fed up with your conferences and conventions.
I want *nothing* to do with your religion projects,
your pretentious slogans and goals.
I'm sick of your fund-raising SCHEMES,
your public relations and image making.
I've had all I can take of *your* ego-music.
When was the last time you sang to me?
Do you know what I WANT?
I want justice—oceans of it.
I want *fairness*—rivers of it.
That's what I want. That's all I want.

—Amos 5:21–24 MSG

Worship is SEEING
what God is *worth* and
GIVING him what he's worth.

Tim Keller

CHAPTER EIGHT

Grace-Full WORSHIP

Does the thought of actually being able to "pleasure" God do anything for you? I am staggered at the very possibility that there is something *we* can do—not to add on to God's perfections or to merit one thing from him—but to bring delight to the one from whom flows the river of all delights (Ps. 36:8–9)—to effect joy in the presence of the God whose joy is our strength (Neh. 8:10)—to cause gladness before the one who transforms our mourning into gladness (Jer. 31:13).

Listen to the words of Haggai: "This is what the LORD Almighty says: 'Give careful thought to your ways. Go up into the mountains and bring down timber and build the house, so that I may take *pleasure* in it and be honored,' says the LORD" (Hag. 1:7–8). Worship that is built upon the foundation of thoughtful reflection and with the right "timber" is designed to pleasure the heart of God and bring him the honor of which he alone is worthy.

So how did we get the idea that worship is for *our* benefit?

CALL TO WORSHIP

"Paul—it's time. Fire away!" We weren't shooting skeet; I was instructing our sound engineer, Paul Burns, to project a chart I had made onto the large screen in our worship center. We were aiming at more than clay pigeons! The house lights went down, and the chart went up.

- I want more theology and less singing on Sunday mornings.
- Now that we enjoyed an Advent choir, can we get rid of the praise band?
- Get rid of the choir. I'm afraid we might lose the kids.
- It's nice to see you preaching in real shoes for a change.
- Where are your Birkenstocks? I like it better when you preach in them.
- If I hear one more "rim shot" on the snare drum, I'm changing churches.
- Your written prayers of confession are too wordy.
- We sing too many weighty hymns. I can't think that fast.
- We sing too many cheesy choruses. I am embarrassed for our visitors.
- Do you dye your hair? As my senior pastor, that would be a bad example.
- Can you just stand behind the pulpit? Less walking around, please.
- You lift your hands in worship. Why doesn't the other pastor do the same?
- I am changing churches because I need a more charismatic worship.
- I need a more traditional worship that takes Reformed theology seriously.

Unmuted laughter erupted throughout the congregation as I read each line of this "call to worship." It felt more like the kind of laughter that is generated by nervous conviction than by well-crafted humor. I was introducing a new series of sermons on worship that would take us through the season of Lent, the seven Sundays leading up to Easter Sunday.

Though the actual language was slightly veiled, I made this chart from real e-mails, letters, or notes slid under my office door between Thanksgiving 2001 and January 2002. Two-thirds of the "constructive worship criticisms" were unsigned. And no one who indicated that they had left the church in search of "better worship" stopped by for prayer and conversation or even a good ole' Southern good-bye.

I share this story to encourage Christians, especially pastors, who may be encouraged to know that theirs isn't the only church dealing with the ongoing and ever-changing conflict of "worship wars." Many people assume that certain churches are removed from the fray of foolishness. It simply isn't so.

Even though our church family has a longstanding reputation for taking worship quite seriously, we are a gathering of sinner-saints just like every other church. As my little chart indicates—when it comes to worship, we are just as capable of being petty, self-centered, and childish as anyone else.

Consumers or the Consumed Ones

We live in a day in which worship has become more of a commodity for keeping consumers happy than a consuming calling by which we are made holy. But the purpose of worship is to love *God*—exclusively and extravagantly—for *his* sake, not our satisfaction.

D. A. Carson writes, "If the heart of sinfulness is self-centeredness, the heart of all biblical religion is God-centeredness: in short, it is worship. In our fallen-ness we constrict all there is to our petty horizons."[1]

The apostle Paul challenges the notion that worship is a *dimension* of the Christian life by presenting worship as a *lifestyle*—a *doxological* lifestyle. The Christian life does not consist of going to great worship services; rather, the Christian life is itself *worship service in response to God's greatness and mercy!* "Therefore, I urge you, brothers, in view of God's mercy, to offer your bodies as living sacrifices, holy and pleasing to God—this is your spiritual act of worship" (Rom. 12:1). In view of God's outrageous grace, mercy, and compassion lavished on us in Jesus, *we* are the living sacrifices to be consumed to the glory of God.

What do we really mean by phrases such as, "I liked the worship today"; "The worship stunk, but the preaching was OK"; "I'm looking for a more contemporary...or blended...or traditional...or neoclassical-postmodern...or a capella-Reformed-without-robes worship"?

Such an approach to worship has more in common with looking for a new, exciting restaurant in which to be served than with the worthy demands of God-centered worship. Instead, our hearts should be asking, "Lord, having found your love to be better than life, how can we most faithfully exist for the praise of your glory and honor? In view of the sacrifice of Jesus, we give ourselves to be consumed as you wish. What is your pleasure, O merciful God? What is your delight, O worthy and generous Lord? What is your joy, O blessed Bridegroom?"

There is a scene in Zechariah that is filled with contemporary relevance. God sent his prophet to ask about the real motivation behind a special season of worship and fasting in which his people engaged *during the whole Babylonian captivity!* "Then the word of the LORD Almighty came to me: 'Ask all the people of the land and the priests, "When you fasted and mourned in the fifth and seventh months for the past seventy years, *was it really for me* that you fasted? And when you were eating and drinking, *were you not just feasting for yourselves?*"'" (Zech. 7:4–6).

What a searching question: "*Was it really for me?*" God asks the same question of us: *"Is it really for me that you engage in all of your worship squabbles and debates? Is it really for me that you close your eyes and lift up your hands with such great emotion? Is it really for me that you sing, dance, kneel, light candles, swing from chandeliers, wear a cross, or cross yourselves?"*

> A little over a century ago, it was not uncommon to find Christians in some traditions asking after a sermon, "How did you get on under the Word?" Now we ask, "How did you enjoy the sermon?" Now the latter question is extended; "How did you enjoy the worship?" (i.e., the rest of the service apart from the sermon). Worship can be rated according to our degree of enjoyment. It is part of the *genus* "entertainment industry."
>
> Should we not remind ourselves that worship is a transitive verb? We do not meet to worship (i.e., to experience worship); we aim to worship God. "Worship the Lord your God, and serve him only"; there is the heart of the matter. In this area, as in so many others, one must not confuse what is central with byproducts....If you seek experiences of worship, you will not find them; if you worship the living God, you will experience something of what is reflected in the Psalms. Worship is a transitive verb, and the most important thing about it is the direct object.[2]

Worship is God's love language—the main dialect he wants us to master, the tongue in which he would have us become most fluent. There is *nothing* in which he finds greater delight than true worship. And there is nothing to which God responds with greater disdain than false worship. Indeed, God does not tolerate our liturgical lies and lethargy. Listen as he speaks through Isaiah:

> "The multitude of your sacrifices—what are they to me?" says the LORD. "I have more than enough of burnt offerings, of rams and the fat of fattened animals; I have no pleasure in the blood of bulls and lambs and goats. When you come to appear before me, who

> has asked this of you, this trampling of my courts? Stop bringing meaningless offerings! Your incense is detestable to me. New Moons, Sabbaths and convocations—I cannot bear your evil assemblies. Your New Moon festivals and your appointed feasts my soul hates. They have become a burden to me; I am weary of bearing them. When you spread out your hands in prayer, I will hide my eyes from you; even if you offer many prayers, I will not listen." (Isa. 1:11–15)

Distorted, polluted, or misdirected worship is the ultimate insult. It is a slap in the face of God. It is the loudest and clearest way we can say to him, "Your love is *not* better than life. I will take my thirst and have it slaked by some other lover. There are others more beautiful and worthy of my affections than you." I can't imagine any of us intending to say such things; nevertheless, our attitudes and actions often reveal this very spirit.

What, then, is a good working definition, or description, of God's favorite love language? Here's one I have found to be helpful, centering, and convicting.

> Worship is the submission of all our nature to God. It is the quickening of conscience by his holiness; the nourishment of mind with his truth; the purifying of imagination by his beauty; the opening of the heart to his love; the surrender of will to his purpose—and all this gathered up in adoration, the most selfless emotion of which our nature is capable and therefore the chief remedy for that self-centeredness which is our original sin and the source of all actual sin.[3]

Try to imagine *this* definition of worship being woven into your life, church family, and ultimately, throughout the universe! For so it shall be on that Day! Until then, how does God respond to worship that is *less* than he deserves? We know that he loves his people perfectly through Christ, but how does he engage us in our most eternal, glorious, and consuming calling? As a passive observer? No way!

Pitiful Worship

During Malachi's ministry, the worship offered by God's people had become so pitiful and polluted that God actually cried out in pained disgust, "Oh, that one of you would shut the temple doors, so that you would not light useless fires on my altar!" (Mal. 1:10).

Worship in the rebuilt Jerusalem temple was so far removed from the adoration and communion the Father sought that it would have been better for the doors of the temple to be locked shut! How bad is that?

An expanded translation of the verse above might read: *"Time out! What...are...you...doing? Turn off the PA and the rear screen projector. Dismiss the choir. Shut down the praise band. Put away the communion elements. Do you really call this worship? Is this the way you feel about me in your hearts? Does this worship represent my worth to you? Please—go on home. Shoo! Be gone. Leave! You might as well be at the food court of the mall."*

You Do Not Honor Me!

> "A son honors his father, and a servant his master. If I am a father, where is the honor due me? If I am a master, where is the respect due me?" says the LORD Almighty. "It is you, O priests, who show contempt for my name.
>
> "But you ask, 'How have we shown contempt for your name?'" (Mal. 1:6)

Translation: *"I fathered you into existence, and I have made you to be my treasured children—forever. Since I have loved you as no other father ever could, am I wrong to expect childlike love and honor from you?*

"Or if you only think of me as your master, where's the respect and love a servant should give a master like me? You have polluted the rivers of my delight. In fact, you priests are the worse contaminators! Instead of loving me, you despise me."

You Bring Me Crippled Animals!

"It is you, O priests, who show contempt for my name.

"But you ask, 'How have we shown contempt for your name?'

"You place defiled food on my altar.

"But you ask, 'How have we defiled you?'

"By saying that the LORD's table is contemptible. When you bring blind animals for sacrifice, is that not wrong? When you sacrifice crippled or diseased animals, is that not wrong? Try offering them to your governor! Would he be pleased with you? Would he accept you?" says the LORD Almighty. (Mal. 1:6–8)

Translation: *"It's not adoration I experience in your worship, but bribery and contempt. You're acting as if I'm your sugar daddy—rather than your Father. Why do you act so surprised when I say this? Take a fresh look at the sacrifices you are offering me. It's bad enough that my people bring blind, crippled, and diseased animals to the temple as 'so-called' offerings of penitence and praise.*

"But you priests, the leaders of my children—the guardians of my Name and forgiveness—you break my heart even more. I trust you to safeguard my worship, but you are the ones who have corrupted it by offering these very animals upon my altar. What should I conclude about your love for me? You have more awe of your governor than your God."

Shut the Doors!

"Now implore God to be gracious to us. With such offerings from your hands, will he accept you?"—says the LORD Almighty.

"Oh, that one of you would shut the temple doors, so that you would not light useless fires on my altar! I am not pleased with you," says the LORD Almighty, "and I will accept no offering from your hands." (Mal. 1:9–10)

Translation: *"You offer me dis-graceful worship and yet you expect me to be gracious to you in the midst of your hardships? What are you thinking?*

That worship is a magic formula or technique to get what you want? That 'grace' means you can live any way you want and I will still be obligated to 'bless' you? Please, somebody, empty the sanctuary! The lights are on, but nobody's really here, but me."

My Name Will Be Great in Spite of You!

> "My name will be great among the nations, from the rising to the setting of the sun. In every place incense and pure offerings will be brought to my name, because my name will be great among the nations," says the LORD Almighty. (Mal. 1:11)

Translation: *"Now don't get me wrong. I'm not looking for pity. I'm not going away with hurt feelings and deep insecurity. Remember my promise to Abraham. A day is coming when men and women from every single family group and all nations will participate in perfect worship—not just here in Jerusalem, but throughout the world. They will offer acceptable sacrifices of praise to me.*

"It's good that I don't solely depend on your worship to make the nations thirsty to know me. Who'd want to drink from this fountain? I have loved you with passion and delight, yet you act prevailed upon and bothered when you 'do your duty.'"

You Are Cynical about Worshiping Me!

> "But you profane it by saying of the Lord's table, 'It is defiled,' and of its food, 'It is contemptible.' And you say, 'What a burden!' and you sniff at it contemptuously," says the LORD Almighty.
>
> "When you bring injured, crippled or diseased animals and offer them as sacrifices, should I accept them from your hands?" says the LORD. "Cursed is the cheat who has an acceptable male in his flock and vows to give it, but then sacrifices a blemished animal to the Lord. For I am a great king," says the LORD Almighty, "and my name is to be feared among the nations." (Mal. 1:12–14)

Translation: *"I am saddened by your reasoning and offended by your attitude. Because life is hard and I haven't performed on your behalf the way you expected me to, you conclude that 'worship doesn't work, so why bother?'*

"What is worse, you have become bored and cynical about the greatest privilege I offer mankind—to fellowship with me in the assurance of my love, to dialogue with me in the chamber of my grace, to serenade one another in the joy of my covenant!

"Why do you offer me worship that costs you nothing and then expect me to respond to your personal whims? You cannot earn anything from me. I freely give, but I just as freely withhold. I am your kind Father, but I am also your glorious King. I love you too much to indulge your childish pouting or idly stand by while you rob me of your heart's affection. You were created to be so much better than you are behaving!"

Indeed, God passionately cares about his worship. We tend to get pretty passionate concerning the issue of worship, too, but not necessarily in the same way God does.

Worship or War?

Just as God is passionate about worship, so are we—who have been made in his image. It is quite noteworthy to realize that the world's first homicide was committed over a difference of opinion about worship! Cain killed Abel because God found his younger brother's worship more acceptable than his own (Gen. 4:1–16). This is the *first* recorded fatality in the worship wars, but not the last.

A closer look at this narrative reveals just how destructive the reign of sin and death has been to God's favorite love language. Both Cain and Abel brought offerings to the Lord that represented the fruits of their labors. Cain was a farmer, so he offered some of his produce as an act of worship. Abel was a shepherd, and he presented the Lord with some of the fat portions of the firstborn of his flock.

The Scripture tells us that God "looked with favor" on Abel's worship, but not so upon Cain's. When God rejected Cain's worship, the older brother's response was quick and harsh—even insane: He murdered his brother.

It's important to understand that the Bible does not present itself as an exhaustive account of every conversation God had with his people, neither does it record every detail in redemptive history. I draw attention to this fact because there's a story behind this story to which we're not privy. It's fair to assume that God had given both of his sons the same instructions concerning worship: the *whats, whys,* and *how tos.*

What, then, can we learn from this story about the warping effect sin has on our whole orientation toward worship? How has the shalom of our most glorious, important, and eternal calling been violated? That Cain became contrary, instead of contrite, when God did not receive his sacrifice is quite telling. Even a brief meditation on this passage renders these observations.

- Sin leads us to worship on our own terms, disregarding God's design and delights.
- Ultimately, worship reveals which dominion has gained practical reign in our hearts—the reign of grace or the dominion of sin.
- Sin creates a utilitarian and consumeristic orientation toward worship—a "What's in it for me?" mind-set. When we don't "get out of worship" what we expect or think we deserve, we get angry at the object of our worship—namely, God, or whatever "god" we may be worshiping. This amounts to the worship of worship, instead of the worship of God.

THE PRIESTHOOD OF BELIEVERS

What implications for us can be found in God's forthright and painful dealings with the priests in Malachi's day? As the Body of

Christ, we no longer look to a priesthood to mediate between us and God. Through his "once for all" sacrifice (Heb. 7:27), Jesus, our great high priest, has perfectly fulfilled the temporal mediation roles of Israel's priests. But more profoundly, he has made their bloody sacrifices obsolete, for "when this priest [Jesus] had offered for all time one sacrifice for sins, he sat down at the right hand of God...because by one sacrifice he has made perfect forever those who are being made holy" (Heb. 10:12, 14).

Therefore, as a priesthood, *our worship must be unmistakably marked by its thoroughgoing Christ-centeredness.* When we can wholeheartedly say, "It's all about you, Lord," we come back to the heart of worship.

And now, in the unfolding drama of his redeeming story, God has constituted his whole family as a *priesthood of believers.* The whole body of Christ has become a *kingdom of priests:* "But you are a chosen people, *a royal priesthood,* a holy nation, a people belonging to God, that you may declare the praises of him who called you out of darkness into his wonderful light" (1 Pet. 2:9).

The privileges we have received through our status as a royal priesthood are staggering—in fact scandalous and blasphemous by the reckoning of orthodox Jews. Because of the finished work of Jesus, "we have confidence to enter the Most Holy Place" (Heb. 10:19). This means that every Christian has free and perpetual access into the heavenly equivalent of the Holy of Holies, the curtained room in the Jerusalem Temple where Israel's high priest was alone permitted to enter.

When Jesus was crucified, the curtain leading into the Holy of Holies was torn *from the top down* (Luke 23:44–45; Heb. 10:20). God has ripped the barrier and thrown open the access into his holy and joyful presence for the whole priesthood of believers.

Therefore, when we come together as a royal priesthood to worship, each member should be fully engaged, joyous, and giving. There is absolutely *no* place in Christ-centered worship for critics, cynics, or consumers; for we have all been made to be lead worshipers and worship leaders!

But the responsibilities, like the privileges of our priesthood, are staggering. As our great high priest, Jesus has completed his once-and-for-all sacrifice; but we are charged to offer new gospel sacrifices *perpetually.* As a royal priesthood, "let us continually offer to God a sacrifice of praise—the fruit of lips that confess his name. And do not forget to do good and to share with others, for with such sacrifices God is pleased" (Heb.13:15–16).

Therefore, as a royal priesthood, *our worship will pleasure the heart of God when it is offered in word and deed, in adoration and action.* Once again hear God as he speaks to us about these matters through Isaiah—with words that need little commentary, just an honest listening:

> "Shout it aloud, do not hold back. Raise your voice like a trumpet. Declare to my people their rebellion and to the house of Jacob their sins. For day after day they seek me out; they seem eager to know my ways, as if they were a nation that does what is right and has not forsaken the commands of its God. They ask me for just decisions and seem eager for God to come near them. 'Why have we fasted,' they say, 'and you have not seen it? Why have we humbled ourselves, and you have not noticed?'
>
> "Yet on the day of your fasting, you do as you please and exploit all your workers. Your fasting ends in quarreling and strife, and in striking each other with wicked fists. You cannot fast as you do today and expect your voice to be heard on high. Is this the kind of fast I have chosen, only a day for a man to humble himself? Is it only for bowing one's head like a reed and for lying on sackcloth and ashes? Is that what you call a fast, a day acceptable to the LORD?
>
> "Is not this the kind of fasting I have chosen: to loose the chains of injustice and untie the cords of the yoke, to set the oppressed free and break every yoke? Is it not to share your food with the hungry and to provide the poor wanderer with shelter—when you

see the naked, to clothe him, and not to turn away from your own flesh and blood? Then your light will break forth like the dawn, and your healing will quickly appear; then your righteousness will go before you, and the glory of the LORD will be your rear guard. Then you will call, and the LORD will answer; you will cry for help, and he will say: Here am I.

"If you do away with the yoke of oppression, with the pointing finger and malicious talk, and if you spend yourselves in behalf of the hungry and satisfy the needs of the oppressed, then your light will rise in the darkness, and your night will become like the noonday. The LORD will guide you always; he will satisfy your needs in a sun-scorched land and will strengthen your frame. You will be like a well-watered garden, like a spring whose waters never fail. Your people will rebuild the ancient ruins and will raise up the age-old foundations; you will be called Repairer of Broken Walls, Restorer of Streets with Dwellings.

"If you keep your feet from breaking the Sabbath and from doing as you please on my holy day, if you call the Sabbath a delight and the LORD'S holy day honorable, and if you honor it by not going your own way and not doing as you please or speaking idle words, then you will find your joy in the LORD, and I will cause you to ride on the heights of the land and to feast on the inheritance of your father Jacob." The mouth of the LORD has spoken. (Isa. 58:1–14)

Which do we choose? To worship as a well-watered garden—bringing the life-transforming waters of the reign of grace to our neighbors and nations? Or to worship as a weed-infested jungle—parading our pettiness, selfishness, and hypocrisy before the watching world? Whose pleasure matters most—God's or ours?

Further Up *and* Further In

Door-*Shutting* Worship

PHILIPPIANS

If the essence of worship is doxology, declaring the worth of the heart's treasure, then Paul doesn't leave us in doubt about either his treasure or his heart. "But whatever was to my profit I now consider loss for the sake of Christ. What is more, I consider everything a loss compared to the surpassing greatness of knowing Christ Jesus my Lord, for whose sake I have lost all things" (Phil. 3:7–8).

But worship is more than impassioned declaration; it also requires appropriate response—a response that is commensurate with the value of one's treasure. Once again, Paul is overtly transparent in sharing with us the only worthy response to the priceless Jesus. "For to me, to live is Christ and to die is gain" (Phil. 1:21). Worship became a lifestyle for Paul, a doxological lifestyle of knowing, loving, enjoying, serving—even dying for—Jesus.

Likewise, *our* primary vocation as the true "circumcision" (Phil. 3:3) is to live the remainder of our lives "in a manner worthy of the gospel of Christ" (Phil. 1:27) to the glory and praise of God. A most worthy Jesus is calling you and me to a worthy worship. There is no issue in our living and dying of greater import. As we consider the sheer privilege of this doxological calling, we would be wise to ask ourselves the same questions generated in Malachi's day:

- Are we engaging in worship that pleasures the heart of God or that makes him want to "shut the doors"?
- Are we offering acceptable worship or "blind, crippled, and diseased sacrifices" to our Bridegroom?

- How can we more faithfully worship God for his sake and delight?

The apostle Paul helps us visualize the demands of the reign of grace on worship with the words he wrote to believers in Philippi. Consider the essential elements of acceptable worship revealed in this one verse: "For it is we who are the circumcision, we who *worship by the Spirit of God,* who *glory in Christ Jesus,* and who *put no confidence in the flesh*" (Phil. 3:3).

The Doors on Our Worship Should Be Shut When It Is...*Heartless*

We are to "worship by the Spirit of God."

Consistent with the startling and welcoming nature of grace, Jesus made his most revolutionary announcement about worship to a promiscuous Samaritan woman. He declared that the Father is seeking worshipers—but not just any kind of worshipers. He is seeking those who worship "in spirit and truth" (John 4:23). To worship "in spirit" or "by the Spirit" is to recognize that we are part of a *new era* in the history of redemption. With the outpouring of the Holy Spirit at Pentecost, the promised messianic age dramatically broke in with Kingdom power. Worship will no longer be centered on Mount Zion or in Jerusalem or within the temple. The shadows of old-covenant, localized worship gave way to the substance of new-creation, universal worship.

Through the preaching of the gospel in the power of the Spirit, the reign of grace will spread well beyond the borders of Israel—from Jerusalem to Judea to Samaria to the uttermost parts of the earth! (Acts 1:8). To worship by the Spirit, therefore, does not merely mean that we are rescued from boring or listless worship; rather, *we are rescued from self-centered and self-serving worship.*

By his Spirit, God replaces our heart of stone with a heart of flesh (Ezek. 36:26–27). This new heart is to beat with a passion for his passions. Spirit-filled worship, therefore, will be decidedly God-centered.

And since God is quite passionate about the revelation of his glory, among the nations and in every sphere of life, Spirit-empowered worship will always be missional and eschatological: *missional,* reflecting God's joy in redeeming his people out of every race, tribe, tongue, and people group; and *eschatological,* reflecting God's promise to transform every sphere of the present fallen world into the new heaven and new earth—the eternal worship center.

This is why our worship services should be Seeker-sensitive, not seeker-sensitive. God is the Great Seeker and Finder! The prophet Zechariah envisioned a day when God's presence would be so powerful among his people that the nations will stream into the expanding new covenant community.

> This is what the LORD Almighty says: "Many peoples and the inhabitants of many cities will yet come, and the inhabitants of one city will go to another and say, 'Let us go at once to entreat the LORD and seek the LORD Almighty. I myself am going.' And many peoples and powerful nations will come to Jerusalem to seek the LORD Almighty and to entreat him." (Zech. 8:20–22)

Paul took Zechariah's contagious missional vision quite seriously as he instructed believers in Corinth concerning the importance of order (decorum) and ardor (delight) when we gather for public worship. The apostle doesn't suggest that churches design special services to accommodate visitors or appeal to cynical seekers; rather, his words presuppose the presence of nonbelievers whenever we worship. Why? Because God has placed us in the culture to live well and to love well among all people, in everything we do. Our worship service begins well before we "come to church."

Priests build bridges, not walls. "In every way," we are to "make the teaching about God our Savior attractive" (Titus 2:10), not by compromising the gospel, but by contextualizing it for our communities and culture. With hearts, hands, tears, and caring, we are to live as "blameless and pure, children of God without fault in a crooked and depraved generation, in which you shine like stars in the universe as you hold out the word of life" (Phil. 2:15–16).

We are poets and potters, homemakers and, sometimes, trouble-makers. We are aldermen and fishermen, worriers and warriors, fellow strugglers, foolish sinners, and famous heroes. We weep as we bury our loved ones and rejoice in a beautiful sunset or a good meal—just like the rest of humanity. But we have also found meaning, purpose, and hope for all things in Jesus. His love compels us to be generous with all men as he has been generous with us.

More nonbelievers will be present in our worship services when we stop labeling them as targets and start loving them in the course of everyday life. Then we will witness, quite naturally, those supernatural times when our neighbors and associates "will fall down and worship God, exclaiming, 'God is really among you!' " (1 Cor. 14:25).

The Doors on Our Worship Should Be Shut When It Is... *Christless*

We are to "glory [boast, exult] in Christ Jesus."

There is nothing about which God is more passionate than his Son. As a central feature of the Philippian epistle, Paul included this Christ-hymn—composed and sung by the early church. It demonstrates the thoroughgoing Christocentricity of worship that pleasures the heart of God.

Who, being in very nature God,
did not consider equality with God something to be grasped,
but made himself nothing,
taking the very nature of a servant,
being made in human likeness.
And being found in appearance as a man,

he humbled himself
and became obedient to death—
even death on a cross!
Therefore God exalted him to the highest place
and gave him the name that is above every name,
that at the name of Jesus every knee should bow,
in heaven and on earth and under the earth,
and every tongue confess that Jesus Christ is Lord,
to the glory of God the Father. (Phil. 2:6–11)

Whether it's Episcopalian, Church of Christ, Pentecostal, Baptist, postmodern, traditional, or contemporary, if our worship is not increasingly centered on Jesus and what he has accomplished on our behalf, then shut the doors and run! In Philippians, Paul identifies believers as those who "glory" in Jesus. What does "glorying in Jesus" look like?

- We glory in Jesus when we are captivated by his beauty and rest fully on his righteousness given to us by faith.
- We glory in Jesus when, as his betrothed Bride, we worship with confidence and astonishment that we are betrothed to the perfect Husband—Jesus.
- We glory in Jesus by living all of life in the hope of the coming Wedding Feast of the Lamb.
- We glory in Jesus when worship becomes a pitcher by which we are poured out as a drink offering to our Great Lover, rather than expecting worship to be a spigot to which we are constantly coming to be filled up.

Peter tells us in 1 Peter 2:5 that we are to offer "spiritual sacrifices acceptable to God through Jesus Christ." In worship, what "spiritual sacrifices" can we possibly give to Jesus, our wonderful Bridegroom?

What do we give him who has everything? The one who has taken us to be his Bride is the fulfillment of the three great offices God established in Israel—prophet, priest, and king.

Jesus testified that he was our *prophet,* when he said of himself "A prophet is not without honor except in his home town and in his own household" (Matt. 13:57 NASB). The writer of Hebrews comments: "In the past God spoke to our forefathers through the prophets at many times and in various ways, but in these last days he has spoken to us by his Son, whom he appointed heir of all things, and through whom he made the universe" (Heb. 1:1–2). Indeed, he is the Father's last and final word to us.

So as we gather to worship *Jesus our prophet,* what spiritual sacrifice can we offer? We can give him our attention. We can listen to him; we can look for him in every scripture. We can believe every word our Husband speaks to us. We can give him our conscience as we submit to his authority, confident that he always and only purposes for our good.

Jesus is also our "great high priest" (Heb. 4:14–16), who constantly intercedes for us and bids us come boldly to his throne of grace. What do we give *Jesus our priest* as we worship him? We give him our weakness, our sin, and our needs. There is no other Husband so caring, tender, gentle, and loving; he takes us at our worst and most needy and intercedes on our behalf.

Not only is Jesus our prophet and priest, he is our *king* (John 18:37)—in fact the "KING OF KINGS AND LORD OF LORDS" (Rev.19:16), and "the ruler of the kings of the earth" (Rev. 1:5). What do we give *Jesus our king?* We give him our obeisance. We bow down before him in awe and adoration. And we give him our obedience. As a well-loved Wife, we willingly submit to our Husband-King in all things.

THE DOORS ON OUR WORSHIP SHOULD BE SHUT WHEN IT IS...*FEARLESS*

We are to "put no confidence in the flesh."

To "put no confidence in the flesh" means that we worship from the posture of humility, rather than hubris. We should not lack confidence when we come before the Lord, but we must decry all cockiness; presumption has been replaced with prostration! Indeed, when it comes to worship, joy and humility are not mutually exclusive; in fact, they are dynamically interrelated! This is why Revelation always depicts the twenty-four elders falling off their thrones as they engage in the joys of heavenly worship (Rev. 4:9–10; 5:8; 7:11; 11:16; 19:4). Reaching for the sky and hugging the carpet go hand in hand!

In the same chapter in which God lamented how his people no longer adored him with the affection of a young bride, he also warned of "how evil and bitter it is for you when you forsake the LORD your God and have no awe of me" (Jer. 2:1–2, 19). To be in awe of our God is to fear him, not to be afraid of him. Where there is no fear of the Lord, there is no worship.

What is "the fear of the Lord?" It is an affectionate reverence for the one who has literally died so that we could be his Bride. The one who made himself our Bridegroom also made the entire cosmos and upholds every single atom by the power of his word! Let us adore him as our Lover! Let us be in awe of him as the Lord!

We are the Bride who is making herself ready (Rev. 19:7) for our Wedding Day. We are the Bride whom Jesus is bathing with his word, as he removes our stains, blemishes, and wrinkles of sin. We are the Bride who is humbled and gladdened to be secure in Jesus' love. We are the Bride who submits to his transforming work in our lives—as painful and thorough as it will be!

Therefore, with joy and faithfulness, let's abandon ourselves to our doxological calling. Let's live as "a fragrant offering, an acceptable sacrifice, pleasing to God" (Phil. 4:18). Let us worship as a Bride whose "citizenship is in heaven," one who "eagerly await[s] a Savior from there, the Lord Jesus Christ" (Phil. 3:20). Let us love as a people who are looking forward to the Day of international knee bending and cosmic transformation—when every tongue will humbly confess and everything in God's new creation will loudly sing that Jesus Christ is Lord, to the glory of God the Father. Amen!

Further Up *and* Further In

The Continuums *of* Worship

The Tension and Balance of Loving God Well

The transforming impact of the reign of grace in sixteenth-century Europe (the Reformation) freed the church to reaffirm many vital truths of the gospel lost in the preceding centuries to traditionalism and corruption. Among these truths is the conviction that God *alone* has the right and delight to regulate the specifics of worship—for it is *his own* doxological celebration! He does so through the testimony of the Scriptures. This affirmation became known as the *regulative principle.*

As Christians, we are to surrender *what we think* about worship and *what we do* in worship to the authority of God's Word. In other words, worship is not a matter of our opinions, (as noble, sincere, and godly as they may be); nor a matter of "what works" (regardless of how effective and successful our efforts).

Rather, worship is always an issue of obedient love—a glad submission to God's pleasure and patterns as revealed in the Bible. God-centered worship will move all of us well beyond our personal preferences and comfort zones. To worship well means that each of us will be humbled and stretched as we offer sacrifices of praise worthy of our God.

Bringing God More Than a Song

Presupposing, then, the *regulative principle,* we find several complementary imperatives (continuums) in the Scriptures concerning the worship of God. Take our first continuum for example, Jesus tells us that "true worshipers" *must* worship "in spirit *and* truth" (John 4:23). The continuum created by this affirmation looks like this:

TRUTH	SPIRIT
Safeguarding God's Truth	**Surrendering to God's Spirit**
Informed mind	Inflamed heart
Didactic (propositional)	Affective (passionate)
Theological (by the Word)	Pneumatological (by the Spirit)
Revelation	Inspiration
1 Timothy 4:6, 11, 13; 5:7	Philippians 3:3
2 Timothy 2:1–2; 4:1–3	Isaiah 29:13

Truth and spirit are complements, not competitors of one another. The truths God reveals in the Word about himself, us, the gospel, art, music, the Lord's Supper, baptism—all things and everything—are foundational to worship. We must be committed to *truthful* worship. But truth is no mere intellectual category. The Scriptures show us that we only *know* something when it has been wrapped around our *hearts*—when what we learn with our minds engages our inner person (spirit) by the work of the Holy Spirit.

Faithfulness to this continuum means that we are not really worshiping in spirit if we are not worshiping in truth, and we are not really worshiping in truth if we are not worshiping in spirit. We are not free to join a "teaching church" just because we prefer thinking to feeling, and we are not free to join an "experiential church" just because we prefer feeling to thinking. An informed mind *must* lead to an inflamed heart for true worship to take place.

Historically, Christians have acted as though we are permitted to select whichever half of a continuum is most appealing to us personally. But to pick one side of a continuum based on personal preference or personality type is to love Jesus on *your* terms, not his. As we would walk into an ice cream parlor and order a scoop or two of our favorite flavor, we tend to treat what the Bible says about worship like a dessert buffet—picking and choosing from an array of delightful elements and tasty styles. In reality, the Scriptures reveal worship to be a well-planned menu served by God in several courses—and he expects us to clean our plates.

With the goal of primarily honoring and pleasing God in worship, let us reflect upon the rest of these continuums in our calling to consuming faithfulness and obedient love. These continuums can be applied to whatever worshiping context of which we are a part. I have included references to many Scripture passages that I encourage you to look up and study, perhaps with a small group. Where do you see yourself and your worshiping community positioned in each of the following?

Object of Our Worship	Subjects in Our Worship
Loving God	**Loving the People of God**
God—the Trinity	The family of God
God, we adore *thee*	God, *we* adore thee
Looking up	Looking around
Vertical	Horizontal
Exodus 20:1–6	1 John 4:7–12
Matthew 22:34–38	Matthew 5:23–24

The most important aspect of worship is the *who,* not the *how to.* True adoration of God is birthed by truly apprehending *him.* To be strong on liturgy but light on theology is to worship *worship,* not worship *God.* Paul confronted this issue while ministering in Athens: "I see that in every way you are very religious. For as I walked around and looked carefully at your objects of worship, I even found an altar with this inscription: TO AN UNKNOWN GOD. Now what you worship as something unknown I am going to proclaim to you" (Acts 17:22–23). To be wrong about God's identity is to be wrong about his worship.

But worship never takes place in the abstract, always in the context of a people, a moment, and a culture. To worship God faithfully will result in relational commitment, scrutiny, and maturity. We have deceived ourselves if we think it possible to worship God well and have no covenant commitment to a local church. Worship is a corporate celebration of the reconciling power of the gospel, not a private exercise in existential fulfillment. Remember Cain and Abel!

John cut to the heart of this issue when he told us that it is impossible to love God whom we have not seen, if we do not love brothers and sisters with whom we share everyday life and the physical elements of the Lord's Supper (1 John 4:19–21). Some of us actually fall into the opposite error. We tend to confuse rich horizontal fellowship, or warm relationships, with biblical community. But if Jesus is not the center of our worship then we may be enjoying the blessing of good friendship, but not engaging in biblical worship.

TRANSCENDENCE	IMMANENCE
Loving God in His Majesty and Mystery	**Loving God with Childlike Joy**
God is above	God is near
Awe and reverence	Confidence and comfort
"Be still and know that I am God."	"Abba, Father!"
Jeremiah 2:13–19; Acts 2:43; Psalm 86:10	Hebrews 4:16

Be honest, which do you prefer—a near God or a faraway God? Actually, he is both, simultaneously—and our worship should reflect respect and experience of both dimensions of this continuum. Many of us, however, have confused respect for God's majesty with pushing him somewhere high in the ceiling of a great cathedral.

We think we love mystery, but in reality we simply want a far-away god—one who is so big and *out there* that no real personal encounter is ever expected. Others of us have confused familiarity with nearness. We want a harmless puppy, not a God who is really near, near enough to meddle with our hearts.

PROSTRATION	CELEBRATION
Loving God as Sinner-Saints "God, have mercy on *me,* the sinner."	**Loving God as Saint-Sinners** "I celebrate God with joy"
"You are a lot worse off than you think."	"You are a lot more loved and accepted than you ever dreamed or imagined."
Isaiah 6	Psalm 30

We must not confuse reverence with rigor mortis or assume that joy is meant to replace tears. An emotionally congruent response in worship is determined by the demands of the Word. Sometimes the Scriptures will call forth silent wonder, sometimes tearful lament, sometimes "pew-jumping joy," and sometimes all of the above in the same service.

Be careful about what you label "dead worship" and "alive worship." What you call "dead" may actually be alive with quiet awe and silencing glory—and what you call "alive" may be deadness to the things that matter most to the heart of God.

LAW	GOSPEL
Loving God's Law God's holiness and righteousness	**Loving God's Grace** God's mercy and grace
His standards, will, and commandments revealed in the Word	His compassion, forbearance, and forgiveness revealed in Christ

This continuum, like the rest, confronts our natural biases and theological prejudices. "Recovering Pharisees" are often confused about the continuing place of law and obedience in the life of a believer. They wrongly assume that calls for commitment, discipline, or repentance promote legalism or works-righteousness.

On the other hand, believers or churches that have assumed the role of being God's "prosecuting attorneys" in the community and culture or his self-appointed change agents are dangerously clueless about the singular power of the gospel of grace to change the heart.

NOETIC	SOMATIC
Loving God with My Mind Reflection, thinking, pondering, meditation, implications	**Loving God with My Body** Kneeling, standing, clapping, lifting hands, prostrating ourselves, dance, movement

The Scriptures decry dualism—putting asunder what God has joined together. We are those for whom the Great Commandment defines our worship, even the whole of life. I have personally lived and worshiped at both ends of this continuum. I have had my "don't give me theology, just give me Jesus" stage. And I've gone through my "deep thoughts and folded hands" stage. Both have smelled more like self-centered idolatry than other-centered adoration of God.

Worship That Reflects Who We Are	Worship That Directs Who We Are To Become
Loving God with Cultural Sensitivity	**Loving God with Kingdom Sensibility**
What is your context and culture? What gifts has God entrusted to your church family? How is the family of believers well represented in the way your worship is structured?	In what ways is God stretching, breaking, changing, and remaking your church family in light of the gospel?
1 Corinthians 12:14	1 Corinthians 5:13

Each congregation is a story within the Story, a scene within the whole movie, a tree within the big landscape. Our challenge is to discover how the gospel of God's grace and the glory of Jesus can be most powerfully expressed through the unique people and setting in which we find ourselves. Our worship services should reflect continuity with the past story of the whole people of God; present reality in our particular moment in the history of redemption; and a taste of the future when the completed story of redemption will find us with the whole diverse family of God—living, loving, and worshiping in perfect, reconciled unity.

CONTINUITY	SPONTANEITY
Loving God as a Participant in the Big Story	**Loving God in This Moment**
Celebrating the continuity of the whole history of redemption	Anticipating the sovereign movement of the Holy Spirit in *our* moment in the history of redemption
Maintaining continuity with your own liturgical traditions	Maintaining openness to new traditions emerging

Zeal for guarding historic tradition can become the soil from which arid traditionalism and the stench of dead orthodoxy grows like kudzu. But freedom and spontaneity in worship can often be another name for poor planning and flying by the seat of your pants, yet again. Our worship should give strong evidence of both roots and wings.

Inreach	Outreach
Loving God in Our Midst	**Loving God among the Nations**
Edification	Missiological worship
Body life, testimonies	Gospel movement, not missionary moment
Responding to the gospel	Deployed by the gospel
Invitations	Commissions
1 Corinthians 14:26–33; 1 Thessalonians 4:18;	1 Corinthians 14:24–25
1 Thessalonians 5:11; Ephesians 4:1–16	Zechariah 8:21

God-centered worship will be missional and transformational. Every time we gather for public worship, we should sense that something awe-fully dynamic is taking place. The gospel changes people and, ultimately, all things. We don't gather like make-believe soldiers to reenact the Civil War. We gather to envision and participate in the greatest victory ever won: Jesus has come to destroy the works of the devil, and he has succeeded! The mop-up operation is under way, and it is a movement of resurrection, not one of memorializing the dead!

MICRO	MACRO
Loving God Well in This Hour and a Half	**Loving God Well 24/7**
Liturgy	Life
Cultus	*Coram Deo*
The service of worship	Worship service
Acts 2:42; 1 Corinthians 10–14	Romans 12:1–2
1 Timothy 2	Amos 5:21–24

We have placed far, far too much emphasis on the "micro" celebration of worship to the near exclusion of any meaningful understanding of the "macro" setting of worship. By micro, I am referring to what we usually call the worship service, our public gathering on the Lord's Day to celebrate the gospel in Word, sacrament, and praise. What's even worse is that we have reduced the category of "worship" to the musical dimension of worship, thus giving the distinct impression that everything else in the worship service is, well, not worship. This is abhorrent! Such a notion, in my estimation, has been most destructive to our contemporary understanding and experience of worship.

An objective reading of the Scriptures will lead to the conclusion that God applies the language of worship far more to the lifestyle of believers in the world than to our lip service in the sanctuary. Indeed, the phrase *worship service* should be synonymous with *the Christian life.*

Lead Worshipers	Worship Leaders
Being Led to Adore Christ by Those Captured by the Gospel	**Being Led to Adore Christ by Those Gifted by the Holy Spirit**
Thirsty adorers	Skilled craftsmen
Heart	Art
Psalms 42; 63	Psalm 150; 1 Corinthians 11:17–34

There is quite an emphasis today on identifying and almost revering "great worship leaders," men and women with unique gifts at leading the music portion of a worship service. But as we work hard to place the right people "up front" to lead worship, let's make sure that we are most concerned to cultivate and deploy a generation of lead worshipers, not just gifted song leaders.

I would far rather be led by an average musician with a convincing and contagious heart for God, than a gifted musician who is capable of creating "moments" and manipulating emotions, who doesn't really demonstrate gospel thirst and humility.

Already	Not Yet
Loving God Imperfectly with Other Sinner-Saints	**Loving God Perfectly with Every Glorified Believer**
Appetizer	Entree
First fruits	Complete harvest
Is our worship *now* making us insatiably thirsty for worship *then?*	Is our worship *then* making us patiently faithful as we worship *now?*
Striving to stir up congregants—provoking their longings for heaven—rather than trying to satisfy them	Filling our hearts with the visions of how others-centered and corporate our worship will be forever
Hebrews 12:22–24	Revelation 4; 5; 7; 19; 21–22

Everything about life in this world is meant to leave us redemptively discontent. We aren't home yet. Even what we would call the best worship service imaginable is meant to make us restless for the perfect worship, which will only be celebrated after the return of Jesus, Bridegroom for Bride. Failure to own and celebrate this truth fuels the wrong kind of discontent. "Your worship is too boring. I'm gonna find a church that really knows how to worship." Or just as tragic, "Our worship is perfect! Don't change a thing. How could the worship of heaven be any better than ours?" Do you really want to know?

Oh, come let us adore him—Christ the Lord, Christ the Lover, Christ our Life!

Further Up *and* Further In

The Triads *of* Worship

Tri-Perspective Models of Our Most Glorious Calling

There is something awe-fully *triune* about the Bible, beginning with the revelation of God as Trinity: Father, Son, and Holy Spirit. The three-beat rhythm and music of the gospel can be heard in so many places in the biblical narrative. To recognize this is to celebrate God's worship as a grand symphony rather than as an inspirational sound bite—a multiverse hymn rather than a mantra-like chorus. Worship is *his-story-cal, new covenantal,* and *incarnational.* Following is a visual image of maturing, tri-perspective worship.

His-Story-Cal Worship: The Ongoing Drama of Redemption

God's worship, like the unfolding story of salvation and re-creation, is progressive. We are not worshiping faithfully unless we see ourselves participating in the whole story. From the echoes of Eden to the first fruits of the new heaven and new earth, our worship is a participation in the whole doxological drama.

As we gather to worship, we worship in the "faith of our fathers," established in real time-space events of the past that must be experienced in *our* moment. This is the essence of what the Bible means by the concept of "remembering." To remember is not merely to recount the facts of a story but to participate in the power and reality of that story! Likewise, when we gather to worship, we do so with an eye to the future. The whole Christian life is decidedly eschatological or future oriented. We are to remember our future into *this* moment—for it is *our* future.

HISTORICAL	CONTEXTUAL	ESCHATOLOGICAL
Past *Faith*	**Present** *Love*	**Future** *Hope*
Anchored to the historic faith	Effectively engaged in this present moment	Anticipating the Day of eschatological fulfillment
Garden The Garden of Eden as the prototype of all worship	*Wilderness* The New Israel living the Exodus of the gospel as our present context for worship	*The New City* The New Jerusalem in the new heaven and new earth as the fulfillment of worship

THE COMMANDS OF GOD	NEW CREATION	THE NEW HEART
The Regulative Principle directing our worship	The New Creation Era defining our worship	The New Commandment delighting our worship
1 Corinthians 7:19	Galatians 6:5; 2 Corinthians 5:17	Galatians 5:6
Roots	Shoots	Fruit

NEW COVENANTAL WORSHIP: A CHRISTOLOGICAL APPROACH

Likewise, acceptable worship is *always* centered on the person and work of Jesus—for "no matter how many promises God has made, they are 'Yes' in Christ" (2 Cor. 1:20). The whole Jesus for holy worship! In every service of worship, Jesus should be honored and experienced as prophet, priest, and king. Every portion of God's Word is to be studied, applied, and celebrated with Jesus clearly in view (Luke 24:36–48).

Jesus As Prophet	Jesus As Priest	Jesus As King
Giving Jesus Our	**Giving Jesus Our**	**Giving Jesus Our**
Attention	Adoration	Obeisance
Listening	Sin	Obedience
Conscience	Groanings	Longings

Jesus As Pursuer	Jesus As Bridegroom	Jesus As Husband
Of His Bride	**To His Bride**	**To His Wife**
In eternity and history	In the present and until he returns	At his return and forever

Incarnational Worship: Who Is Our Audience?

Lastly, for our worship to be God-centered—faithfully and passionately designed for his pleasure and purposes—we will keep three audiences in mind and heart.

Upreach	Inreach	Outreach
1st Audience	**2nd Audience**	**3rd Audience**
God	The covenant family	Neighbors and nations

Majestrial	Medicinal	Missional
We Minister	**We Minister**	**We Minister**
To the Lord	To one another	To the lost and least

If sex is for MARRIAGE, what does the Bible say about singleness? First, it reminds us that Jesus himself was *single,* although he is also set before us as God's MODEL for humanness. The world may believe that sexual experience is *indispensable* to being human; the Bible flatly disagrees.

John STOTT

Eros ceases to be a DEVIL only when it *ceases* to be a god.

C. S. LEWIS

LET HIM KISS ME WITH THE KISSES OF HIS MOUTH—FOR YOUR LOVE IS MORE *delightful* THAN WINE.

—SONG OF SONGS 1:2

Anything that rubs man's nose in his MORTALITY is also capable of *lifting* his heart to God, and probably no other phenomena on earth are so EFFECTIVE in this respect as are that great trio of death, *prayer,* and sex.

Mike MASON

CHAPTER NINE

Graced SEXUALITY

God has designed us for deep connection—for rich, mutually fulfilling relationship. To be utterly naked in intimate relationship and to feel no shame whatsoever—what words can adequately express the longing each of us has for such shameless connection and fulfilling intimacy?

But of course, Satan has corrupted our sexuality. Of course, he has targeted sex, with all its mystery and majesty. Of course, there is perversion, incest, sexual abuse, sexual addiction, pedophilia, pornography, infidelity, and sexual immorality of any and every form. Of course.

HEARTBREAKING

I could hardly believe what I was hearing. Sitting in a small Italian house church, just outside of Turin, near the base of the Italian Alps, I was dumbfounded, heartbroken, and incredulous.

Aurora, the wife of a former Roman Catholic priest, was sharing stories and calling—stories of sexual abuse, the likes of which I'd never heard, and her calling to walk, weep, and work with the growing number of victims that are surfacing in her circle of life. Who are the ones so tragically sinned against? Nuns—in her homeland and neighborhood.

"Please pray for these precious, damaged sisters. Many of them have been raped by priests, some forced to have abortions, others turned out of their convents and parishes with no place to go, no one who believes them, and no money to live on."

"How do they deal with such horror?" a member of our visiting missions team asked.

"They generally go in one of two directions," Aurora responded, her eyes now glistening with fresh tears—evidence of both compassion and anger. "They either run back to the system, losing themselves in a life of busyness, shame, and denial, or they repudiate any knowledge of God. For in our country and culture, there isn't any separation between church and state or between God and anything. For some of these women, it's easier to try to live life without God than to try to live life with a God who abuses nuns."

ENRAGING

I opened an e-mail from a longstanding friend.

> *Dear Scotty,*
>
> *It finally came! I am so happy with the thoroughness and integrity of the report. I will be there to represent myself and the many others who have prayed so long for this day. I'm just sorry some of us gave up praying years ago.*

She was rejoicing over a long-overdue report—a report signaling that a certain Protestant denomination was finally responding to a great tragedy. Years ago on the continent of Africa, my friend lived in a Christian boarding school that served as home for many other MKs (missionary kids) like herself. While their parents were serving Christ in the field, these children were entrusted to a staff of fellow-called and -commissioned disciples of Jesus.

However, one of the pastors on staff had a severe problem. His problem resulted in manifold problems for over twenty children whom he sexually molested over the course of several years. He hypnotized many of the children before abusing them.

No one took the children's stories very seriously. In time, this pastor was called off the mission field to serve in a local church, against the protest of former victims. In his new location, the abuse resumed and continued until he died. Finally, the children, some of whom are now grandparents, were believed.

NUMBING

"Honey, you won't believe this article on sexual activity among young girls." Darlene didn't hand me a copy of *Christianity Today* or *Discipleship Journal,* but *O,* the Oprah magazine. Written by Michelle Burford, the article was simply titled "Girls and Sex." Here's the opening paragraph: "When I was 12, having nerve meant calling my math teacher by her first name—not attempting fellatio before study hall. So you can understand why I was appalled when I clicked on Oprah's show last spring to hear seventh-grade girls barely out of training bras reveal to a stunned Oprah that they were offering oral sex as cavalierly as they would a good-night peck."[1]

In research for her article, Ms. Burford interviewed twenty-five young women and found that Oprah's show was neither exaggerated nor were her guests an anomaly. One of her own seventeen-year-old interviewees offered this account. "In seventh grade, I was one of the only virgins among my friends. The friends I have now who are still virgins have oral sex without intercourse because it's as close as they can get to sex without intercourse. The majority of the girls at my school are both giving and getting oral sex—they just aren't talking about it."[2]

Disturbing

A growing number of youth pastors are reporting that these same sexual attitudes and practices are found among a great percentage of middle-school and high-school students who are vitally involved in their ministries. More pastors and professional Christian leaders than ever before are losing their pulpits, jobs, and families as a result of affairs or sexual misconduct.

In the last decade, *Leadership* magazine conducted a survey to which three hundred pastors responded. It revealed that "23 percent indicated that they had done something sexual with someone other than their spouse. Twelve percent reported having intercourse with someone other than their spouse, and 61 percent admitted to fantasizing occasionally about having sex with someone other than their spouse. Twenty-five percent indicated that they sexually fantasized weekly or even daily."[3]

In an increasing percentage of evangelical churches, right alongside of grief support groups, we are finding a growing proliferation of sexual-abuse and sexual-addiction recovery groups. Let's celebrate and multiply this kind of caregiving. But let's also examine the exponential increase in the need for such ministry among believers.

Sin has vandalized shalom everywhere, but nowhere more obviously or destructively than in the intricate and beautiful sphere of our sexuality. But the problem of sexual immorality is not a new one.

Broken Faith

Malachi witnessed this malicious thievery of intimacy and the contamination of covenantal beauty among the worship leaders of his day:

> Another thing you do: You flood the LORD's altar with tears. You weep and wail because he no longer pays attention to your offerings or accepts them with pleasure from your hands. You ask, "Why?" It is because the LORD is acting as the witness between you

> and the wife of your youth, because *you have broken faith with her, though she is your partner, the wife of your marriage covenant.* (Mal. 2:13–14)

God's worship is often sabotaged by misplaced passion. When his magnificent design for the marriage bed, or the sanctuary, is replaced with our maniacal demand for personal fulfillment, the implications are far-reaching.

The marriages among the priests and populace were under great duress. But their marriage problems weren't rooted in poor communication skills. It's not as if all they needed were a few good seminars on "How to Really Love the Wife of Your Youth, Wrinkles and All." Theirs was a heart issue, a worship issue. Because the men in the community had "broken faith" with their wives, God ignored their make-believe worship, their insincere offerings (appeals for grace without repentance), and their self-centered tears and wails. He found no pleasure in that which is to be the doxological equivalent to sex (v. 13).

The worship leaders in Jerusalem had traded in their aging wives for younger pagan models (pun intended). They married women whose hearts did not belong to Yahweh, but to other gods. The sad thing is, the priests weren't acting as though their hearts belonged to Yahweh either. For this generation of men, marriage, to a wife or God, didn't reveal the beauty of covenant faithfulness and mutual pleasuring; it was more like the ugliness of adult-bookstore exploitation and addiction.

THE SEX OF WORSHIP

As creatures created for intimacy, we long for connection and closeness. Made in God's image and redeemed to be his covenant children, we are never more alive than when we can joyfully bow our knees with Paul before the Father, "from whom all fatherhood derives its name" (Eph. 3:14–15, Greek translation from NIV footnotes). God, alone, can father us the way we long to be fathered. In repudiation of Sigmund

Freud's charge, we haven't projected on God our need for a perfect father. He is the perfect Father who has brought the analogy to us!

Likewise, marriage is not an institution that we project on our relationship with Jesus; Jesus is the One who brings the meaning and purpose of marital intimacy to us. It's just as fair to say that Jesus is the *one from whom all marital intimacy derives its name.* What's the significance of this affirmation?

Let's recall this pristine scene in the Garden of Eden. When Adam first saw Eve, "the man said, 'This is now bone of my bones and flesh of my flesh; she shall be called "woman," for she was taken out of man.' For this reason a man will leave his father and mother and be united to his wife, and they will become one flesh. The man and his wife were both naked, and they felt no shame" (Gen. 2:23–25).

As the Father of the bride, God presented Eve to Adam. The first marriage established a defining relational principle: Marriage is to have the highest priority over any other familial relationship. A man is to *leave* his parents when he enters into the covenant of marriage. There is a severing of the parent-child relationship so that loyalty to one's parents is superseded by allegiance to one's spouse.

Notice, as well, that a man is commanded to *cleave,* or *cling,* to his wife. This intense embrace only further underscores the priority, passion, and perpetuity of this bond. However, the mystery and intimacy of this relationship is most profoundly spelled out in the phrase, "and they will become *one flesh.*" Clearly, the sexual union between a husband and wife is indicated here, but so much more as well. The union that God has designed in marriage is unlike any other. The playfulness and purity of the first marriage is summarized in this tantalizing image—*"the man and his wife were both naked, and they felt no shame."* Such a feast of harm-free vulnerability and full-gaze enjoyment is to be celebrated nowhere else than in covenant marriage—between a husband and wife.

Well, there is one other place this love feast is to be celebrated. Major lights should go on within us when we return to Paul's letter to the Ephesians and read these words: " 'For this reason a man will leave his father and mother and be united to his wife, and the two will become one flesh.' This is a profound mystery—but I am talking about Christ and the church" (Eph. 5:31–32).

The relationship that was shared between the first Adam and his wife, Eve, is now redemptively superseded by the relationship that exists between the second Adam, Jesus, and His wife, the Church. This is a profound mystery indeed! We are made for shameless, passionate, out-in-the-open, glorious intimacy with our Savior, Jesus! What Adam and Eve enjoyed before the Fall has become a symbol and type for the relationship we are to enjoy with Jesus. Talk about grace!

Consider some of the implications of this truth:

- Our relationship with Jesus is to supersede all other human relationships in terms of priority, allegiance, and intimacy—including the relationship we enjoy with the members of our families—even our spouse. (Luke 14:25–26)

- The only love "better than life" is the love Jesus has for us, Bridegroom for Bride. We are under an idolatrous illusion if we think such love can be found in any other relationship or embrace.

- To Jesus, alone, will we be married in the new heaven and new earth. Only Jesus can fulfill the good longing, and sometimes, obsessive demand we have for oneness and intimacy.

- Where is our shameless intimacy and oneness with Jesus most visually, fully, and profoundly celebrated this side of heaven? *In worship.* Indeed, as stated in our discussion on idolatry—worship

> is to our marriage with Jesus what sexual intercourse is to marriage with a spouse.

Doesn't it stand to reason, then, that Satan will do anything he can to infiltrate, pollute, and distort marriage—the very relationship that is designed as a model and means of the love of God? Doesn't it make all the sense in the world that Satan will vigorously target worship for corruption—our most important, defining, glorious, and eternal of all acts? For it is in worship that we most intimately connect with our God and reveal the astonishing beauty of Jesus and the wonder of the gospel. And isn't it obvious, more so than ever, why Satan pours out all of his venom, multiplies his schemes, and releases his demons for the perversion and pollution of the good and dangerous gift of sex?

The Worship of Sex

The intrigue and pleasure of sexual experience outside of marriage, especially intercourse, may be the most insidious, counterfeit, and tantalizing substitute there is for Christian worship. Can we make an idol of a wife, a husband, of marriage itself? Of course—we do it all the time. Can we worship sex? If that question is not one of the all-time most rhetorical questions, what is?

Richard Winter writes,

> Sex is a wonderful gift that is intended to be expressed and experienced in the context of a lifelong, committed relationship between a man and a woman. Sexual orgasm is one of the most intense pleasures known to human beings. It has the greatest potential of giving us a foretaste of heaven and the greatest potential for leading us toward hell! As is the case with most good gifts that God has given us to enjoy, we are never satisfied with sexual pleasure and always want more....In every era sex has been used as a "fix" to relieve boredom, to give a sense of taking control and to find release from anxiety, anger and frustration. But because of the tech-

nology at hand today, we probably live in the most erotically stimulated culture of all time.[4]

Where does all of this extreme erotic stimulation lead? To the building of more and more altars for the adoration and service to the gods and goddesses of sexual experience—chiefly seen in the pornography industry. The *New York Times Magazine* published these numbing numbers in May of 2001:

> The $4 billion that Americans spend on video pornography is larger than the annual revenue accrued by either the National Football League, the National Basketball Association, or Major League Baseball. But that's literally not the half of it: the porn business is estimated to total between $10 and $14 billion annually in the United States, when you toss in the porn networks and pay-per-view movies on cable and satellite, Internet Web sites, in-room hotel movies, phone sex, sex toys and that archaic medium of my own occasionally misspent youth, magazines....People pay more money for pornography in America in a year than they do on movie tickets, more than they do on all the performing arts combined.[5]

These heartbreaking statistics underscore how much we need a *reign* of grace through righteousness in our hearts, churches, and culture, and not merely *guilt-free* Christians running around celebrating how good it feels to be forgiven.

John Eldredge muses,

> The older Christian wedding vows contained these amazing words: "With my body, I thee worship." Maybe our forefathers weren't so prudish after all, maybe they understood sex far better than we do. To give yourself over to another, passionately and nakedly, to adore that person body, soul, and spirit—we know there is something special, even sacramental about sex. It requires trust and abandonment, guided by a wholehearted devotion. What else can this be

> but worship? After all, God employs explicitly sexual language to describe faithfulness (and unfaithfulness) to him. For us creatures of the flesh, sexual intimacy is the closest parallel we have to real worship. Even the world knows this. Why else would sexual ecstasy become the number one rival to communion with God. The best imposters succeed because they are nearly indistinguishable from what they are trying to imitate. We worship sex because we don't know how to worship God.[6]

Oh, come let us adore him, Christ the Lord, Christ our beloved Bridegroom, who is making all things new. The vandalism of shalom will be redeemed, and a shalom that is beyond all we can ask, hope for, or imagine will be established forever. Pornography will be replaced with poetry. Where adult bookstores once stood, children will play with once-wild, now-tamed beasts. In the place of sexual predators there will be dancing mountains and clapping trees. The bluest skies and the greenest grass will simply eliminate any need for black, ever again. The tears of abuse and abusing will be wiped out of our eyes, and we will dance and touch and be known without shame or harm forever.

A Prayer Walk

Perhaps in reading this chapter, many different emotions have surfaced in your heart: the shame of your own "misspent youth," the ongoing pain of having been sexually abused, the fear of being exposed as a sexual addict, the anger and frustration born of a commitment to stay sexually pure while not having a redemptive outlet for your passion, fear for your children, conviction about joining other reformers in the battle against the pornography industry, an intensified longing for Jesus to return… For all of us, I think it wise to conclude this chapter with a prayer walk, applying the powerful and healing truths of the gospel to our hearts.

Many of our greatest regrets, deepest wounds, and emotional chains were generated in our sexual stories. How does the gospel help us to respond to sexual sin, guilt, and struggle? Where can we find power and hope to fulfill our calling to sexual purity and faithfulness? Pray with me in the light of the *justification, sanctification,* and *glorification* we are given in Jesus.

GRACE REIGNING IN JUSTIFICATION

Gracious Father, I praise you for setting me free from the guilt of all my sexual sin—past, present, and future! I have not been a good steward of this precious gift, and I praise you for your forbearance and mercy. Jesus, I worship you for living a life of perfect sexual purity in everything you thought, said, and did—not just to be my model but to be my righteousness. You have done what I could never do but what the law required of me: You loved your Father and others, perfectly—all the time. Your obedience has earned the Father's blessing for me. You never misused your sexuality.

And I praise you for taking the death that my impurity earned. The cross looms larger and larger as I consider the waywardness of my lustful heart. Because of your cross, I will never be condemned for my sin, sexual or otherwise. The Father dealt with you according to my sexual sin, and he now relates to me according to your righteousness.

Amazing! This encourages me like nothing else, especially when I fail or compromise myself. When I am condemned by Satan for my sin, I will remember you and your life and death for me. Jesus, this makes me want to honor you all the more with my body and passions. I want a pure heart—not just a forgiven one.

GRACE REIGNING IN SANCTIFICATION

Glorious Father, now that you have declared me to be righteous *in* Jesus, I submit to your purpose to make me pure *like* Jesus. I want his beauty to overtake my heart. Fill me, Father. Fill me with the joy, freedom, and goodness of your Son.

You are so generous with me! Not only have you given me the status of being righteous, you have promised to make me sexually whole, pure, and perfect on the astonishing Day when Jesus returns to glorify me and all of your creation. .

Until then, I no longer have to fear the reign of sin and death in my life—for it has been broken by the work of Jesus. I am no longer a prisoner to sexual sin or any sin. I trust in your promise to complete the good work you have begun in me! I know that I cannot change myself. Your promise offers me great hope as I seek to obey you and trust in the work of your Spirit in my life.

Because I don't have to fear that you are ashamed of me or disgusted with me, I am free to be honest before you. I confess that there is still a lot of foolishness and weakness in my heart. Sometimes—when I catch myself thinking, fantasizing, and planning to sin sexually—I wonder if I know you at all.

I praise you for teaching me in your Word about the war that is going on in my heart and in the hearts of all your children. I'm so glad I am not alone in this struggle. I trust you, Father, to wage a mighty battle by your Spirit. I want to be less and less naive about my sinful nature.

You command me to give you my body and its parts as instruments of righteousness. By faith, I do so right now. However, I will not trust in my surrender, but in your Son, to change me. Because of your love, Father, I purpose to obey whatever you teach me about sex and purity.

Father, as the reign of grace advances in my heart, I am learning how growth in holiness involves a deeper repentance of sin and a greater boasting in Christ. You have freed me to grieve over my sin without putting my conscience back under the law. For this I praise you. I know I will only be completely free and whole when Jesus returns; nevertheless, Father, I trust you when you tell me that the power of the gospel is great enough to change me. When I am disobedient, I will seek to blame no one, and I will fall again upon your mercy.

I cannot merit anything from spiritual disciplines like Bible reading, prayer, fellowship, worship, meditation, and service; nevertheless, these conduits of grace profit me greatly as I desire to become sexually healthy, whole, and pure. Thank you for giving me everything I need for a life of godliness. I purpose to use these good gifts diligently.

Father, thank you, as well, for freedom to enjoy your good and passionate design for my sexuality and sex. And thank you for helping me become wiser about the corrupting and destructive power of the wrong kind of sexual images, influences, and propaganda that confront me everywhere. As a sign of freedom, I will be quicker and more consistent in making good choices for myself in these matters and more conscious of what is needful and best for others.

Though I am prone to forget every day, I purpose to remember that Jesus' righteousness is what makes me an object of your affection. When I sin sexually, I will rely on my union with Christ and not on my strivings, promises, penance, or rigorism to regain a sense of holiness.

GRACE REIGNING IN GLORIFICATION

What a Day it's going to be, Lord Jesus, when you return and everything is made perfect, including me! I will fill my heart as full as I can with the vision of the Day when all sexual temptation will be gone, every semblance of sin and death forever swallowed up! My damaged and deceitful heart will finally be free and whole. This is a powerful hope, Lord Jesus: Never again to be hurt sexually; never again to hurt anyone sexually.

I am so thankful that you will glorify me and your family and the whole cosmos instantaneously! I will be so ready for sanctification to be over! No more having to crucify the flesh. No more sin to confess. No more residue of my sexual abuse. No more forgiveness to extend. No more walking by faith; for Jesus, we will see you and be made like you!

Father, I so look forward to being with the whole family of God as we begin living together forever in the perfections of the new heaven and new earth—loving perfectly, even as we are perfectly and passionately loved by our great Bridegroom, Jesus.

Because marriage will not exist in that state, the fulfillment of my sexuality and your design for sex will find consummate completion in my living as a part of the beloved Bride of Jesus...forever. The great longing I have for intimacy and rich connection will be magnificently celebrated without limitation, corruption, or disruption. Hallelujah... what a Savior! Hallelujah...what a salvation!

Sex and *the* City

1 THESSALONIANS

The HBO TV show *Sex and the City* could just as well be set in the ancient city of Thessalonica. When the reign of grace came to Thessalonica, the enemy set about to destroy its dominion. He already had a strong foothold there—a sexual foothold. The Thessalonian Christians had come from a background of paganism. The idea of limiting sexual intercourse to marriage was ludicrous to a culture shaped by the prevailing Greco-Roman world-view:

> It was widely accepted that men either could not or would not limit themselves to their wife as their only sexual partner.…A man might have a mistress who could provide him also with intellectual companionship; the institution of slavery made it easy for him to have a concubine while casual gratification was readily available from a harlot. The function of his wife was to manage his household and to be the mother of his legitimate children and heirs.[1]

Do we really believe that the sexual insanity, abuse, and perversion of our day can change? Paul did! There is hope, great hope, but only through the power of the gospel. Consider how Paul applied grace to sex in the city of Thessalonica.

CHASTISEMENT GROUNDED IN LOVE

In answer to the "Macedonian call," the apostle Paul took the reign of grace through the preaching of the gospel into the cosmopolitan city of Thessalonica. Though only there for three weeks on his first visit, a great love affair was secured.

Writing to encourage and further establish these new converts in a gospel-defined lifestyle, Paul composed his first letter from Corinth. With stylus in hand, he was surrounded by a world of insatiable sexual insanity. John Stott describes the setting:

> In Corinth, Aphrodite, the Greek goddess of sex and beauty, whom the Romans identified with Venus, sent her servants out as prostitutes to roam the streets by night. Thessalonica, on the other hand, was particularly associated with the worship of deities called the Cabiri, in whose rites gross immorality was promoted under the name of religion.[2]

Paul's opening words to the Thessalonians expressed the depth of his affection for the young church: "We loved you so much that we were delighted to share with you not only the gospel of God but our lives as well, because you had become so dear to us" (1 Thess. 2:8). Laying a foundation of sincere friendship and authentic care, Paul built a bridge that could sustain the weight of some very pointed instruction on sexual matters:

> For we know, brothers loved by God, that he has chosen you, because our gospel came to you not simply with words, but also with power, with the Holy Spirit and with deep conviction. You know how we lived among you for your sake. You became imitators of us and of the Lord; in spite of severe suffering, you welcomed the message with the joy given by the Holy Spirit. (1 Thess. 1:4–6)

Indeed, the reign of grace took hold in these believers' hearts! The gospel came with "power and deep conviction" (v. 5).

As a man always alive to his own story of failure and redemption, Paul sought to be gentle with these pagan converts, "like a mother caring for her little children" (2:7). He was glad to care for them "as a father deals with his own children, encouraging, comforting (2:11–12). Paul was careful to secure the roots of the Thessalonians deep into the soil of the *delights* of God's love; for without this foundation, the *demands* of God's love are simply too overwhelming.

Paul's love urged the believers "to live lives *worthy of God,* who calls you into his kingdom and glory" (1 Thess. 2:12). So what is a life "worthy of God"? First of all, it is a life lived in response to the worth of God's Son and his gospel. If we are not *compelled* by God's grace, we will not be *empowered* to live for Christ's glory. Secondly, it is a life given to the advancement of God's kingdom—*the reign of grace.*

PAUL'S INSTRUCTIONS

These infant Christians had given their hearts to Jesus but needed further teaching on how to live out their newfound faith. So the fatherly Paul lays out these instructions:

> Finally, brothers, we instructed you how to live in order to please God, as in fact you are living. Now we ask you and urge you in the Lord Jesus to do this more and more. For you know what instructions we gave you by the authority of the Lord Jesus.
>
> It is God's will that you should be sanctified: that you should avoid sexual immorality; that each of you should learn to control his own body in a way that is holy and honorable, not in passionate lust like the heathen, who do not know God; and that in this matter no one should wrong his brother or take advantage of him. The Lord will punish men for all such sins, as we have already told you and warned you. For God did not call us to be impure, but to live a holy life. Therefore, he who rejects this instruction does not reject man but God, who gives you his Holy Spirit. (1 Thess. 4:1–8)

Here's a summary of Paul's instruction to young believers who lived in a hostile and sexually amoral culture—much like ours.

LIVE IN ORDER TO PLEASE GOD

> Finally, brothers, we instructed you how to live in order to please God, as in fact you are living. (v. 1)

God's grace calls and empowers us to live more and more for God's pleasure. This is freedom at its best! A real sign that the gospel has penetrated our hearts is that we begin to find more joy in "pleasuring" God than in pleasing ourselves. We need instructions in this way of life, because God's ways are not our ways! Therefore, we are to...

Submit to the Revelation of Scripture

> For you know what instructions we gave you by the authority of the Lord Jesus. (v. 2)

Paul reminds us, along with the Thessalonians, to receive the Scriptures as the will of God and to submit to them as the authoritative revelation of the life that is pleasing to him. A heart alive to the love of God will be alive to the Word of God. The Bible is the perfect law that gives liberty to those who are living under the reign of grace.

Be Sanctified

> It is God's will that you should be sanctified. (v. 3a)

It is God's will and pleasure that we become holy—that we live by his design and in his delight. The essence of holiness is to discover and surrender to the purpose for which God originally designed anything in creation—like sex! A heart under the reign of grace is always asking the Father to reveal his will—especially regarding design and purpose.

Avoid Sexual Immorality

> ...that you should avoid sexual immorality (v. 3b)

Expounding on his instruction to be "sanctified," or holy, Paul tells the Thessalonians to avoid sexual immorality. What does it mean to live a sexually holy life? First, it means *knowing* God's purposes for sex and what he says is and is not sexually appropriate. The Scriptures are our storehouse of wealth and wisdom on this issue. Secondly, it means *obeying* God in the power and beauty of the gospel.

The word Paul uses here for "sexual immorality" is *pornea.* At the time of Paul's writing, *pornea* meant sexual intercourse outside of marriage, but it also referred to any form of illicit sexual activity deviating from God's standards (thus we have the word *pornography*). The immediate implication is that sexual intercourse is *only* appropriate in the context of marriage.

Paul wasn't being a curmudgeon or a frozen Pharisee with sexual hang-ups. He really believed that God's design for everything is good, pleasing, and perfect. It's only in light of God's original design and redeeming purposes in Jesus that such an admonition makes any sense at all.

The sexual mores of the reign of grace required a radical readjustment for the believers in Thessalonica—as for many of us. Indeed, the implications of grace are huge for sexual purity. This is why we must continually blast our hearts with the beauty and bounty of Jesus found in the reign of grace.

Learn to Be a Good Steward of Your Body (and Its Sexual Passion)

> ...that each of you should learn to control his own body in a way that is holy and honorable, not in passionate lust like the heathen, who do not know God. (vv. 4–5)

This admonition reveals an important dimension of Paul's worldview. Paul equates sexual irresponsibility with the absence of the knowledge of God, not merely with the violation of rules and taboos.

Those who "do not know God" are driven by a "passionate lust" to get sexual gratification—however, whenever, and with whomever. Our hearts are never neutral or passionless. Elsewhere, Paul describes what happens when God simply removes the restraints on the hearts of those who reject his glory and design: "Therefore God gave them over in the sinful desires of their hearts to sexual impurity for the degrading of their bodies with one another" (Rom. 1:24).

In contrast, Paul says of believers, "You were bought at a price. Therefore honor God with your body" (1 Cor. 6:20). Here, Paul states and then directly applies the implications of the gospel. To paraphrase, he says: "God graciously bought you out of the destructive dominion of sin and death. You are no longer your own. Mercifully, you belong to him. Therefore, use 'your' body (and whatever else he has entrusted unto you) as a demonstration of the wonder of the gospel, as a living symbol and expression of the unimaginable intimacy Christians enjoy with Jesus."

Don't Take Sexual Advantage of Someone Else

> ...in this matter no one should wrong his brother or take advantage of him. The Lord will punish men for all such sins, as we have already told you and warned you. (v. 6)

The idea here is that of crossing a boundary—trespassing (sexually) on someone else's territory. We must not exploit another person's body for our own sexual pleasure, whether through seduction, manipulation, fantasy, or abuse. Neither are we to be careless about the seemingly "innocent" and "harmless" ways we may incite someone to sin sexually by the way we dress, speak, "innocently flirt," or physically touch one another. From preadolescent days of "playing doctor" to current moments of a "holy kiss" that is a little less than holy—let's purpose to honor one another. Without becoming hostage to the *professional weaker brothers and sisters in our midst,* let's be careful to love well and exercise discretion.

One of the clearest evidences of the reign of grace in our hearts is the movement toward other-centered living. Paul puts it like this: Because of the encouragement that comes from your union with Christ and because of the comfort you receive from his love, "do nothing out of selfish ambition or vain conceit, but in humility consider others better than yourselves" (Phil. 2:1, 3). Only the reign of grace can effect such a radical redirection of our sinful hearts!

Paul underscores this admonition against sexual exploitation with a sober warning. "The Lord will punish men for all such sins, as we have already told you and warned you....He who rejects this instruction does not reject man but God, who gives you his Holy Spirit" (1 Thess. 4:6, 8).

Perhaps these words of Jesus were reverberating in Paul's mind when he wrote to the Thessalonians:

> If anyone causes one of these little ones who believe in me to sin, it would be better for him to have a large millstone hung around his neck and to be drowned in the depths of the sea. Woe to the world because of the things that cause people to sin! Such things must come, but woe to the man through whom they come! (Matt. 18:6–7)

So how do we honor God with our bodies sexually? Knowing that we are bought with the blood of Jesus, his grace enables us to live changed lives.

ENABLING GRACE, AND SEX FOR THE CHRISTIAN

1. GRACE ENABLES US TO RESIST SEXUAL TEMPTATIONS

Grace Gives Us Speedy Feet

Paul further admonishes us to "flee from sexual immorality" (1 Cor. 6:18). There are times when faced with temptation we are to *run,* like Joseph ran from Potiphar's house! (Gen. 39). As Potiphar's wife stood before him buck naked, having already perfumed the bed in which she planned to seduce him, Joseph wasn't called to hang around and share the gospel with her—spiritual maturity wouldn't have been manifest in standing tall and praying for strength not to lust—no, it was time to get out of Dodge!

Can you think of current or past scenarios in which running, literally or otherwise, is exactly what the situation calls for?

Grace Gives Us Steadfast Hearts

"No temptation has seized you except what is common to man. And God is faithful; he will not let you be tempted beyond what you can bear. But when you are tempted, he will also provide a way out so that you can stand up under it" (1 Cor. 10:13). With the command comes provision. God does not expect us to resist temptation without his assistance, and his assistance is sufficient and sure.

Always remember that none of our sexual temptations are unique to us. None of us will ever be able to cry "Unfair! I was singled out for an unbearable trial." It's simply not true. We are surrounded by men and women who face the same intense pressures and opportunities to compromise sexually that we do. Let's take heart and warning, and let's learn from one another even as we lean on one another!

The promise of 1 Corinthians 10:13 presupposes that we will be faithful to take advantage of the "way out" provision God gives us in the face of sexual temptation. His generosity does not guarantee our obedience. What are some of the "routes out" that God may give us when we are tempted?

- A strong finger to push the channel-change button on the remote.

- A cell phone to call a friend for help as you feel an impossible-to-overcome urge to drive to a massage parlor on the way home from work.

- A powerful vocabulary with the word "No!" in it, to be employed when your girlfriend or boyfriend is pressuring you to cross sexual boundaries.
- An understanding pastor to whom you can confide when you are finally able to admit that in the past, or right now, you are sexually abusing someone.
- An understanding counselor who can help you and your spouse deal with sexual dysfunction, awkwardness, and pain in your relationship.
- A welcoming support group for sexual addictions or pornography addictions.
- A gentle Christian, strong in grace, with whom you can share your story and struggles with homo-emotional attraction or a lifestyle of homosexuality.
- A wise and loving counselor and/or support group that will help you begin the healing journey for sexual-abuse issues in your past.

Grace Gives Us Firm Resolve

"Put to death, therefore, whatever belongs to your earthly nature: sexual immorality, impurity, lust, evil desires and greed, which is idolatry" (Col. 3:5). Resisting Satan's temptations calls for strong measures: Nothing short of *death* to our earthly nature will free us from its hold.

If you should open your car door and find three or four diamondback rattlesnakes occupying the driver's seat, coiled up and ready to strike, I assume it would not take you very long to determine an appropriate course of action. Firm, decisive, and immediate response is called for. Sexual immorality is no less venomous or less needful of an immediate response. Grace enables us to do the hard thing with the right motive—to the glory of God.

2. Grace Enables Us to Fully Engage Sexually with a Covenant Partner in Marriage

The Biblical View of "Marital Duty"

> The husband should fulfill his marital duty to his wife, and likewise the wife to her husband. The wife's body does not belong to her alone but also to her husband. In the same way, the husband's body does not belong to him alone but also to his wife. Do not deprive each other except by mutual consent and for a time, so that you may devote yourselves to prayer. Then come together again so that Satan will not tempt you because of your lack of self-control. (1 Cor. 7:3–5)

These verses need to be interpreted carefully. Paul is not giving spouses the right to demand sex of one another or permission to exploit one another's bodies at will. Just the opposite! Grace leads us to be far more preoccupied with understanding and meeting our spouse's sexual needs than our own. The reign of grace will never lead me to say to my spouse, "Your body is mine! Give it to me." Rather, it will always lead me to say, "My body is yours. How can I serve you with it?"

Paul's phrase "marital duty" is not meant to convey a utilitarian, flat-line service orientation toward sexual expression in marriage. Contrary to some Victorian misconceptions, God does not turn his head in embarrassment when Christians have sex in marriage! Read the Song of Songs—an Old Testament book revealing a level of sexual passion, joy, fun, creativity, spontaneity, and pleasure that may surprise, if not embarrass, some of us!

The Biblical View of Sexual Passion

Sexual passion and pleasure between committed spouses is likened unto a refreshing fountain in the Book of Proverbs.

> Drink water from your own cistern, running water from your own well. Should your springs overflow in the streets, your streams of water in the public squares? Let them be yours alone, never to be shared with strangers. May your fountain be blessed, and may you rejoice in the wife of your youth. A loving doe, a graceful deer—may her breasts satisfy you always, may you ever be captivated by her love. (Prov. 5:15–19)

Some may wrongly argue that this portion of Scripture confirms how male-centered sexual experience and pleasure are in the Bible. So, in fairness, listen to how the woman in the Song of Songs describes her lover's beauty.

> My lover is radiant and ruddy, outstanding among ten thousand. His head is purest gold; his hair is wavy and black as a raven. His eyes are like doves by the water streams, washed in milk, mounted like jewels. His cheeks are like beds of spice yielding perfume. His lips are like lilies dripping with myrrh. His arms are rods of gold set with chrysolite. His body is like polished ivory decorated with sapphires. His legs are pillars of marble set on bases of pure gold. His appearance is like Lebanon, choice as its cedars. His mouth is sweetness itself; he is altogether lovely. This is my lover, this is my friend, O daughters of Jerusalem. (Song of Songs 5:10–16)

How free, how alive, how sensuously intimate is this woman's description of her lover's body! Now, if you are squeamish or timid, you may want to skip the rest of this paragraph! "Once again the English translations are reticent and here intentionally obscure the more explicit Hebrew text. It is not his body that is like a slab of ivory, rather his sexual organ (Hebrew, *me'eh*, "member") which is like a tusk of ivory."[3]

Indeed, the Scriptures are a lot more "colorful" and liberated than some of us have imagined! Obedience to God's design and delight for sexual passion doesn't just restrict us, it also releases us!

As a youth pastor, I used to have teenagers ask after sex and dating talks, "So, just how far *can* we go?" As a senior pastor, the question has changed. Christian couples or individual husbands and wives occasionally ask me, "So what are the boundaries of sexual expression in our marriage bed?" I have enjoyed giving them pastor Tommy Nelson's response:

> Men and women tend to have different parameters about what they consider to be appropriate sexual behavior. How far can a man go? [And I would add, wife.] As far as he wants as long as his wife doesn't feel demeaned in the process. If a woman has a problem with a specific sexual act or position, then a man [or woman] needs to stop immediately.
>
> When I conduct premarital counseling sessions, I make couples talk about what they believe is appropriate sexual behavior. I ask, "How would you feel about this? What about that?" Some of the couples are embarrassed, but they generally admit to me later that this is a very helpful part of our counseling time. It's better to give some serious thought to what you like and don't like, what you'd like to try and not try, and so forth before your wedding night.
>
> Years ago, young women in England were instructed that on their wedding night, they should lie on their backs and think of the queen, meaning that they were to endure sex so that they might conceive babies who would be loyal citizens to the queen and loyal soldiers in her army. What a terrible image! What an unfortunate lack of pleasure for women and for the men who had sex with them....Thank goodness, the Song of Solomon gives us a much different impression of sex. The Lord desires for His people to experience joyful and mutual sharing and giving.[4]

3. Grace Enables Us to Be Restored and to Repent

If you are a victim of sexual abuse, the reign of grace can restore and bring great healing to your heart as nothing else can. My wife is a childhood victim of sexual abuse, and her journey of healing is a strong testimony to me. Out of her pain has come much sorrow but also a gift of mercy that welcomes others onto the healing path. Please be encouraged to begin this hard and courageous journey of proving the reign of grace hyper-abundant to meet you where you are.

On the other hand, if you have sinned against another sexually, repentance is your first step toward healing. It is no small thing to realize how frequently sexual sin by God's people is recorded for us in the Bible. Think of King David (2 Sam. 11; Ps. 51), "the woman caught in adultery" (John 8), Samson (Judg. 14–16), the list goes on—all were welcomed and forgiven by the God of grace. That same welcome is extended to us today. Does your story include unresolved sexual insanity from earlier days? Are you currently paralyzed by obsession, if not addiction, to sexual sin. Please know that you are not outside the reach of grace; in fact, you are a prime target for the reign of grace.

As loving and grace-full as our Father is, he still demands that we have a healthy fear of him—not the fear of a slave, but the fear of the beloved, a passion for the honor and glory of the one who loves us so wondrously. Although Jesus has completely exhausted God's judgment against our sin by his death on the cross, let's remember an earlier study in this book—our Father continues to discipline those he loves. To be indifferent to the will of God (sexually or otherwise) is to invite his…shall we say…*fatherly correction.*

If you or someone you care about has been a victim of sexual abuse, I encourage you to visit Dr. Allenders's Web site (thepathlesschosen.com) for helpful information.

A new command I give you: LOVE one another.
As I have loved you, so you *must* love one another.
By this ALL men will know that you are my disciples,
if you *love* one another.

—John 13:34–35

When Jesus Christ CRUCIFIED is not proclaimed and lived out in love, the Church is a *bored* and boring society. There is no power, no challenge, no fire—no change. We make DRAB what ought to be dramatic.

Brennan Manning

Whereas Christ turned water into wine, the CHURCH has succeeded in doing something more *difficult;* it has turned wine into water.

Søren Kierkegaard

In the presence of a PSYCHIATRIST I can only be a sick man; in the presence of a Christian brother I can *dare* to be a sinner.

Dietrich Bonhoeffer

CHAPTER TEN

The Witness *of* RELATIONSHIPS

Do you ever wonder how those outside our Christian communities experience us and our subculture? No doubt, many view us as isolated and insulated from the real world—perhaps as if we are floating safely detached from the rest of humanity, oblivious to their cries and needs—like Noah and his family aboard the buffet-filled, entertainment-laden, gift-shop-abounding Ark.

However, as those called to be living epistles read by all men (2 Cor. 3:2), giving faithful expression to the glory of God and the grace of the gospel, let us weep if this is the way our lifestyle interprets the story of Noah's ark for our contemporary cultures. For the ark wasn't an extended Carnival cruise for a self-indulgent, self-righteous family—and their *many* pets.

Just consider its captain—a weak man, righteous only by faith—who entered the blessings of the new postflood world and proceeded to get drunk, get naked, and curse his own son! (Gen. 9:18–27). If anything, the ark was a sure sign and profound symbol of God's covenant faithfulness to save the whole world through the life of another Captain one Day.

Indeed, Noah's ark (Gen. 6–9) floated through the history of redemption as a demonstration of God's judgment against sin but also as a bold declaration of his commitment to redeem. For the primary destination of the greatest love boat of all time was always a Person not a place. Jesus, himself, is the greater Noah who, in taking the flood of God's judgment on the cross, has secured the salvation of men and women from every single race, tribe, and people group—and the glories of the new heaven and new earth.

This is why God memorialized the story of Noah's ark by the redeeming and welcoming promise of a rainbow. And yet it seems that we have put an altogether different spin on "ark life."

Ark Culture and Malled Christianity

One of my associate pastors recently shared a somewhat disturbing and convicting article from *GQ* magazine. It was the reflections of a journalist written after a recent encounter with contemporary Christian culture—or as he terms it "ark culture."

> Ark culture is mall Christianity. It's been malled. It's the upshot of some dumb decision that to compete with them—with N'Sync and *Friends* and Stephen King and Matt and Katie and Abercrombie & Fitch and Jackie Chan and AOL and *Sesame Street*—the faithful should turn from their centuries-old tradition of fashioning transcendent art and literature and passionate folk forms such as gospel music...and instead of all that head down to Tower or Blockbuster and check out what's selling then try to rip it off, on a budget if possible and by employing artists who are either so devout or so plain desperate that they'll work for scale.
>
> What makes the stuff...so thin, so weak and cumulatively so demoralizing (even to me, a sympathetic journalist who'd secretly love to play the brash contrarian and rate the *Left Behind* books above Tom Clancy) has nothing to do with faith. The problem is lack of faith. Ark culture is a bad Xerox of the mainstream, not a truly distinctive or separate achievement. Without the courage to lead, it numbly follows, picking up the major media's scraps and gluing them back together with a cross on top.[1]

"Ark Culture"—what a telling image. Does our presence in the culture seem as though we're on a club-like cruise for insiders only? "Mall Christianity"—ouch! What *does* all of our merchandise and media convey to those visiting our "mall"? "Without the courage to lead, it numbly follows"—tell me it ain't so!

In doing research for this article, Walter Kirn entered the "ark" for a week and tried on the world-view and paraphernalia of conservative Christian America. He ate from the *What Would Jesus Eat?* cookbook, watched "lame" alternative versions of Christian TV programming, listened to "parroted" Christian music, was introduced to action figures like *Bibleman,* and listened to the many ways Christian educators try to make a rational explanation of where dinosaurs fit into the story of a world that is only six thousand years old, and... I think you get the point.

One part of me wants to be arrogantly dismissive: "Big deal. He's not describing me and my church." Another part of me wants to be cool and hip and say "Right on! Bash those 'fundy,' anticulture, cocoon types who make the rest of us look so bad." And then I'm tempted to put on my inside-the-ark defensive cap, "What'd you expect from the editorial department of *GQ*?"

Should we even care about the impressions of *GQ* journalist Walter Kirn and others like him? God certainly does—not because he's into Gallup polls or Nielson ratings but because he's God, and he loves and cares for those who live outside our modern-day ark. And God cares very much about the calling he has given us to represent him *to* the world and *in* the world. The real issue is not "What can we do to be taken more seriously by non-Christians?" The issue is "When are we going to take our God more seriously and his commitment to bring healing to the nations by the leaves of the tree of life?" (Rev. 21:22–22:2).

The tree of life once stood tall in the Garden of Eden as a symbol of God's glory and grace (Gen. 3:22), but its life-giving fruit has been withheld from a fallen Adam and Eve until we join them in another City. The many trees felled to build Noah's ark of redemption all pointed toward the ultimate tree of redemption, the cross of Jesus.

It is *that* tree that will give rise (quite literally) to the "tree of life" as it will tower in "the New Jerusalem," "the new heaven and new earth." This giant tree of perpetual grace will yield its leaves "for the healing of the nations," and its multimonth fruit will nourish God's forever-family forever! (Rev. 22:2). But even *now* the healing shade of that tree of redemption is to be manifest as we extend the welcoming heart of God to our neighbors and the nations all around us.

What are *we* building with the timber of the cross? Are we constructing bad culture and a members-only ark, or are we building "a city set on a hill" (Matt. 5:14) whose light is a reflection of the city "whose architect and builder is God" (Heb. 11:10) and "the Holy City, the new Jerusalem, coming down out of heaven from God, prepared as a bride beautifully dressed for her husband"? (Rev. 21:2).

A Witness to the Nations

As the covenant people of God, we are to reflect God's glory, love, and grace in everything we do (including eating and drinking—1 Cor. 10:31). God's generous and welcoming heart is to be the hallmark and benchmark of all our relationships, for it is through our relationships that we represent God to the world.

God is never more adored, honored, or pleasured than when we love one another as he has loved us. He has created every human relationship to reveal his magnificent glory and extol the wonders of his grace. As his image bearers, we are to show what God is like to the watching world.

But when, instead of imitating God's selfless and generous nature, we turn our relationships into feeding troughs for our own consumption, we violate the shalom. Worse than that, we blaspheme—by misrepresenting God's likeness to the nations. Whether it's the way we relate to our world and culture, how we relate to one another in the Body of Christ, or how we live our married lives—all our relationships are to be lived to the glory of God, not primarily for our own benefit.

We're either a light to the nations or a blight to our communities. Which is it for us? The implications are huge!

> Krishna once said, having examined the lives of Christians for many years, "Christians claim that Jesus Christ is the Savior of sinners, but they show no more signs of being saved than anyone else." There once was a period when Gandhi was spiritually restless, and he began to attend a church regularly. He found the sermons boring, the congregation not very devout, sometimes he slept, and woke up feeling guilty. But then he noticed that several Christians were sleeping too, which eased his conscience. Worst of all, he was snubbed by the Europeans because of the color of his skin. He left that church, and abandoned his enquiry into the Christian faith for good.[2]

Worship As a Witness to the Nations

The longer I study the unfolding story of the reign of grace, the more I see just how unselfish the God of glory really is. He *exists* to be generous. There's simply nothing utilitarian about God—nothing selfish, nothing self-serving, nothing of self-interest associated with our Father in any way, shape, or form.

God's passionate concern for his worship isn't born out of his need to be appreciated or given a vote of confidence. He isn't codependent or insecure, like you and I. Rather, God's worship is one of the primary ways by which the reign of his grace is taken to the nations of the world: "'My name will be great among the nations, from the rising to the setting of the sun. In every place incense and pure offerings will be brought to my name, because my name will be great among the nations,' says the LORD Almighty" (Mal. 1:11).

Worship is the primary means of spreading God's fame, and when God's fame increases, his family enlarges, his people mature, and his world is transformed. This proposition requires that we accept the broader definition of worship given by the Scriptures. Worship is not just what takes place in the sanctuary of the local church—it's also what takes place in every sphere of life and culture where God has placed us. The corruption of God's worship is the corrosion of evangelism and missions. God appropriately gets angry when we use worship primarily for our own medicinal purposes rather than as a celebration of his missional passions.

The same redemptive anger and generous heart is revealed when God rebukes his people for poor stewardship of their relationships and callings.

LIVING AS CALLED AND CARING PEOPLE

Our resident prophet Malachi has something to say about how we are to love others. Turning his attention to relationships in the covenant community, Malachi first drew his bead on the priests and their love lives. Why were the priests targeted? Not simply because of how poorly they loved the whole family of God, but because of the implications of their actions. A priest was called to be a "bridge builder" (the meaning of the Latin word for "priest," *pontifex*)—a primary conduit of the mercy and grace of God pouring from heaven into this world. When priests love poorly, *everyone* gets robbed—God, believers, and nonbelievers.

These priests were the chief architects and builders of their own version of ingrown ark culture. Consider the rebuke God leveled at them:

> "And now this admonition is for you, O priests. If you do not listen, and if you do not set your heart to honor my name," says the LORD Almighty, "I will send a curse upon you, and I will curse your

blessings. Yes, I have already cursed them, because you have not set your heart to honor me.

"Because of you I will rebuke your descendants; I will spread on your faces the offal from your festival sacrifices, and you will be carried off with it. And you will know that I have sent you this admonition so that my covenant with Levi may continue," says the LORD Almighty. "My covenant was with him, a covenant of life and peace, and I gave them to him; this called for reverence and he revered me and stood in awe of my name. True instruction was in his mouth and nothing false was found on his lips. He walked with me in peace and uprightness, and turned many from sin.

"For the lips of a priest ought to preserve knowledge, and from his mouth men should seek instruction—because he is the messenger of the LORD Almighty. But you have turned from the way and by your teaching have caused many to stumble; you have violated the covenant with Levi," says the LORD Almighty. "So I have caused you to be despised and humiliated before all the people, because you have not followed my ways but have shown partiality in matters of the law." (Mal. 2:1–9)

Here is a list of grievances we find in this passage:

- You don't listen to me.
- You haven't set your heart to honor me.
- You disregard my covenant.
- You don't speak for me.
- You cause many to stumble.
- You are shoddy in obeying and applying my Word.

In short, these priests were guilty of living as though they were neither loved by God nor called by him to a particular way of life. For all practical purposes, they had become atheists.

How are we to apply these strong words to the family of God in our generation? Do we think (hope!) that God is only addressing the pastors, elders, and deacons? Actually, the audience is much wider.

THE UNIVERSAL OFFICE OF EVERY BELIEVER

When we come to the New Testament, we find two dramatic shifts with respect to the priesthood. First of all, Jesus fulfills all of the temporal types represented in God's gift of the Old Testament mediatorial priesthood. The Book of Hebrews is a grand celebration of this good news. By shedding his own blood upon the cross, Jesus once and for all put an end to the need for a priesthood that offers atoning sacrifices for the sins of the people of God.

But secondly—as discussed in chapter 8—with the outpouring of the Holy Spirit on the day of Pentecost, we find that *the whole Body of Christ becomes a priesthood.* During the Protestant Reformation, the radical implications of the reign of grace were articulated and formulated as the foundation upon which God will redeem his world. Among the doctrines given expression during the Reformation are the *priesthood of the believer* and *vocation.* These truths stress that, by virtue of the work of Jesus, every Christian is called to great intimacy with God and significant kingdom work for him. As Luther argued, the work of the priest is no more holy than the labors of the farmer, tinker, or artisan craftsman. All of life matters to God, and God places his servants in every sphere of life.

These liberating insights were given fuller expression as the Scriptures were studied and the Reformers began fearlessly to proclaim that *every* Christian is called to live and serve as a prophet, priest, and king. While not disregarding the particular offices and authority structure God has established in the church, the Reformers reaffirmed the creation and cultural mandates given to Adam and Eve at the time of creation. As God's image bearers, we have an amazing commission—each of us! Tim Keller comments:

> This doctrine is called the "universal office" of believer, and *it is nothing short of revolutionary*. . . . Jesus himself said that the least in the kingdom of God is greater than John the Baptist (Matt. 11:9–11).
>
> We are all prophets (Joel 2:28–29; Acts 2:14ff.). Every believer is to exhort (Heb. 3:13), counsel (Rom. 15:14), evangelize (Acts 8:4), and teach (Col. 3:16) with the word "dwelling richly" within. *You must speak!*
>
> As a priest (1 Pet. 2:9), you have access to the presence of God, as did the priests of old (Matt. 27:51; Heb. 4:14–16). You have the responsibility to offer spiritual sacrifices and deeds of mercy (Rom. 12:1–2; Heb. 13:2, 16). *You must serve!*
>
> As a king (Rev. 1:5–6), you have authority over the world (1 John 5:4), the flesh (Rom. 6:14ff.), and the devil (Luke 10:19). We all have divine weapons to demolish strongholds and obstacles to the kingdom of Christ (2 Cor. 10:4–5). *You must take charge!*[3]

We, Too, Are Responsible

What an overwhelming privilege and responsibility we have as God's covenant people! In a most profound sense, the rebukes and invitation directed at the priests in Malachi's day are directed at us. God has gifted, empowered, and deployed his people into every sphere of life to be conduits of the reign of grace. This is the essence of missional living—the same calling Adam and Eve enjoyed in the Garden of Eden: To live well and to love well to the glory of God.

- We must listen to God as he speaks to us through his Word and through his creation.
- We must set our hearts to honor him through obedience to the Great Commandment (loving God with all of heart, soul, mind,

and strength), through obedience to the new commandment (loving others as Jesus loves us), and by obedience to the Great Commission (loving God and others "out loud" among our neighborhoods and nations of the world).

- We are to have the highest regard for God's covenant with us and for all of our covenant relationships (in the family, in the church, in the culture).
- We are to speak for him by sharing the gospel and by "filling up" the culture with evidences of the grace and truth of Jesus.
- We must work hard not to cause anyone to stumble, whether in or on the outside of the covenant community.
- We must study and faithfully apply his Word to all areas of life—humbly, justly, and with hearts full of mercy!

To live this way is to become the magnificent and magnetic people God has commissioned us to be and to live for the Day when the knowledge of the glory of the Lord will cover the earth as the waters cover the sea! Remember: Adam and Eve were to fill up creation with the light of God's glory, reigning as prophets, priests, and kings. Likewise, Israel was to be a light of God's glory to the nations—a revelation of his covenant of redemption and commitment to re-creation. And now we, the Bride of Christ, are called to do the same until the Day when the nations stream into the final luminous city, the New Jerusalem. All the history of the world, the history of redemption, is moving from a Garden to a City.

Richard Mouw writes:

> Jesus came to rescue a creation which was pervasively infected with the curse of sin—an infection not limited to the psychic territory populated by "human hearts." The curse of sin touches the

natural realm, reaching into art and economics, affecting family relationships and educational endeavors, holding thrones and budgets in its grip....

Jesus died to save sinners—but he is also the Lamb who serves as the lamp in the transformed City. As the Lamb of God he draws all of the goods, artifacts, and instruments of culture to himself; the kings of the earth will return their authority and power to the Lamb who sits upon the throne; Jesus is the one whose blood has purchased a multinational community, composed of people from every tribe and tongue and nation. His redemptive ministry, as the ministry of the Lamb, is cosmic in scope....

The God who declares here and now that it is "well" with my soul is the same creating Lord who once looked at the whole world which he had made and proclaimed, "This is good!" This God wants once again to say that things are "well" with his entire creation—and he will someday do so when he announces, "Behold, I make all things new....It is done! I am the Alpha and the Omega, the beginning and the end" (Rev. 21:5–6). "It is well with my soul" is only a first step, an initial fruit of God's redeeming activity. We must share in God's restless yearning for the renewal of the cosmos....

Our conviction—our sure hope—that the Lord will bring these things to pass in his own time should lead us to express our discipleship boldly. Our present efforts as citizens of Zion will culminate in the final victory of the Lamb whose light will fill the city.[4]

Marriage As a Witness to the Nations

As witnesses to the nations of the world, we must realize that God has designed all relationships for *his* ends, and this is most true of marriage—the ultimate of all human relationships. Marriage does not exist primarily to make me happy, but holy! There is astonishing joy in marriage, but its purpose is greater than our joy! From healthy covenant marriages in Judah, God sought "godly offspring" (Mal.

2:15)—covenant children sent into the world under the creation and cultural mandate. The same is true today—God is seeking vital covenant marriages and healthy children who will invade the world as joyful witnesses to the reign of grace!

It's really a "no brainer." Why does God hate divorce? Because divorce is the ultimate repudiation of his intent for marriage and a contradiction of the essence of the gospel. Divorce misrepresents the glory and the grace of God as few things can.

The priests in Malachi's day had rejected a God-centered approach to marriage and were divorcing the wives of their youth (Mal. 2:15). Apparently, their reasoning went something like this: "My wife is getting old. She is nagging and sagging. I deserve better than this. I will divorce her and choose another. Then I will be happier as a husband. So what if she is a worshiper of another god? I want to be happy." They were preoccupied with self-fulfillment and a utilitarian approach to their relationships.

You Complete Me!

As Christians we all too easily slip into the deceptive mode of using a marital wish list shaped more by Hollywood than by our holy God. Nothing more clearly reveals an individual's belief about the main purpose of marriage than the criteria he or she uses in choosing a mate. Any of God's good gifts can become matters of obsession.

Personal taste and convictions about things like body types, sexual aesthetics, financial security, social standing, educational accomplishment, and athletic prowess are not inherently wrong.

There is a problem, however, if our primary commitment in life (and in marriage in particular) is to find someone to whom we can speak that memorialized line from the movie *Jerry McGuire*—"You complete me!" Or in other words, "I believe you are the one who can fill up this deep cavern in my soul!" I assume the priests in Malachi's day said something like this in Hebrew to their new younger pagan models!

We must guard ourselves in our spirit and not break faith (Mal. 2:16) with respect to marriage and all our relationships.

Marriage Reveals Both Our Depravity and Our Dignity

Marriage, as designed by God, has more power than any other human relationship to reveal both a man's dignity and his depravity. There simply aren't very many places to hide in marriage—at least not for very long.

> To put it simply, marriage is a relationship far more engrossing than we want it to be. It always turns out to be more than we bargained for. It is disturbingly intense, disruptively involving, and that is exactly the way it was designed to be....Like God Himself, then, marriage comes with a built-in abhorrence of self-centeredness....It attacks people's vanity and lonely pride in a way that few other things can, tirelessly exposing the necessity of giving and sharing, the absurdity of blame. Angering, humiliating, melting, chastening, purifying, it touches us where we hurt most, in the place of our lovelessness....There is nowhere to hide in marriage, no way to escape its searing demands.[5]

But marriage is also designed by God to reveal our dignity and the true end for which we have been made.

> One of the most profound ways in which the Lord touches us and teaches us about Himself and His Own essential *otherness* is through the very limits He has placed upon our relationships with one another. It is an enormous source of human frustration that our need for intimacy far outstrips its capacity to be met in other people. Primarily what keeps us separate is our sins, but there is also another factor, and that is that in each one of us the holiest and neediest and most sensitive place of all has been made and is

> reserved for God alone, so that only He can enter there. No one else can love us as He does, and no one can be the sort of Friend to us that He is....And so the very distance we feel from the person we love most dearly may be, paradoxically, a measure of the overwhelming closeness of God....To know the Lord is to be brought into a personal relationship so dramatic and overwhelming that marriage is only a pale image of it.[6]

An Open Invitation to an Outdoor Wedding

God has designed marriage to convey the enormity of the blessing of covenant relationship—a blessing even greater than the Father-child relationship we share with him. As the new covenant people of God, we are to order our whole lives in response to the unparalleled honor of being given to Jesus as his Wife. We are the Bride of Christ! Consider the staggering implications of such grace.

Taking Malachi's concerns very seriously, I have a proposal to make. Let's live the Christian life as though we are planning a huge outdoor wedding with an open invitation. At the wedding we will share a huge buffet of God's grace and the beauty of committed and passionate love. Before the watching world, all of our relationships will be marked by the sacred and joyful romance that Jesus has secured with us in the new covenant. However, this outdoor wedding must be more than *consideration,* for the Scriptures are clear: This is our *calling.*

Think about how your relationships would be affected if you chose to faithfully live as the Bride of Christ. The new commandment of Jesus gives us much more than a hint of what this entails. "A new command I give you: Love one another. As I have loved you, so you must love one another" (John 13:34). To learn how profoundly Jesus loves, we must study how he loves his Bride—us! And then we are to purpose to live and love, in private and in public, with this same love—to his glory!

Further Up *and* Further In

The Church *As* Magnetic Matrimony

More on Ephesians 5:25–33

What if… I thought to myself as another creative advertisement from Madison Avenue reeled me in. What if the church could reveal this kind of beauty, spontaneity, and love before the watching world?

An obviously smitten husband is thrilled to take his beloved into a crowded public square to celebrate their anniversary. There he begins loudly to proclaim for all to hear, "I love this woman…I love this woman…I love her!" Birds scatter, while some bystanders are amused, some irritated, and perhaps many more, envious of this public display of a man's unashamed rejoicing over his beloved.

Stunned, shy, and obviously moved…his wife's amusement becomes astonishment as he presents the object of his affection with a magnificent diamond ring. Melting, she throws her arms around his neck, and exulting in the wonder of being desired and enjoyed, she responds with wholehearted sincerity, "I love this man…I love this man…I love him!"

Oh that our public life as the Church would be as mesmerizing and magnetic a display of how Jesus rejoices over his Bride and takes great delights in us—and an equally authentic and compelling expression of how we are learning to love him in return. There is no other way we could bring more glory to our covenant Husband or be more effective in fulfilling our commission to take the gospel to every nation.

Becoming this kind of church in our generation will require each of us to intensify both our love for Jesus and for his Bride. To love Jesus with wholehearted sincerity is to love what he loves, and there is nothing that this Bridegroom loves more than his Wife. Indeed, we are no more committed to our covenant Husband than we are committed to cherishing and nourishing his Beloved.

A foundational passage, referred to earlier in the book, deserves—no, demands—a deeper look as we consider the Church's calling to contagious living and loving in the public squares:

> Husbands, love your wives, just as Christ loved the church and gave himself up for her to make her holy, cleansing her by the washing with water through the word, and to present her to himself as a radiant church, without stain or wrinkle or any other blemish, but holy and blameless. In this same way, husbands ought to love their wives as their own bodies. He who loves his wife loves himself. After all, no one ever hated his own body, but he feeds and cares for it, just as Christ does the church—for we are members of his body. "For this reason a man will leave his father and mother and be united to his wife, and the two will become one flesh." This is a profound mystery—but I am talking about Christ and the church. However, each one of you also must love his wife as he loves himself, and the wife must respect her husband. (Eph. 5:25–33)

If our churches are to have a profound drawing effect in our neighborhoods and among the nations—we must become a communiqué and conduit of Jesus' incomparable love for the Church. Here are some of the most telling marks of this love highlighted in this portion of God's Word:

Sacrificial Love

Remarkable love is costly love. The remarkableness of Jesus' love for the Church is captured by a simple yet profound phrase. He "gave himself up for her." The cross of Jesus is the new measure and true means of loving well. The cross compels us out of the "ark" and "mall" and into each other's messy lives *and* into our broken culture.

It's quite expensive to live this way because it draws on our most guarded accounts. Though including our money, the currency we spend to love each other well is of a far greater worth and cost to us because it taps into the resources and reserves of our hearts—the bullion of our brokenness, the wealth of our weakness, the jewels of our "junk."

But when the "debt to love" (Rom. 13:8–10) we owe Jesus and one another is faithfully paid, an aroma of life arises to the praise of God and the drawing of the nations. We become a corporate expression of the beloved "sinner" who washed Jesus' feet with her tears—incredulous that such wondrous love would be ravished on an otherwise deceived and despised prostitute like herself. Such a church will love much because they have been forgiven much (Luke 7:36–50).

David Watson gives us a vision of community secured by the wealth of the cross:

> Since the cross is at the heart of all fellowship, it is only by way of the cross that fellowship is deepened and matured. This will involve the frequent and painful crucifixion of all forms of self—self-seeking, self-centeredness, self-righteousness—and the willingness to remain weak and vulnerable in open fellowship with other Christians. Often we try to meet each other from positions of strength. We talk about our gifts, blessings and achievements in the name of Christ. Mutual encouragement along these lines may sometimes be necessary and helpful. But true fellowship, which binds our hearts together in love, begins when we meet at the point of weakness. When I am willing to be open to you about my own personal needs, risking your shock or rejection, and when I am willing for you to be equally open with me, loving you and accepting you with unjudging friendship, we find ourselves both at the foot of the cross, where there is level ground, at the place of God's healing and grace.[1]

When the culture and our communities can look at us and say, "Behold, how they love one another," then the right questions begin to follow. "What explains this attractive way of life? Why do these people care for one another and us? Who or what is responsible for the beauty radiating in their midst?"

The Grace of a Cleansing Bath

Be honest: Have you ever attended a wedding and, noticing a significant disparity between the "glory" of the groom and bride, found yourself privately thinking, "What in the world does he see in *her?* How did she ever land *him?*" If so, you have tasted the heart and wonder of the gospel—Jesus has chosen a Bride who needs a bath. Paul says that Jesus has "cleansed" the Church "by the washing of the water through the word," and he continues to do so.

To love as Jesus loves means we assume and accept that relationships with other members of the Bride of Christ are going to be marked by dirt, grime, sin, and brokenness. But they will also be marked by ongoing cleansing in the waters of God's redeeming grace—which are refreshing, but no mere bubble bath!

If you are looking for a church in which there is already "perfect hygiene," an antiseptic environment free from the contaminating influence of sinners, don't waste your time. Join a spa for Pharisees, not a church where Jesus' Bride gathers to worship. The world is going to take the gospel more seriously as they observe *us* authentically needing and loving the Jesus we keep insisting *they* desperately need. The world needs to see us taking each other to the river of Jesus' cleansing and healing love, just like the friends who took their paralyzed friend to Jesus, lowering him through the roof on his pallet.

Who are we as the Bride of Jesus? Among other things, we are paralytics taking other paralytics to Jesus. We all belong on the pallet and at the corner of each other's pallets.

A View to Each Other's Glory

Jesus sees us as we are, and as we will be—a radiant church. He is preparing us for the Day when we will be presented in splendor as his Bride, at the biggest outdoor wedding that has ever taken place! To love each other well requires that we begin to look for and draw out one another's glory—in our marriages, in the fellowship of our local churches, with our children—even as we relate to nonbelievers. No one has captured a vision of this costly way of loving better than C. S. Lewis:

> It may be possible for each to think too much of his own potential glory hereafter; it is hardly possible for him to think too often or too deeply about that of his neighbor. The load, or weight, or burden of my neighbor's glory should be laid on my back, a load so heavy that only humility can carry it, and the backs of the proud will be broken. It is a serious thing to live in a society of possible gods and goddesses, to remember that the dullest and most uninteresting person you can talk to may one day be a creature which, if you saw it now, you would be strongly tempted to worship.... There are no *ordinary* people. You have never talked to a mere mortal.... It is immortals whom we joke with, work with, marry, snub and exploit.... Next to the Blessed Sacrament itself, your neighbor is the holiest object presented to your senses. If he is your Christian neighbor, he is holy in almost the same way, for in him also Christ *vere latiitat*—the glorifier and the glorified, Glory Himself, is truly hidden.[2]

Let's consider, then, how we can reject ark culture and malled Christianity and live the Christian life, quite literally, planning a huge outdoor wedding with an open invitation. One that requires that we go into the highways and byways, compelling gloriously grimy people—people we don't even like—to be a part of our own bridal party! Much like the parable Jesus told of the Wedding Banquet (Matt. 22:1–14). In this parable those most committed to ingrown ark culture, the Pharisees, refused the invitation of the king to the marriage of his son—being preoccupied with "more important things."

So the king said to his servants, "'The wedding banquet is ready, but those I invited did not deserve to come. Go to the street corners and invite to the banquet anyone you find.' So the servants went out into the streets and gathered all the people they could find, both good and bad, and the wedding hall was filled with guests" (Matt. 22:8–10).

This is the vision with which we are to live and love before the watching world—Jesus' Wedding Banquet will be filled with the "good and the bad," all deserving to be there only because we have been given the wedding garment of the righteousness of our Bridegroom. In the culture, in our neighborhoods, and among the nations, all of our relationships are to be marked by the sacred and joyful romance that Jesus has secured with us in the new covenant. There is to be a magnetic and compelling light emerging from our involvement in the world as a "little city" destined to become a glorious Bride.

Mercy and Compassion for the Stained, Wrinkled, and Blemished

It's one thing to offer forgiveness, but quite another to get significantly involved in each other's lives. To love with Jesus' love is to love by word and deed—to love those who are stained and wrinkled and blemished. We are to love our fellow idolaters and adulterers, to love over the long haul, and to love when it's the hardest thing in the world to do. What does this entail? Is God's welcoming heart obvious in our churches? Consider a few searching questions:

- Do alcoholics and other addicts feel more understood, loved, and accepted at AA meetings than in the religious subculture of our churches? Have you ever attended an AA meeting or a similar group designed to care for addiction-related issues? I encourage you to do so and take note of what you observe that seems to be very right.
- What strategy does your church have for getting involved in messy marriages, affairs, and separation and divorce proceed-

ings? Are these things talked about openly and consistently, not just after a crisis emerges?

- Think about the parable of the Prodigal Son (Luke 15). Do the leaders of your church conduct themselves more like the restored younger brother or like the self-righteous older brother? More importantly, which of the brothers are you more like as you experience the sin and failures of those in your church family?

- Do people of various racial, ethnic, and economic backgrounds feel welcomed into your church family? How do you know? How would you feel if a group of Hispanic or Afro-Americans started visiting your church? What if they moved into your neighborhood?

Never forget that we are to live as each other's wedding attendants, as we help one another get ready for our shared wedding to Jesus! This requires a long obedience in the same direction and freedom from the idolatry and naiveté of what we think life in the Body of Christ is *supposed* to be.

In his classic volume on community, *Life Together,* Dietrich Bonhoeffer comments:

> Innumerable times a whole Christian community has broken down because it had sprung from a wish dream. The serious Christian, set down for the first time in a Christian community, is likely to bring with him a very definite idea of what Christian life together should be and to try to realize it. But God's grace speedily shatters such dreams. Just as surely as God desires to lead us to a knowledge of genuine Christian fellowship, so surely must we be overwhelmed by a great disillusionment with others, with Christians in general, and, if we are fortunate, with ourselves....
>
> Every human wish dream that is injected into the Christian

community is a hindrance to genuine community and must be banished if genuine community is to survive. He who loves his dream of a community more than the Christian community itself becomes a destroyer of the latter, even though his personal intentions may be ever so honest and earnest and sacrificial.[3]

In a day when the average American Christian is a member in 1.6 to 2.2 churches, (so the polls tell us), it's time for each of us to reexamine our commitment (or lack thereof) to the local church and to repent of our idolatrous ideals and self-serving notions.

Nourishing and Cherishing Affection

As an earthly husband "feeds and cares for" his own body, so we are to love one another with a tangible and transforming love. *Objects of His Affection* was an extended reflection upon and application of an amazing passage found in the prophecy of Zephaniah:

> Sing, O Daughter of Zion; shout aloud, O Israel! Be glad and rejoice with all your heart, O Daughter of Jerusalem! The LORD has taken away your punishment, he has turned back your enemy. The LORD, the King of Israel, is with you; never again will you fear any harm. On that day they will say to Jerusalem, "Do not fear, O Zion; do not let your hands hang limp. The LORD your God is with you, he is mighty to save. He will take great delight in you, he will quiet you with his love, he will rejoice over you with singing." (Zeph. 3:14–17)

While maintaining the appropriate individual dimensions of this scripture, a more faithful application is found as it is applied to our corporate life as the Bride of Jesus. The lyric and music of these astonishing promises are to swell with great volume and skill in our worship centers, small-group fellowships, short-term mission trips, mercy-ministry outreaches, youth groups, elders' meeting—wherever we gather as the people of God. It is through the daily, dull, and demanding routines of our relationships that we are to give each other a taste of God's great delight *in us,* the quieting power of his love *for us,* and the almost unimaginable song of his rejoicing *over us.*

When the watching world sees us loving and caring for one another in extravagant and extraordinary ways, they will believe that God has sent his Son to be the Savior of all men. Love is the final apologetic (confirmation) of the beauty, truth, and reality of the gospel.

Always As a Revelation of Jesus' Beauty and Glory

Above all things, our love is to reveal the "profound mystery" of Christ and the church. We are to be zealous, committed, and joyful in our calling to present the beauty and love of Jesus as faithfully as we can, wherever we are.

Is it possible? Is it really feasible to believe that all of our relationships, and especially our corporate life as the covenant Bride of Jesus, can be marked by such beauty? Yes! As the reign of grace continues to wage war against the defeated dominion of sin and death, we must expect and work hard to ensure that substantive expressions of the wondrous love of Jesus show up in all of our relationships. Love is the greatest and most authentic validation of the beauty and truth of Christianity. When we love one another as Jesus loves us, the world will be convinced that God has sent his Son to be the Savior of the world—indeed, that he has sent his Son to turn a whore into his queen!

Tithing is GOD'S catechism for *sacrificial* giving.

George MALONE

NO ONE CAN SERVE TWO MASTERS. EITHER HE WILL *hate* THE ONE AND LOVE THE OTHER, OR HE WILL BE DEVOTED TO THE ONE AND DESPISE THE OTHER. YOU CANNOT *serve* BOTH GOD AND MONEY.

—MATTHEW 6:24

He who has God and EVERYTHING has *no more* than he who has God alone.

C. S. LEWIS

There are TWO ways to get enough. One is to continue to *accumulate* more and more and the other is to DESIRE less.

G. K. CHESTERTON

It is GOOD for a man's soul to *know* what he can do without.

ARISTOTLE

Our Father REFRESHES us on the journey with some pleasant inns, but will not encourage us to *mistake* them for home.

C. S. LEWIS

CHAPTER ELEVEN

Romantic GENEROSITY

It was big news—a real shock to a culture jaded by divorce suits and legal sharks circling about in a great sea of financial settlements. Shortly after the announcement of his engagement to be remarried, Sir Paul McCartney made it clear that there would be no prenuptial arrangement. He *is* a Sir, and a very atypical twenty-first–century man.

If there is any chance you don't recognize the name Paul McCartney, he is a founding member of a musical group that redefined the whole landscape of the pop music scene—and in many ways, a whole generation and culture. I will never forget the Sunday evening in 1964, as a fourteen-year-old kid, hearing Ed Sullivan introduce Paul and his three friends to America. "Ladies and gentleman, please welcome the Beatles!"

And then the now familiar refrain, "Oh yeah Ieeyah tell ya sumpthin', I think you'll understand....I wanna hold your haaaaaand; I wanna hold your hand."

Now a widower, thirty-eight years later, with a net worth of *one billion dollars,* Sir Paul (knighted by the Queen Mother) was about to take another bride to himself with no "prenup" to safeguard his fortunes against the what ifs. Many thought him careless, if not unwise. His choice actually made me think about Jesus a little—but only a little, because our Bridegroom has proven to be much more generous with *his* Bride.

The only prenuptial agreement Jesus made was one that enriched his Bride-to-be with a net worth beyond calculation. Those married to Jesus receive the wedding garment of his perfect righteousness and inherit the entire earth. But, as the Bride of Christ, we must be ever aware that we are stewards, not owners, of the things God has entrusted to our care!

Living as a steward rather than an owner gets wondrously translated into living without a prenuptial contract with Jesus. Everything Sir Paul McCartney has is legally Mrs. McCartney's and vice versa. Likewise, Jesus has given *everything* to have us as his bride! *And, therefore, whatever he possesses is ours and whatever we possess is his!* In *this* marriage, the possessive pronoun that predominates is neither mine nor yours, but ours. How untenable a thought that we would withhold anything from such a generous lover. Stewardship becomes a romantic expression of love for those betrothed to Jesus!

Stewardship ceases to be an annual lecture about "tithing" (is that before or after taxes?), and it becomes the exchange of vows in which Jesus says to us and we say to him, "With everything that I have and with everything that I am, I honor you."

Stewardship ceases to be pressure to give more to missions and mercy ministries, and it becomes the response of a cherished Bride to her Bridegroom's passions and concerns. We become generous *with* him, not *for* him.

Stewardship ceases to be fruitless discussions about how many square feet you can have in your home or how much you can pay for a new car or how often you can frequent restaurants and *still* be considered godly. It becomes a betrothed Bride's lifestyle of getting ready for the Wedding Supper of the Lamb! We learn to spend and invest our possessions in light of our marriage to Jesus rather than squandering them as though we are single and free.

If you haven't been tempted to skip a chapter in this book yet, my guess is you're on the verge just about now. What is it about the topic of stewardship that automatically throws many of us into a defensive, rolling-of-the-eye mode? "Oh no, here comes another big-hair televangelist after my money" or "You're not going to put me under the law again. Grace has freed me from all that tithing talk." Please hang around a little longer.

Grace Doesn't Guarantee Generosity

One of my greatest regrets, in over two decades of professional ministry, has been my naiveté in assuming that the more I preach and teach about the grace and love of God, the more our hearts, as God's people, will instinctively choose to live unselfishly and generously. That simply is not the case; if it were, I would be a far more generous man myself. There is nothing automatic when it comes to living other-centeredly, generously, and sacrificially. Whatever led me to think that preaching grace coupled with preaching against legalism was the same thing as preaching grace coupled with the call to obedient love?

One of the most grace gifted of all churches, Corinth, was one of the most ingrown, petty, narcissistic, and selfish—to the point that Paul referred to them as "worldly," mere "babes in Christ." Grace, in and of itself, does not generate or guarantee the dethronement of greed. It is only as we see grace as a dominion to which we are to submit—a transforming reign under which we are to gladly live—that we will increasingly live as cheerful givers instead of selfish takers.

The truth is, we are always looking for reasons and excuses not to give. Personally, I have always retreated from any form of high-pressure salesmanship or skilled oration from guilt meisters manipulating me to give more money to anything—whether it's the local church, the Protect the Rainbow Trout Society, Mothers Against Bad Hair Days, or even world missions. Likewise, I have been repelled by formula-based discipleship programs that promote—wittingly or unwittingly—righteousness by financial accountability. Perhaps you can relate. What are the most successful excuses you have found for not living a more generous life, perhaps for not even taking the issue of tithing seriously?

Malachi's Malcontents

Our friend Malachi pressed home the issue of generosity to a group of God's people who were much more challenging than defensive Christians. Malachi's audience would have been a fund-raiser's worse nightmare. They weren't just stingy—they had fallen prey to an *entitlement* mentality of consuming proportions. Worst of all, they charged God with failure to be God.

"You have wearied the LORD with your words…by saying, 'All who do evil are good in the eyes of the LORD, and he is pleased with them' or 'Where is the God of justice?'" (Mal. 2:17). Malachi's contemporaries—rather than being defensive about their lack of giving—accused God of treating them unfairly! In essence they said, "God, you're falling down on your job. Evil people prosper while we languish. You are more pleased with them than with the righteous ones—us! You're supposed to bless us, not them! It feels as if we're being robbed. You aren't really the just God you claim to be."

Honestly, how would you respond to this charge if you were God? We don't have to guess. Malachi delivered God's reply: "You have *wearied* the LORD with your words." Stop and think about it. This was a very generous response on God's part. It's a good thing he was just *weary* and not some of the other options available to him. Indeed, it's a good thing the God of justice showed up as the God of mercy—or there would have been a bad case of consumption! In so doing he turned the tables on his ungrateful, wearisome people.

"So you think there's been some injustice and inconsistency going on? That I haven't blessed you the way you deserve." He continued, "'I the LORD do not change. So you, O descendants of Jacob, are not destroyed. Ever since the time of your forefathers you have turned away from my decrees and have not kept them. Return to me, and I will return to you,' says the LORD Almighty" (Mal. 3:6–7).

It's a good thing God *is* consistent! It's the only reason his covenant people weren't consumed. God blessed an ill-deserving people based on the righteousness of another (Isa. 53). And he had been *very* consistent with *that* promise of all promises—forbearing his people's incredulous charges and years of disobedience, unfaithfulness, and blatant sin.

God had continually called the postexilic family to repentance. "Return to me," he cried. But their hearts were just as far away from him as their ancestors' had been *before* the Babylonian captivity! Their response brings to mind a scene in the story of the Prodigal Son, recorded in Luke 15. The invitation to the gospel party through the door of repentant faith was extended to the petty older brother who was filled with self-pity, just as sincerely as was the Father's welcome extended to the wildly irresponsible younger brother. But contempt encrusted the heart of the elder, just as it had Malachi's malcontented elders.

I'm reminded of Paul's words to the Romans: "Or do you show contempt for the riches of his kindness, tolerance and patience, not realizing that God's kindness leads you toward repentance?" (Rom. 2:4). Kingdom kindness is meant to produce king-size repentance.

WHO'S ROBBING WHOM?

There had been some robbing going on, alright, and now it was time to expose the real thieves:

> "Will a man rob God? Yet you rob me.
> "But you ask, 'How do we rob you?'

> "In tithes and offerings. You are under a curse—the whole nation of you—because you are robbing me." (Mal. 3:8–9)

Once again Malachi had to deal with obese obliviousness. "What do you mean we've been stealing from you?" In the face of God's grand mercy, his people had been committing grand larceny, and they didn't even realize it.

But let's think about God's response. Robbery is taking something that isn't yours in the first place. In what sense, then, is *not* tithing thievery? There's only one answer, and it's been given over and over throughout the history of redemption: *All that we have belongs to God!*

God has loaned us everything we have, and he has commissioned us to live as good stewards of his trust and stuff. But sin has revolutionized our choice and use of pronouns. Instead of "You and yours, Lord," we cry, "My-me-mine!" Someone has recognized, quite appropriately, that at the center of sin is "I"—S"I"N.

Stewardship or Consumership?

One of the surest signs that the reign of grace is gaining presence and influence in the lives of God's people is the measure of our generosity. But an even more fundamental sign is when we give up our perceived right of ownership and take up the freedom of stewardship. Such an attitude is reflected in the prayer of King David when gifts for building the Temple were offered. Notice how many times he ascribes the ownership of all things to God. David made it clear: Even what we give to the Lord is already his!

> Yours, O Lord, is the greatness and the power and the glory and the majesty and the splendor, for *everything in heaven and earth is yours.* Yours, O Lord, is the kingdom; you are exalted as head over all. *Wealth and honor come from you;* you are the ruler of all things. In your hands are strength and power to exalt and give

> strength to all. Now, our God, we give you thanks, and praise your glorious name.
>
> But who am I, and who are my people, that we should be able to give as generously as this? *Everything comes from you, and we have given you only what comes from your hand.* We are aliens and strangers in your sight, as were all our forefathers. Our days on earth are like a shadow, without hope. O LORD our God, as for all this abundance that we have provided for building you a temple for your Holy Name, *it comes from your hand, and all of it belongs to you.* (1 Chron. 29:11–16)

Consider how contrary Malachi's contemporaries were to David's spirit and world-view. Their lives were a tragic testimony to conspicuous consumerism. Everything was measured in terms of their own personal benefit and profit. God wanted to shut the door on their worship because they had turned the most sacred of all encounters into a device for manipulating God unto more blessings.

They approached marriage in the same way. What else can explain their crass indifference to the marriage covenant, which led them to trade in aging wives for idol-worshiping pagans? And now, their approach to money and possessions was, "Why tithe if all we've gotten in the past is injustice (being interpreted as lack of personal blessing)?"

THE TRUE OFFENSE OF POOR STEWARDSHIP

Why did the selfishness of the Israelites bother God so much? God is not an uptight CPA preoccupied with balancing the books.

It disturbed him because he is a compassionate Father who cares for the lost and the least of the world. Malachi's whole discussion about tithing, offerings, and stewardship was born out of God's heart for righteousness and justice: "'I will come near to you for judgment. I will be quick to testify against sorcerers, adulterers and perjurers, against those who defraud laborers of their wages, who oppress the widows and the fatherless, and deprive aliens of justice, but do not fear me,' says the LORD Almighty" (Mal. 3:5).

God associates sorcery, adultery, and lying with not paying a common laborer what he deserves, not showing compassion and mercy to widows and orphans, and failure to provide advocacy for those without citizenship and a friend.

Who really gets robbed by the breakdown in tithing and offerings? Is it God? Yes, in the sense that he owns everything. But just as profoundly, and so central to the context of these verses, it is the poor who are robbed, it is the widow, it is the orphan, it is all victims of the reign of sin and death. A large part of the prescribed tithes and offerings were used to care for those needing daily bread, clothing, a drink of cold water—the dignity of knowing someone cares.

The issue of tithing is more a matter of the heart than a biblical tenet to be debated. Good stewardship is meant to reveal the mercy, generosity, and tender heart of God; it is a concrete demonstration of the beauty and bounty of the reign of grace.

To work for righteousness and justice is to *sic the reign of grace on the reign of sin and death!* It is to declare war on all the inequity, racism, poverty, oppression, favoritism, hunger, political corruption, materialism, and systemic darkness and evil associated with the Fall.

The Worship of Stewardship

Jesus teaches us that the way we relate to money indicates the true master of our hearts—it is a practical revelation of who or what has gained the adoration and worship of our souls.

> Do not store up for yourselves treasures on earth, where moth and rust destroy, and where thieves break in and steal. But store up for yourselves treasures in heaven, where moth and rust do not destroy, and where thieves do not break in and steal. For where your treasure is, there your heart will be also....

> No one can serve two masters. Either he will hate the one and love the other, or he will be devoted to the one and despise the other. You cannot serve both God and Money. (Matt. 6:19–21, 24)

If we choose to steal *from God,* there are any number of thieves that can providentially break in and steal *from us.* But if we spend and invest on behalf of the reign of grace, God is worshiped. It behooves us to see the vital connection between worship and stewardship. Jesus could not have made it any clearer.

TITANS OF GRACE

Are we, then, as grace-saved Christians, to tithe? Yes and more! Consider this vignette of how the reign of grace breaks into a community of God's people.

> And now, brothers, we want you to know about the *grace* that God has given the Macedonian churches. Out of the most severe trial, their overflowing joy and their *extreme poverty* welled up in *rich generosity.* For I testify that they gave as much as they were able, and even beyond their ability. Entirely on their own, they *urgently pleaded with us for the privilege of sharing in this service* to the saints. And they did not do as we expected, but they gave themselves first to the Lord and then to us in keeping with God's will. (2 Cor. 8:1–5)

Every time I read this passage I think about the ending of the movie *It's a Wonderful Life.* Do you remember the last scene? George Bailey, the character played by Jimmy Stewart, becomes the object of a magnificent outpouring of gifts, money, love, and mercy. Men, women, children, the rich, the poor, blacks, whites, alcoholics, police officers, bank examiners—representation of the whole diverse community of humanity—they all show up for the *privilege* of giving on behalf of a man who nearly lost his life because of his own sacrificial generosity for them!

That last scene, really the whole movie, can be seen as the reign of grace having a violent face-off with the reign of sin and death—*Potterville!* This is what righteousness and justice are all about—putting life, people, culture, and society in the order God designed for them. This was certainly happening in Macedonia among a group of Christians not characterized as tithers, but as Titans of grace!

These Titans of grace were actually Gentile converts to the faith, commonly referred to as "dogs" by many Jews. Amazingly, the ones they sought to help were *Jewish* converts. Paul, himself, is overwhelmed as he describes this group of Christians, who "urgently pleaded" for the "privilege" of participating in the famine relief offering for Jewish Christians in Jerusalem. Paul recorded for us the reality of what *It's a Wonderful Life* merely symbolizes.

Jesus is the destroyer of all hostilities brought about by the reign of sin and death, and he is the reconciler of the formerly irreconcilable. The reign of grace leads to a Day in which everything will be summed up in Jesus and reconciled and reconstituted through him!

To Tithe or Not to Tithe—That Is Not the Main Issue!

The gift of these Macedonian believers was more than the prescribed tithe—it was an indication of a far more generous and fundamental gift. Paul said they "gave themselves first to the Lord" (v. 5). What does this mean? No doubt it means that they reaffirmed the stewardship of all of life, including the stewardship of their *lives.* "Lord, here we are. Everything we have and are is yours. How would you have us respond to this crisis among our brothers and sisters in Jerusalem?"

Tithing isn't the primary measure of our generosity; rather, it is a symbol of our joyful surrender to a lifestyle of stewardship and a refusal to be seduced by the illusion of ownership. When we live like a people who have been bought with a price, the main ownership we celebrate is the privilege of being owned by Jesus.

The tithe was designed as a first-fruit offering—a partial gift, symbolic of the whole. Therefore, to offer the first fruits of your corn crop did not just mean "All the corn is yours, Lord"; rather, "All the corn, the land, my tools, my oxen, my hands, my sweat, my hunger, my cornmeal, my family, the rain, my sin, my hopes, me—it's all yours, glorious and gracious God."

Romantic Generosity

Consider what happens when we bring the stunning truth of being bought with the life of our Savior within the story line of being the Bride of Christ. The price of our redemption, the death of Jesus upon the cross, is the payment that satisfies the justice of God as our holy judge, but it is also the dowry price Jesus paid to the Father to purchase his betrothed and cherished Bride! "Do you not know that...you are not your own? You were bought at a price: therefore honor God with your body" (1 Cor. 6:19–20). What if Jesus only "tithed" his blood for us?

A life that is "not our own" is a life lived *right now* as the legal bride of Jesus—awaiting our Wedding Day at his return. We are able to proclaim and experience this exquisite affirmation, "I am my beloved's, and His desire is for me!...His banner over me is love!" (Song of Songs 2:16, 4). And we are enabled to sing great love songs and translate them into generous living:

> "Jesus, priceless treasure, source of purest pleasure, truest friend to me; Long my heart hath panted, 'til it well-nigh fainted, thirsting after Thee, Thine I am, O spotless Lamb, I will suffer nought to hide Thee, ask for naught beside Thee."[1]

> "Riches I heed not, nor man's empty praise, Thou mine inheritance, now and always; Thou and thou only, first in my heart, High King of heaven, my Treasure Thou art."[2]

Giving to Get?

Getting back to Malachi and his malcontents: After God exposed their robbery, he offered his miserly people an amazing challenge.

> "Bring the whole tithe into the storehouse, that there may be food in my house. Test me in this," says the LORD Almighty, "and see if I will not throw open the floodgates of heaven and pour out so much blessing that you will not have room enough for it. I will prevent pests from devouring your crops, and the vines in your fields will not cast their fruit," says the LORD Almighty. "Then all the nations will call you blessed, for yours will be a delightful land," says the LORD Almighty. (Mal. 3:10–12)

If there has ever been a portion of God's Word more misused and abused than this, please let me know! A superficial reading of this text leads one to assume that God is promising a get-rich-quick scheme. *"Give me ten percent of your income, and I will fill your barns so full of stuff that you'll have to tear them down and build bigger ones!"* Is this really what's being promised here, especially in light of the conversations surrounding the text? I think I remember Jesus telling a story in Luke 12 about the peril of bulging barns and building bigger ones to replace them.

As a Bribe or unto the Bride?

The promises attached to tithing aren't offered as a bribe to motivate us; they are addressed to a Bride to thrill us! Look carefully at what is promised. As we bring the "whole tithe" into the storehouse, there will be food in God's house. Why food? Because God is mercifully attacking hunger in a world affected by the reign of sin and death. He is doing so as the reign of grace advances in the hearts of the Bride of Jesus and as we become generous with our Bridegroom.

As I write these few words, an estimated fifteen million Africans are facing starvation in the southern countries of the continent. A horrible famine has wrought destruction in a land already devastated by AIDS. The prosperity and blessing associated with Malachi's discussion about tithing is associated with our Bridegroom's commitment to be gracious and great among the nations (Mal. 3:12), "even beyond the borders of Israel" (Mal. 1:5). Jesus is gathering his Bride from every nation, about whom he says, "they will be mine" (Mal. 3:17), "my treasured possession" (Mal. 3:17). As his mercy is extended through us, his Bride, Jesus is made famous among all the nations!

The Measure of Stewardship

God has established forever the meaning and measure of our stewardship: "For you know the grace of our Lord Jesus Christ, that though he was rich, yet for your sakes he became poor, so that you through his poverty might become rich.... You will be made rich in every way so that you can be generous on every occasion, and through us your generosity will result in thanksgiving to God" (2 Cor. 8:9; 9:11).

God delights in our tithes when our hearts say, "Jesus, by this offering I gladly acknowledge that everything I have and am is yours, as my covenant Bridegroom. I own nothing, yet I own everything because I belong to you."

Indeed, we are not blessed to increase the boundaries of our property lines, but to participate more fully in the expansion of the territory of the reign of grace. Where George Bailey nearly took his own life just to pay an eight-thousand-dollar mortgage debt in Bedford Falls, Jesus freely had his life taken from him to pay the sin debt of his whole Bride—throughout history and from all nations. And yet, because of Jesus' generosity, our generosity, like that modeled by George Bailey, takes on Kingdom significance. The gospel doesn't make us philanthropists, but transformationalists—not altruists, but realistic about the dire needs of the world and God's delight to meet these needs through us.

Is the reign of grace freeing *us* to live lives consumed by the love of Jesus, or is the reign of sin and death enslaving us to simply consume our way through life? This was *always* Paul's concern: Which dominion has captured the adoration and submission of our hearts? Who is our lover?

As the Bride of Christ, we can join with Agur—a contributor to the book of Proverbs—in this prayer:

> Two things I ask of you, O LORD; do not refuse me before I die: Keep falsehood and lies far from me; give me neither poverty nor riches, but give me only my daily bread. Otherwise, I may have too much and disown you and say, "Who is the LORD?" Or I may become poor and steal, and so dishonor the name of my God. (Prov. 30:7–9)

Let us have done with all prenuptial nonsense! Let us love Jesus with passion and delight and wild generosity!

To learn more about a freeing and focused lifestyle of stewardship and generosity, I encourage you to visit my friend Dave Ramsey's Web site at Daveramsey.com.

Further Up *and* Further In

Thanks—Living *and* Giving

2 Corinthians 9

How then are we to live and give as the Bride of Jesus? When it comes to stewardship and generosity, let's make sure we are not "hopeless romantics" but "faithful lovers." As the Bride of Jesus, all of us are called to a life of grace-full giving and our Bridegroom gladly "giveth more grace" to free us unto this very end. Practically speaking, what does this lifestyle look like? Many of us remain ignorant, irresponsible, or indifferent about this matter, but Paul's instructions for believers in Corinth are all we need to get started.

Before exegeting (unpacking, drawing out, making clear) the apostle's sound advice given in 2 Corinthians 9, let's "exegete" our moment in world history. Though the issue of stewardship is always central to the Christian life, why especially now as we move into the twenty-first century?

A Cry for Help

I recently received a letter from a good friend of over thirty years that underscores why we must take the issue of stewardship more seriously than ever as the people of God. My friend's name is Larry Warren, the founder and director of a mission's organization called African Leadership. His words and numbers boggle my mind and convict my heart—as I trust they will yours as well.

But his letter also greatly encourages me, because it was from *him*—from a man I've watched the gospel radically change over the past three decades from being an angry cynic to a success-driven businessman to a generous lover of Jesus and the African people. Though he permanently carries a strain of the malaria virus in his system from his involvement in world missions, he also permanently carries the only hope for the African crisis—and for the whole cosmos—the reign of grace.

Two summers ago Larry took me to South Africa and Kenya where I saw, smelled, tasted, and touched the reality of hunger and the devastation of the AIDS/HIV crisis firsthand. Though the testimony of the Scriptures should be sufficient, many of us remain filled with unbelieving and uncaring hearts. Like "doubting Thomas," unless we "touch" we will not trust.

Until Larry took me to a small hospital built for the sole purpose of caring for babies and young children dying of AIDS—until he put one of these little ones in my arms—I didn't really understand or care. Until he walked me through a village/ghetto of ten thousand image bearers of God—whose male population is already 40 percent HIV positive—it was easy to remain suburbanized in the ghetto of my own indifference.

Please read Larry's letter carefully, before we conclude by applying Paul's directives to our hearts and our brief moment in the ongoing reign of grace. I think you will agree with me—the big question is not "What do you think about tithing?" rather it is "Do you love me?" If we answer yes, the impassioned reply quickly comes—"Then feed my sheep."

Dear Scotty,

Thanks for your ongoing concerns about the crisis in Africa and what we can do to help. I just returned a few days ago from my most recent visit to the continent, and my sense of urgency and hope is intensified. I've probably given you more information than you've asked for, but whatever we can do in the last third of our lives (we're getting old, brother), let's do it—for Jesus' glory and kingdom. By the way, are you ready to go back with me yet?

Where do I start? The year 2003 begins with the continuing famine in Southern Africa that threatens the life of over 15 million people. I just saw thousands of people in Zimbabwe line up peacefully to receive food after walking eight to nine miles in 90 degree heat, hoping they can walk that far again in the afternoon with an additional fifty pounds of food to take care of their families for a month. James Morris of the United Nations World Food Program says "the African food shortage is the worst humanitarian crisis in the world today."

Predictions for later this year and into 2004 indicate that over 40 million people in Africa will be at risk of starvation if the international community does not significantly increase food shipments. In Ethiopia alone, 20 million people need food their country cannot obtain, says the BBC. Yet Westerners, especially Americans, don't even know about the problem. Unlike the media coverage of the 1985 famine in Ethiopia when over 1 million people died of starvation and diseases related to malnutrition, we've seen very little international coverage or financial response to the current desperate need in countries like Zimbabwe, Malawi, Zambia, and Mozambique.

Five hundred million dollars has been pledged for disaster relief in these countries by the U.N., $100 million of that from the U.S., but the total is less than half of what is needed and much of what has been pledged has not been delivered. Christians especially should be informed and challenged to help as our book of faith directs us to "do good to all men, especially those in the household of faith." The overwhelming majority of those in need of food in Eastern and Southern Africa profess to be Christians.

Why are we so unresponsive? Mainly because most Christians in wealthy countries don't know of the problem—aren't informed on the biblical mandate to help, or are conformed to the materialism of their culture, their local church, and the racism and self-interest of their governments. In a southern Sudanese village, near Nimole, the village elders asked me, "When will the Americans save us? We know you have the power to save us. You saved the Moslems in Kuwait and the white people in Bosnia. When will you rescue the black Christians from this conflict that has taken the lives of over 2 million?"

The current HIV/AIDS pandemic in Africa is another example of why we need to be informed. The U.S. spends over ten thousand dollars per person, annually on the 1 million Americans infected with AIDS. Less than 3 percent of the Evangelicals in America say they will do anything to help AIDS victims in Africa, says George Barna. Over 40 million people have AIDS worldwide and 75 percent of those infected live in Sub-Sahara Africa. The first two groups of people Jesus said we should minister to are the hungry and the sick. Jesus said as we minister to the least of these we minister to him!

We've defeated infectious disease before, says Senate Majority Leader Dr. William Frist. Over 300 million people died of small pox in the twentieth century and as late as the 1950s it affected up to 50 million people per year; but to wipe out small pox there was an aggressive global and concentrated effort. Christians should lead that effort and many are, like Dr. Frist, Bono from U2, and other high-profile believers, but each of us must consider our personal responsibility in the stewardship and areas of influence God has given us. Let's not wait to organize our caring response until epidemic levels reach the U.S. college campuses, as is predicted.

International response and American lack of awareness is not just a problem for Africa. Americans spend as much on advertising our products, $300 billion annually, as was given to all Christian causes combined. Income for global foreign missions, meeting physical and spiritual needs outside the U.S., was $17 billion in 2002. But we spend that much annually on chewing-gum and the same amount in a fifty-two-day period on pet food. The comparisons aren't fair, of *course, since fewer American citizens are giving to the fulfillment of the Great Commission than are buying pet food. But even so, we American Christians spend more on annual audits of our churches and agencies (810 million) than on all their missionaries in the non-Christian world, (according to the World Evangelization Research Center).*

The stock market isn't the only institution that is taking a dive. The Barna Research Group's annual survey on giving shows that while churches still receive a majority of people's donations, loyalty to churches has been declining for several years. They report that 78 percent of all American adults donated money to a nonprofit organization or church in 2000, but that represents a 6 percent decline from the previous year and a 9 percent drop from 1998 when 87 percent of all adults donated. In 2000 six of ten adults gave money to one or more churches but only $649 per person, down from $806 the prior year. Evangelicals gave more; $2097 per person in 2000, but that was 19 percent less than a year ago.

While many Christian churches teach the principle of tithing, or giving 10 percent of one's income to the church, few people follow the practice. Only one of six adults attending church claim to tithe (17 percent) but only 6 percent actually give 10 percent of their pre- or posttax income to their church. The U.S. Department of Labor says that the average American household spends about two thousand dollars annually on health care, not including insurance and almost the same amount on entertainment. Our spending indicates evangelicals give our personal entertainment equal value to the support of the work of our church and put entertainment far above our giving to global Christian causes.

God's children have always actively identified with the poor, the oppressed and the needy. Biblical good is never content with lip service. True righteousness expresses itself in obedience that concerns itself with the needs of others, and the godly rich relate to the poor, and to their possessions according to principles which are detailed and modeled in the Scripture. Our call, as the body of Christ, is to be World Christians—people who understand the mandates of Scripture and the needs of the world. These values and information must shape our relationships, our vocation, and our investments.

Love,

Larry

A Generous Response

With these startling statistics in mind, let the words of 2 Corinthians 8:1–7 sink in once again—this time as Eugene Peterson has translated this passage in *The Message:*

> Now friends, I want to report on the surprising and generous ways in which God is working in the churches in Macedonia province. Fierce troubles came down on the people of those churches, pushing them to the very limit. The trial exposed their true colors: They were incredibly happy, though desperately poor. The pressure triggered something totally unexpected: an outpouring of pure and generous gifts. I was there and saw it for myself. They gave offerings of whatever they could—far more than they could afford!—pleading for the privilege of helping out in the relief of poor Christians.
>
> This was totally spontaneous, entirely their own idea, and caught us completely off guard. What explains it was that they had first given themselves unreservedly to God and to us. The other giving simply flowed out of the purposes of God working in their lives. That's what prompted us to ask Titus to bring the relief offering to your attention, so that what was so well begun could be finished up. You do so well in so many things—you trust God, you're articulate, you're insightful, you're passionate, you love us—now, do your best in this, too.

How can we "excel in this grace of giving" (NIV), in the face of the current international relief crisis? Paul gives us clear instructions.

Instruction for Today

Give toward Equality

> Our desire is not that others might be relieved while you are hard pressed, but that there might be equality. At the present time your plenty will supply what they need, so that in turn their plenty will supply what you need. Then there will be equality, as it is written: "He who gathered much did not have too much, and he who gathered little did not have too little." (2 Cor. 8:13–15)

Larry opened my eyes to Paul's genius and the miracle of grace in this text. Even if we "only" gave 10 percent of our incomes to the expansion of the reign of grace, it would go a long way toward fulfilling the biblical vision of "equality." Paul is not mandating communism or socialism in this text—rather, community and unselfishness! For less than 10 percent of what we spend on our housing, food, and education for our children, we can provide the same real dream and real needs for the poor who inhabit two-thirds of the world. In fact, in Africa a family of five can be fed for less than ten dollars a month; yet in the U.S., we spend more on bird food than we do feeding the starving peoples (Jesus' lambs) of the world!

Equality doesn't mean we all have the same income, but it does mean that God's provisions are to be shared, not hoarded; invested, not squandered; given, not worshiped.

Give Generously

> Remember this: Whoever sows sparingly will also reap sparingly, and whoever sows generously will also reap generously. (2 Cor. 9:6)

As Paul crafted this warning and promise using an agricultural metaphor, images of poor Jewish Christians suffering the effects of a famine in Judea during the reign of Emperor Claudius (A.D. 41–54) filled his heart. He wasn't teaching a seminar on how to safeguard your 401K during times of economic upheaval. No, the principle of "sowing and reaping" was chosen to convey the idea of farming generously and harvesting bountifully *on behalf of others*—not to get more for ourselves! Paul was challenging believers in Corinth with a vision of how much good they could do by simply investing more sacrificially in the ultimate farming enterprise—the reign of grace!

Grace giving always flows from and models Jesus' giving: He exchanged *his* riches for *our* poverty. We are to do the same as we confront poverty on every level—whether we are giving the "widow's mite," a mighty stock, or sweat equity from our own brows. We must never forget: Because Jesus has taken us to be his Bride, a great harvest of a new heaven and a new earth will be reaped from the seed of his life and our union with him.

Give Cheerfully

> Each man should give what he has decided in his heart to give, not reluctantly or under compulsion, for God loves a cheerful giver. (2 Cor. 9:7)

Grace giving is hearty, specific, guilt free, and cheerful. How are we to decide in our hearts what to give? First of all, we need to make a commitment to get intentional and specific in our giving. As the saying goes, "If you aim at nothing, you will hit it every time."

Are you convinced that the Scriptures continue to affirm the principle of tithing? If so, then I specifically challenge you to give at least 10 percent of your income to your local church and its kingdom outreach—at home and abroad. I say at least 10 percent because, in actuality, the Old Testament saints "tithed" an average of 22 percent, when you calculate the required offerings they made on an annual basis.

If you are *not* convinced that tithing is still affirmed by the Scriptures for members of the new-covenant community, then I challenge you to make a case for why you would give less than 10 percent of your income to your local church and its missions outreach. Shall we, who are no longer under the rule of law but under the reign of grace, be *less* generous? Or less cheerful? Cheerful givers don't earn more of God's love—they simply demonstrate it more clearly and boldly for all to see. God loves cheerful givers because he loves himself! We are never more Godlike than when we are generous "as unto him."

Being married to Jesus, let us regularly offer the first fruits of whatever he provides as a way of saying, "I withhold nothing from you, blessed Lover of my soul. I own nothing but being owned *by* you and *for* you!"

Let Your Giving Abound

> And God is able to make all grace abound to you, so that in all things at all times, having all that you need, you will abound in every good work. As it is written: "He has scattered abroad his gifts to the poor; his righteousness endures forever." (2 Cor. 9:8–9)

Grace giving will lead to grace abounding, which leads to more grace giving—ad infinitum. Generosity is the spigot by which God empowers us for a life of good works, and the means by which he enriches the poor.

God's grace gifts don't just meet the real physical needs that we have in *this* world—there is an even larger work going on. Through the reign of grace, God is reconciling men unto himself and to one another—all sin-created barriers are being broken down! Therefore, one of the most important motivations Paul had for collecting the famine relief fund from Gentile churches was to demonstrate the power of the gospel to destroy all hostilities between people groups, races, and nations—beginning with the intense racism, bigotry, and nationalism that kept Jews and Gentiles so separate from one another.

It was an *enormous* statement for converted Gentiles to come to the aid of converted Jews, thus demonstrating the power of the gospel in word and deed—"You are all sons of God through faith in Christ Jesus, for all of you who were baptized into Christ have clothed yourselves with Christ. There is neither Jew nor Greek, slave nor free, male nor female, for you are all one in Christ Jesus" (Gal. 3:26–28).

The reign of grace is committed to the same reconciling agenda today. We, who are many, have been made one in Jesus. We are to work hard to implement this miracle of reconciliation wherever we live—until the Day this work will be completed!

Live Thankfully

> Now he who supplies seed to the sower and bread for food will also supply and increase your store of seed and will enlarge the harvest of your righteousness. You will be made rich in every way so that you can be generous on every occasion, and through us your generosity will result in thanksgiving to God. (2 Cor. 9:10–11)

What is the ultimate goal of grace giving? Thanks-living!—an entire creation reoriented for the praise and worship of God! Indeed, little generosities lead to sure evidences of the reign of grace, which lead to greater assurance about the coming Day of perfect righteousness and cosmic shalom! Every hungry child fed and clothed, every AIDS baby held and loved in the name of Jesus, every grace seed sown is one step closer to the harvest of global reconciliation and peace-full transformation.

Serve Worshipfully

> This service that you perform is not only supplying the needs of God's people but is also overflowing in many expressions of thanks to God. Because of the service by which you have proved yourselves, men will praise God for the obedience that accompanies your confession of the gospel of Christ, and for your generosity in sharing with them and with everyone else. And in their prayers for you their hearts will go

> out to you, because of the surpassing grace God has given you. Thanks be to God for his indescribable gift! (2 Cor. 9:12–15)

Indeed, to live all of life with doxological generosity—that is, as *worship servants*—meets real needs of others and begets spontaneous praise to God. But it also is one of the most powerful ways we confirm the power and beauty of the gospel. When the obedience of love accompanies our confession of the gospel, Jesus and his grace become intelligible and real to nay-sayers, agnostics, skeptics, and cynics—leading many to cry out, "Thanks be to God for the indescribable gift of his Son, Jesus, and the surpassing grace which changes the hearts of men." There is *nothing* more important than for Jesus to be made famous and glorious in the hearts of mankind.

Surely, this is what St. Francis of Assisi intended when he charged his followers to "preach the gospel, and use words if you must." Isn't it true—our words *about* grace only have meaning if they are accompanied, and many times preceded by, demonstrations *of* grace—the reign of indelible and irresistible grace.

Never tire of hearing it—never get used to it—never stop pondering the implications of it, "For you know the grace of our Lord Jesus Christ, that though he was rich, yet for your sakes he became poor, so that you through his poverty might become rich" (2 Cor. 8:9).

Let us labor with faith, love, and hope and worship God for his outlandish generosity in giving Jesus for us and in giving us to Jesus as a cherished Bride.

I encourage—no I lovingly dare—you to visit my friend Larry's Web site at Africanleadership.org. As you do, consider how you can get personally involved in extending the reign of God's grace and the riches of his mercy in the face of the unimaginable HIV/AIDS and famine crises in Africa, and learn how you can invest in training national Christian leaders on the continent.

THE KINGDOM OF THE WORLD HAS BECOME THE KINGDOM OF OUR LORD AND OF HIS CHRIST, AND HE WILL *reign* FOR EVER AND EVER. AND THE TWENTY-FOUR ELDERS, WHO WERE SEATED ON THEIR THRONES BEFORE GOD, FELL ON THEIR FACES AND *worshiped* GOD.

—REVELATION 11:15–16

If someday we SIT in the rocking chair of our old age and look back with regret, with a sense of having *wandered* aimlessly over a faceless terrain, it will be because we never stopped long enough to ASSESS our direction or because we chose to *give* ourselves to empty dreams.

Stacy RINEHART

We always PAY dearly for *chasing* after what is cheap.

Aleksandr SOLZHENITSYN

Think of Handel's *Messiah.* Now IMAGINE the whole oratorio as just one of many lines of music, with hundreds of other lines being sung alongside, and all blending together into a huge swelling harmony. And imagine every *creature* in heaven and on earth—penguins and peacocks, guinea pigs and gorillas, as well as children, women, and men—all SINGING this extraordinary song. This is how Easter is celebrated in God's dimension of reality. What we Christians do on earth is to *add* our line to that total harmony. We celebrate together the fact of a world reborn.

N. T. WRIGHT

CHAPTER TWELVE

Finding Your Place in *the* REIGN OF GRACE

Though I wish I could have written a treatise for immediate glorification, the best I could offer was a travelogue for our glorious destination—the new heaven and new earth. The Christian life is, as Eugene Peterson said, "a long obedience in the same direction"—not simply grace for our fifteen minutes in the spotlight. The good news—" 'Tis grace hath brought [us] safe thus far, and grace will lead [us] home." The honest news—grace will bring us home *safe,* but *not sedated.*

As we have seen, God's grace is not an anesthetic for our personal pain or a first-class carriage ride into paradise; it's the antibiotic that destroys the disease of sin and the curse of death that has infested the whole world. It is the mustard-seed-size kingdom planted in the contaminated soil of the human heart that one Day will reap a harvest so bountiful and peace-full that angels will shout with astonishment, "The kingdom of the world has become the kingdom of our Lord and of his Christ, and he shall reign forever and ever!" (Rev. 11:15).

What's next in the journey home? It would be robbery to conclude this book without stressing and pressing God's generous invitation to *you.* The sum of all we've discussed has important implications for what you do with the rest of your life, as well as what you do with your past. It also has great ramifications for the lives of the people you care most deeply about, for none of us lives as a private novel. God has made us for community, and he changes us in community. All of our stories intersect and are being woven into an intricate tapestry of stupefying beauty and bedazzling artistry. I believe this more today than I ever have before.

Right now, however, life may appear to you more like a painful travesty than a magnificent tapestry. That is certainly how it seemed to many people in our church family and in the Christian music community when the news broke about Grant Cunningham's "untimely" death. I heard comments like, "What a waste." "What was God thinking?" "How could he do this to Kristin and those precious little boys?"

But a very wise woman once challenged me to remember: In this world we view the underside of God's loom of providence—with dangling strings and knots betraying both the design and the delight of his handiwork. Paul put it like this: "Now we see but a poor reflection" of what one Day we will fully see and fully enjoy—the perfect (1 Cor. 13:12) ending to the history of redemption. But the weight of glory (2 Cor. 4:16–18) requires that we *wait* for glory in the face of many inglorious things—like death.

But, as God would have it, Grant's death brought life to many who were stunned into considering the difference between their story line and the story by which he lived and died. Count me in that number. Standing by his hospital bed the last night Grant spent in this world, I witnessed Kristin and their three sons offer the hardest and sweetest good-bye. I wanted to be there more than anywhere else, and I wanted to be anywhere else but there—my heart was resting in my calling but racing in my chest.

Then, in that sacred moment it hit me—my mom was only several months older than Grant when she died. *Of course* God would put me with Grant in his final hours to witness young sons facing death and saying good-bye as best they could. *Of course* my heart was racing. I never got that chance with Mom. *Of course* facing Grant's death would help me finally put a face on that little "faceless orphan" I drew for my counselor. *Of course* God read my letter and heard my cry to Mom—"I refuse to stay dead on the inside." *Of course* God would bring me to life—for he *alone* can bring resurrection and restoration.

Grant's story pushed me further into my story and into God's Story, and God's Story is freeing me—slowly but surely—to love as he loves, beginning with my dad. That's exactly what the reign of grace does—that's what it's all about! *Objects* of God's affection become *agents* and *conduits* of his affection—in our neighborhoods and among the nations! Grant and Kristin gain a heart for fatherless children. Larry and his wife, Mary, gain a heart for the poor and HIV/AIDS-devastated peoples of Africa. My wife, Darlene, gains a heart for victims of childhood abuse and trauma. God is making all things new—in his time, in his way, and for his purposes.

This is where you take up your "laptop" and write the next chapters of this book. God longs to be gracious *to you* (Isa. 30:18) and *through you.* The invitation requires coming and staying alive to two stories—yours and his. Can you think of a better time than now? What are you waiting for—glory or your next paycheck?

Where Are *You* in Your Story?

Some of us are alive to *neither* our story nor God's Story. With no story to give bearings or boundaries, life is simply a series of unrelated events, moments, people, and experiences. We are in constant need of redefining ourselves and finding new gods to "bless us" and to deliver us from "curses."

Some of us are alive only to *our* story. We are committed to personal growth, but within the confining orbit of our own narrative. Life goes well as long as our narrative doesn't experience planetary collision with some other person vying for the same air space.

Some are alive only to *God's* story. We love the promise, beauty, and music of God's story, but we cannot locate ourselves in his narrative. We love to worship more than we love God. We are more comfortable using "god speak" than engaging in normal conversation with the people in our world.

Others are alive to *both stories,* but don't *connect* the two. We live a dualistic life—in two minds and in two worlds: one sacred and one secular. Whichever identity serves the moment wins the day. We are chameleons on Scotch-plaid, cultural schizophrenics—engaging but confused, confident but ambivalent.

Finally, some of us are alive to *both stories,* and *experience them synergistically.* This is where the gospel takes us. In this state, we bring the *reign of grace* to bear wherever God places us—in relationships and in the culture. We are nostalgic for Eden, engaged in the present, and homesick for heaven. We make people thirsty to know Jesus. May God increase this tribe!

How to Come Alive to the Integrated Story

Coming Alive to Your Own Story

If you are one of those people who is not yet alive to your own story, you can join me on my journey and come to know new depths and joy. Coming alive to your story requires that you take some very specific steps. You must gather data, dialogue, reflect, integrate, and share in community.

Gather Data

Gather all the information you can about your family of origin and compile as complete a history as possible of every season of your life—from infancy until today, from the mundane to the great pains.

Become a genealogical newshound. Look for photographs, letters, diaries—anything you can find that contains information about your life and times.

Dialogue

Talk with significant people from your past and present. Interview those who can tell stories and who are willing to interact with you about your family system, their memories of you, descriptions of your community, the times of crises, transition, and joy. Be bold in your pursuit and attentive as a listener. Expand the conversation to include peers, neighbors, teachers, coaches, extended family, etc.

Reflect

Make time for rumination and meditation. Journal as many of your feelings and thoughts as you can. As you reflect upon the information you are gaining, ask yourself these questions: For what and whom are you profoundly grateful? What makes you sad or angry as you remember certain people and places? What are you learning about your heart, longings, fears, and foolishness? How does God fit into your world and story, if at all? How do you wrongfully medicate your pain, instead of dealing with it constructively? What new questions are emerging? Be ruthless and honest and not in a hurry.

Integrate

This is where you begin to connect the past, the present, and the future. To come alive to your story is to participate in an ongoing journey. You aren't writing a research paper, a third-person novel, or a litany of excuses for why you are such a mess! You're learning how to live. How will you integrate what you are learning and feeling into this present season of life? What will it cost you to grow? When and where will you get help for your wounded heart? Who can help you sort out the God issues?

Share in Community

For this process to become more than a dusty monologue or self-centered soliloquy, you must be part of meaningful community. Who are the people in your life with whom you can share what you are learning about yourself and your life context? From whom are you willing to receive honest feedback and loving accountability? To whom are you committed to share the same costly involvement?

Coming Alive to God's Story

Coming alive to God's Story requires the same steps as coming alive to your own.

Gather Data

Commit to learn as much about God's Story as you possibly can. That Story is faithfully recorded for us in the Bible. Seek to become familiar with the contents of all the books of the Bible. Get to know each book and author as they emerge in the context of the overall story God is developing in history. Begin the discipline of reading the Bible all the way through, over and over.

Dialogue

Like any other story, God's Story comes alive through rich conversation. Get to know the people in your community who love the Bible and are vitally involved in the fabric of its story. Learn from them. Learn with them. There are no dumb questions!

But the most important dialogue we can develop is with God himself, and the most vital and powerful context for this dialogue is worship. Every time we gather to worship as the people of God, we are called into a dynamic conversation, not a one-sided monologue. God graciously speaks to us in Word and sacrament, and we respond in confession, faith, adoration, and obedience. Remember, worship is a covenantal conversation—a doxological dialogue between the Creator-Redeemer and his people. Learn to prepare yourself for worship as one coming to give Jesus everything you have and are—as a beloved Bride looking forward to a special time of intimacy with her passionate and present Bridegroom.

Reflect

There is no way we will be able to come alive and stay alive to God's story if we do not learn how to reflect upon the glory, beauty, and grace of Jesus. The more we learn about the story of redemption, the more we will begin to see ourselves as a part of the sacred romance—the great love affair between Jesus, the loving Bridegroom, and ourselves, his ill-deserving but beloved Bride. The truth and grace of Jesus are to penetrate into our hearts, deeper and deeper. There is no substitute for significant and focused times of communing with the Lover of our souls.

Integrate

It's at this junction that our participation in God's Story either heads in the direction of passion or pastime. Will the drama of his Story invade the rhythms our daily life? Will the knowledge of having Jesus as our loving Bridegroom find us living as his faithful, impassioned, submissive Bride? Or will we choose to keep our knowledge of God's story as devotional bookends to an otherwise self-contained life or as inspirational material for good, conservative morality?

Share in Community

Becoming a committed member and servant-participant in the church, in a local expression of the body of Christ, is vital to coming alive and staying alive to God's Story. It is "together with all the saints," as Paul has said, that we come to know "the height, width, breadth, and length of the love of Christ."

Grace Reigning through the Good and the Bad

One of the evidences of grace's advancing reign in our lives is gospel vision—the gift of seeing behind the scenes to what is sometimes imperceptible for many years, the ability to gain perspective on hard-to-understand providences that seem incongruent with a God who is both good and in control.

Grace is reigning when we are able to say with Joseph—in the face of perplexing conundrums and cruel crises—"You intended to harm me, but God intended it for good to accomplish what is now being done, the saving of many lives" (Gen. 50:20). Grace is reigning when we seize, or are seized by, Paul's bold exclamation of faith—"And we know that in *all* things God works for the good of those who love him" (Rom. 8:28). Grace reigns when we start processing the inclusive claims of the "all" in "all things"—one by one. And grace reigns when we can look back over the chapters, paragraphs, and sentences of our complex stories and sing with tears of growing assurance, "Great is thy faithfulness, O God, my Father...great is thy faithfulness!"

A Personal Testimony to Grace Reigning

Writing this book has led me "further up and further in" the process of being able to affirm these freeing truths and sing this profound song. Jesus continues to be most patient and persistent in opening the eyes of my heart to see how "the increase of his government and peace" has been underway long before I even knew him.

As you can tell from reading this book, this process hasn't been easy for me. Author Pat Conroy expressed my feelings well:

> As a boy, I had constructed a shell for myself so impenetrable that I have been trying to write my way out of it for over thirty years, and even now I fear I have barely cracked its veneer. It is as roughed and polished and burnished as the specialized glass of telescopes, and it

> kept me hidden from the appraising eyes of the outside world long into manhood. But most of all it kept me hidden and safe from myself. No outsider I have ever met has struck me with the strangeness I encounter when I try to discover the deepest mysteries of the boy I once was.[1]

But a recent and unexpected opportunity to teach a small Bible class in my hometown of Graham, North Carolina—face to face with the folk who were a part of my childhood story—opened my eyes to God's providential nurturing even during my early childhood and the painful years after my mother's death, years that prepared me for who I am today and who I will become. I can see better than ever how God has been at work in my story, just as surely as he has been at work in yours.

It's typical of God's wild sense of humor and unsearchable wisdom that the Bible class I taught was in my old home church—the church I *despised* while growing up. It is the church where Mom's funeral was held...where I preached my first "fiery" sermon as an arrogant freshman in college...where I married Darlene.

A letter I sent Dad after that revealing visit testifies to the overarching reign of grace in my life and the pursuing and persistent love of God. As I close with it, I pray it will encourage you to see God at work in all the dimensions of your story. And I pray that many such visits, memories, insights, and redeeming moments will define this season of your life, as they have mine.

> *Dear Dad,*
>
> *It was great being with you and Ruth last weekend. There is no way I could have anticipated what God decided to cram between two sunsets.*
>
> *Believe it or not, I'm writing primarily to thank you for arranging for me to teach your Sunday school class last Sunday. It may surprise you, but being in the Brotherhood class was one of the more*

important moments in my recent life. To be honest, when you first asked me Saturday afternoon if I'd be up for it, I was trying to think of a good reason to decline. I've been working feverishly to finish a book, and I was looking forward just to hanging out with you for the day. But God seems to find great pleasure in interrupting my itinerary. We make our plans, and he orders our steps.

Being a former navigator, I know you can relate to the critical importance of position and perspective. It still boggles my mind that you could direct huge ships across the oceans of the world with only a sextant and without the aid of radar.

Dad, I relate to your stories of having to depend on clear nights to know the location of your ship in the middle of a huge, sometimes threatening sea. Likewise, God has to lift the clouds of my earth-bound vision for me to see where I've been in the storms of life and, more importantly, my location in the story of his transforming love. It's a gift to know we're a part of a story larger than our own—to see how seemingly "little people," random acts, cruel setbacks, and small mercies fit into his bigger plan for our lives.

God gave me more than a glimpse of the big story this past Sunday, Dad. He opened the eyes of my heart to see years of his faithful handiwork. As we walked into that small classroom together, I really didn't know what to expect. I wasn't all that thrilled with being assigned to teach from Proverbs 16—preferring to choose my own text. But God knew what he was up to. One of the verses we looked at in Proverbs 16 sums it up pretty well: "The Lord works out everything for his own ends." (16:4). God was at work—and with his ends very much in mind.

As the class started gathering, I began to realize that this experience was going to be more than me simply being a guest speaker for your class. Just when I got comfortable in my seat, I nearly fell out of it. I couldn't believe it when I recognized the pianist for our opening hymns—Mrs. Virginia Caruthers! Dad, she must have started giving Moose piano lessons nearly fifty years ago when we lived in our little green house on Melville Street! And there she was, still at it!

And who should the song leader prove to be but you. Hearing your singing voice reminded me of one of my happiest memories I have as a child. We had just moved into our new home on Oakwood Lane. I was sitting in the den watching TV—I was probably nine or ten at the time. You and Mom were in the dining room.

Though I couldn't see you, I remember hearing you break out into some song to Mom, probably a Mario Lanza tune. That felt so cheesy and corny to me, Dad...and yet, so good, so right for you to sing to Mom. You were alive. There was joy in our home. I guess she died only about a year and a half later. I'm so sorry, Dad.

It was an unexpected treat when the "sisters" started piling into the Brotherhood class. After being introduced, I walked to the podium, opened my Bible, and looked out at the thirty or forty people who were gathered there.

It felt as if I were in an orchestra pit, standing in front of an eclectic assembly of musicians. Looking around the class that morning, I saw so many people whose hands and hearts, together, have been instrumental in bringing the music of God's providential care to me. Dad, I realized once again that our lives aren't just random notes and noise.

I can only shake my head, confessing my unbelief, that this particular group of people could have been assembled in that one Sunday school class. Right in front of me sat Francis Allen, "Ma Allen," as I had called her. Her son "Foogie" had been one of my closest friends (as close as I would allow anyone into my heart in those days). Upon seeing her, I remembered the smell of her homemade biscuits, the welcome I always felt as I walked through her front door, and the twin bed over which she put my name. Dad, even when I didn't have eyes to see it, God was being so generous with me.

A little to my left on the back row sat Jerry Holt—my Boy Scout troop leader and our back-door neighbor. Dad, you remember how close Mom and Carolyn, Jerry's wife, were. She gave me my first babysitting job, and Jerry gave me a love for the outdoors and some important involvement when I could have gotten involved in destructive stuff. I was still pretty stupid with fireworks—but at least I developed a little common sense.

To my right was Dr. Allen "Bunky" Tate, my childhood doctor who faithfully walked me through first shots, first stitches, poison ivy epidemics, and a host of other medical traumas. Dad, I first went to Dr. Tate when I was four or five, and there he was, listening to me well over four decades later. To Dr. Tate's left were Bill and Louise McAdams. Bill waited on me regularly and patiently in Hal's Men's Shop. His kindness and smile are just as inviting today as they were thirty-five years ago.

To my immediate left were J. L. and Patt Williams, my first spiritual parents. J. L. taught the first Bible study I ever attended, gave me a love for reading and learning, took me on my first missions trips, performed my wedding, and preached my ordination sermon. He still looks about thirty-five, though he just turned sixty. Close to J. L. and Patt were George and Betty Webb, Troy Woodard, Dr. Robert Johnson, my Sunday School and Vespers leaders, customers on my paper route—what a gathering.

Looking out at those tender, loving faces, I felt as if I were caught in an episode of that old show This Is Your Life. *The same vibe continued throughout the day.*

Sharing lunch around your little kitchen table, I suddenly felt great thankfulness for Ruth. Have I ever told you that I am glad you married her? I am, Dad, I really am. If you were ever in doubt, be free of those concerns. She's been a great stepmom to me, and she has been such a good wife to you.

Later Sunday afternoon, after leaving your home, Darlene and I stopped by to see the Comptons, Charlie and Zonie—"Ma" and "Pa" as I've called them for as long as I can remember. Garrison Keillor, one of my favorite storytellers and humorists, described a feature of life for young school-age children in the cold winters of Lake Wobegon, Minnesota, that has arrested my heart ever since I first heard it. Visiting with Ma and Pa on Sunday, I now understand why.

Should a violent snowstorm blow in unexpectedly to Lake Wobegon before the school children could be safely taken home, each child was assigned a "storm family." A "storm family" was a family who lived close enough to the school so individual children could be taken in until the storm passed or until the roads leading to the children's homes became passable again.

Dad, the Comptons became my "storm family" when the violent winter storm of Mom's death closed down the road between our two hearts. When we both shut down emotionally, they became a vital part of God's provision for my wounded soul.

It was never my intent to hurt you by spending so much time with Ma and Pa. They gave me what I desperately needed during those years—the words, "We love you and are so proud of you, son"; the physical touch of understanding hugs; and a place to go away from the haunting world of my grief. Dad, the Comptons have always and only encouraged me to move toward you and to respect you. Because of their love and care for me then, I am able to love you more and more today.

All day long, everywhere I looked, there were bold reminders—not just of how many nice and important people have been woven into my story—but more importantly, Dad, a reminder that there is a story. We don't have to make one up. God is writing a score for the symphony, He is conducting the orchestra. We don't have to be able to read all of the notes or even like all of the music. It is enough to know that "the Lord works out everything for his own ends."

God isn't just at work in human hearts. He has committed himself to the ultimate restoration and renewal project. The Bible calls it the "new creation"—God's plan to make a new world out of the broken one we live in.

I don't fully understand everything this means, Dad, but one day "the knowledge of God's glory is going to cover the earth as the waters cover the sea." Wolves and lambs, leopards and goats, lions and calves will all live safely together—and a small child will tend them (Isa. 11:6). One day the whole city of Graham is going to come alive with love, color, joy, and perfect relationships—just like the whole world is going to be perfect forever. What a great story to live by!

Dad, it's true, all the dear people and memories I experienced on Sunday weren't ultimately about me. I'd be pretty self-centered if I only saw the special events of that day as me starring in the movie It's a Wonderful Life. *I'm not sure what I'd call a movie of last Sunday. All I can say is, my eyes and heart have been opened afresh to see how massive God's plan is for all things—you and me and his world. He has been at work in the past, he is at work today, and he's going to finish the whole generous plan one Day in the future.*

Oh yeah, how could I forget…the last thing Darlene and I did before heading back to Tennessee was to stop by Mom's grave. It's the third time I've been back since that first breakthrough visit. It gets easier each time, Dad. I do miss her more than ever, but it's getting okay. I am so glad that one Day there will be no more death, sorrow, crying, or pain.

Once again, thanks for asking me to teach your class. The truth is, your classmates were the ones God used to teach me on Sunday.

I can't tell you too often how thankful I am for what has already happened between us. Let's keep the conversation going. Let's keep processing our stories together. From the seemingly random act of death that wrought destruction in our hearts, God is bringing forth very nonrandom acts of grace, healing, and life. All praise to the One who is making everything new.

I love you more than ever,

Scotty

Questions for Discussion and Reflection

CHAPTER ONE: THE IMPLICATIONS OF GRACE

1. What in this chapter impacted you most? What encouraged you? What proved timely? What called for more clarification?
2. What's your story of grace? If a friend asked you about your spiritual journey and wanted to know "What's so amazing about grace?" how would you respond? Using God's story recorded in the Bible and your own experience, how would you define God's grace to someone who is just beginning to evidence spiritual hunger?
3. When you think about the phrase "reign of grace," what images come to mind? What kind of dominion do you suppose grace exercises?
4. "Further up and further in"... What will that look like for *you* as you proceed to read this book, either by yourself or with a small group of friends?
5. Go back through the bulleted points on page 16. Does reading this list stir any particular emotions or notions within you? Did you find yourself marking any particular Scripture references that warrant more reflection? Make sure to follow through!
6. Look at the "continuums of grace." Which of these intrigue you, perhaps inviting a deeper look? Take a pencil and put a dot where you would place yourself on each of these continuums. Do you tend toward the left or the right of center? (This isn't a political ID!)

CHAPTER TWO: HOW HAVE YOU LOVED ME?

1. What in this chapter impacted you most? What encouraged you? What proved timely? What called for more clarification?
2. When have you felt the most deeply loved? What people (or person) in your life story have given you the most profound taste of acceptance, delight, welcome, and encouragement? How did they show this affection? What effect has their heart investment had on you?

3. When has your experience of God made you feel deeply loved? Are you able to sing sincerely, "Love so amazing so divine, demands my soul, my life, my all"? How can love demand something of us and still be love?

4. Scotty used the phrase "faceless orphan" to describe how it felt to grow up in his home. What phrase(s) would you choose to describe your experience? The goal in this exercise isn't to blame or find fault with anyone, rather to help you see the difference between posing your way through life and positioning yourself as a candidate for more grace.

5. Do you ever ask God the same questions Malachi's contemporaries asked: "How have you loved me? I'm not sure you really care for me at all. If you really love me, wouldn't you________?" What, if any, experiences in your life have made you feel that God doesn't really care about you?

6. What do you suppose makes some people think that God owes us mercy, grace, and compassion? What, after all, is the difference between being a *choice* people and a *chosen* people? If you could choose, which would you prefer God to give you—fairness or grace? Explain.

CHAPTER THREE: FINDING FACE—GAINING HEART

1. What in this chapter impacted you most? What encouraged you? What proved timely? What called for more clarification?

2. At this season in your spiritual journey, does the thought of making eye contact with God cause you more fear or joy? Explain. What would it be like for you to be all alone with God in a heart-to-heart encounter?

3. Tell your life story by identifying some of the "veils" hanging in your closet. How have you tried to hide from God, others, and yourself?

4. Read through the Band-Aids list on pages 41–42. Either as a practitioner or participant, with which of these examples do you resonate? In what ways have you dressed your own wounds as though they are not serious?

5. What would you like to see the grace and power of Jesus change in your life? With respect to your relational style? Your attitudes? Your habits and, perhaps, addictions?

6. Close with a season of prayer for three of your closest friends. What would you love to see God do in their lives?

CHAPTER FOUR: SHALOMED BY GRACE: THE GOAL OF HEALING

1. What in this chapter impacted you most? What encouraged you? What proved timely? What called for more clarification?

2. What do you think about when you hear the phrase "healing journey"? What images come to mind? How would you describe a spiritually healthy person? In your estimation, what are some of the most important signs of heart health?
3. What is the difference between relating to peace as the quest for having certain blessings and guarantees, versus the calling to wholeness? How does this distinction confront some of your notions about life, God, and grace?
4. Are you able to affirm that you are a sinner-saint—that is, can you affirm that though you are justified completely by the righteousness of Christ, you still have a sinful nature that is capable of great foolishness and evil? In light of that concept, think about this statement: "If we are wrong about sin, then it will be impossible to be right about grace." Why is this so?
5. Slowly walk through the questions on pages 54–55. I encourage you to write out your responses in a journal. Think of someone you trust enough to share your responses with, then do so.
6. As you look forward to the Day of perfect health, what are you most looking forward to? Describe the heart you long to have. Thank God that one Day you will indeed love perfectly as Jesus loves.

CHAPTER FIVE: THE KING TAKES A BRIDE

1. What in this chapter and the "Further Up and Further Ins" impacted you most? What encouraged you? What proved timely? What called for more clarification?
2. Reflect on this statement: "To move from piecemeal living to the peace of healing requires the heart to risk more of the pain and joy that come from knowing and being known." Why is this so? What are the pains associated with knowing and being known? What are the joys?
3. Of all the movies, novels, fables, and real-life relationships you have witnessed—what are your favorite love stories? Which ones draw you into their beauty and passion, or perhaps, make you envious and/or angry for not having experienced this kind of a love life? What do you usually do with good longings for intimate relationship?
4. How would you describe your experience of the greatest of all love stories—Jesus' passionate love relationship with his Bride? Is your heart able to say, "Your love, O Lord, is better than life?" If so, what has God used to bring you to this place of resting in his love?

5. How has tracing marriage through the four phases of redemptive history proven to be helpful or at least enlightening? If you are married, what unrealistic expectations of this relationship did you bring into your covenant? What adjustments in your attitude and actions would be required to live your marriage "as unto the Lord"?
6. If you are single, how might the truth of being married to Jesus affect your attitude toward your singleness? What is most difficult about being single? What is most beneficial? Are you actively praying for God to keep you from compromising his design and your heart as you wait upon him?

CHAPTER SIX: THE GRACE OF GOD'S DISCIPLINE

1. What in this chapter and the "Further Up and Further Ins" impacted you most? What encouraged you? What proved timely? What called for more clarification?
2. Having read this section, how would you explain the concept of the "discipline of the Lord" to an immature believer? To a nonbeliever? To a legalistic believer? To a rebellious believer?
3. Which of the false forms of grace listed on page 98 have you witnessed, either in your own life or in the Christian community where God has placed you? How have these been manifested?
4. What's the difference between viewing grace as unconditional love versus undeserved favor? What's the difference between the conditional enjoyment of God's love and being conditionally accepted by him? How can clarifying these concepts help guard against "sloppy agape" and presumptive living?
5. Looking back over your spiritual journey, can you identify ways the disciplining hand and heart of God have been evident? Remember, we are not to look for a tit-for-tat correlation between every sin and difficulty in life, but we are implored to look for and love the correction of our Great Lover.
6. If Jesus were to discipline you at this season in your life on one or two issues, what would those issues be?

CHAPTER SEVEN: FREEDOM FOR IDOLATERS AND ADDICTS—LIKE ME

1. What in this chapter and the "Further Up and Further Ins" impacted you most? What encouraged you? What proved timely? What called for more clarification?

2. Where has there been a collision(s) between painful events and your sinful heart? Describe the damage. How would you describe your own sense of brokenness?
3. What parallels are there between your story and Scotty's? What idols have you chosen for blessing and protection? What substances have you abused to feed and prop up your idols?
4. After reading this section, how would you explain the relationship between sin and addiction to a friend? Discuss the concept of addiction as "worship dysfunction." How does all addiction ultimately relate to idolatry?
5. If you were to faithfully apply Paul's advice given in Galatians 5, what would be required of you? Where are you still in bondage? What war do you need to declare? Are you convinced that the power of the gospel is your only hope for a free and changed heart? How so?
6. As a follow-up to this section, do you sense the need for some good counseling or to get involved in a support group? If you do, I encourage you to do so and, perhaps, help some of your friends to do the same.

CHAPTER EIGHT: GRACE-FULL WORSHIP

1. What in this chapter and the "Further Up and Further Ins" impacted you most? What encouraged you? What proved timely? What called for more clarification?
2. Describe your current experience of worship when you gather with the people of God? Are you bored, engaged, distracted, satisfied, disgruntled, full of anticipation? As far as you can tell, what is driving these responses and emotions?
3. When have you felt the presence of God in worship most profoundly gripping your heart? Describe, accordingly, the ideal worship service. What elements would such a service of worship include?
4. Having read this section, what would worshiping God for his sake and pleasure require of you? What shifts in your understanding, motivation, and practice are called for? In all honesty, do you see yourself more as a demanding consumer of worship or as one being consumed with the glory and grace of Jesus in worship? How is this manifest?
5. Do you find yourself complaining about the worship of your church family more than you are committed to praying for the worship and for those responsible for leading you each Lord's Day? I encourage you to find ways of serving and encouraging those charged with cultivating and leading the worship of God in your congregation. How can you "wash their feet"?

6. As you take another look at the continuums of worship, which ones stand out to you personally? Where do you place yourself in each of the continuums? What convicts you? About what do you need to repent as you give Jesus the worship of which he alone is most worthy?

CHAPTER NINE: GRACED SEXUALITY

1. What in this chapter and the "Further Up and Further In" impacted you most? What encouraged you? What proved timely? What called for more clarification?
2. From your vantage point and perspective, how do you see overt sexualization and "sexual insanity" manifest in our culture today? Describe the changes you have noticed in the past ten years.
3. Where did you get most of your information about sex growing up? What would you have changed, if anything, about the way you were informed and prepared sexually to move into adolescence and married life?
4. In what ways have the scriptures studied in this section informed and illumined you? Be specific.
5. There are no scars that are more damaging than sexual ones. Are you at a good place in your healing journey regarding any sexual sin or abuse that has been a part of your story? Are you aware of the need for more grace and, perhaps, counseling and ministry? Is there someone with whom you can discuss these issues?
6. Having read this chapter, do you believe yourself to be either obsessed or addicted sexually? Or are you currently taking advantage of or abusing anyone sexually? Will you share your struggle with a trusted friend? There is grace and help for you.

CHAPTER TEN: THE WITNESS OF RELATIONSHIPS

1. What in this chapter and the "Further Up and Further Ins" impacted you most? What encouraged you? What proved timely? What called for more clarification?
2. As a priesthood of believers, how can we effectively and faithfully build bridges into the culture and into the lives of nonbelievers by the way we worship God? What changes would you suggest in your own worship service to make the gospel more accessible to nonbelievers—changes that would neither compromise the integrity of worship nor misrepresent the gospel?
3. Just how intentional are you when it comes to sharing the gospel with non-

believers? Are there any friends, neighbors, or family members that you are regularly praying will come to Christ? Have you ever been trained in personal evangelism, and if not, would you welcome the opportunity? Do you have some good models of personal evangelism in your circle of friends or in your church family? Consider having them pray with you and help you become active in sharing your faith.

4. Reflect on the doctrine of "the universal office of the believer." What are the implications of this great truth for *you?* How might you discharge your calling into your vocation, neighborhood, church, and the broken places in your community that are in need of the transforming power of the gospel?
5. Meditate on the coming new heaven and new earth. What particular elements of the perfected cosmos are you most looking forward to? How might you help "push back the effects of the Fall" in those very areas today as you wait for that Day?
6. Close with a season of praying for the missionaries that your church supports or those that you know personally.

CHAPTER ELEVEN: ROMANTIC GENEROSITY

1. What in this chapter and the "Further Up and Further In" impacted you most? What encouraged you? What proved timely? What called for more clarification?
2. Who or what has influenced you the most when it comes to the topic of money? As a Christian, what are the fundamental convictions you have already developed about a biblical world-view of money and possessions? That is, what is already in place in your heart about these matters?
3. Reflect on the image of a prenuptial contract with Jesus. Do you think this is a valid way of helping us think about stewardship? How so? Are you convinced that the Scriptures teach stewardship as opposed to ownership as the prevailing category for how we are to relate to money and possessions? What are the implications of this truth for you personally?
4. Who are your models of generosity in life? Name some of the people whose open-heartedness and open-handedness are visible expressions of the generosity of God. Would you like to be more like them? What obstacles are keeping you from doing so?
5. Have you spent any time faithfully considering what the Bible has to say about tithing? What are your personal convictions about this matter?

6. When you think about the poor, what comes to mind? Do you know any poor people, or can you locate the sections in your town or community that are quite impoverished and in need of God's mercy? Have the Scriptures impacted your understanding about our responsibilities to the widow, the orphan, and the poor? How so?

CHAPTER TWELVE: FINDING YOUR PLACE IN THE REIGN OF GRACE

1. Where do you go from here? What is the next stage in your growth in grace, in your submission to its reign?
2. What painful events in your story (like the deaths of Scotty's mom and his elder/friend Grant Cunningham) stand out as targets for more processing and grace? How would your family and friends say these events have affected you? How has God already brought a measure of healing to your heart? What do you long for and expect God to do next in your life story?
3. How do you connect with Scotty's closing letter to his dad? Are there visits you need to make in order to fill in the gaps of your own story? What might that look like? What risks of love will this require of you?
4. Who are the people with whom reconciliation is still a possibility—the people and relationships in your story that are still unresolved. The Scriptures call us to "be at peace with all men," as far as we are able within our own power to do so. What are some of those broken relationships that the reign of grace alone is sufficient to offer any hope of change or closure before one of you dies?
5. Looking back over the whole book, what are the most valuable things you have learned about God, his grace, the Christian life, yourself, and the journey ahead?
6. Close with a season of prayer, for yourself, your friends, and the nations of the world. Pray in light of the consummation of the reign of grace in the new heaven and new earth. Pray with hope, boldness, and joy.

Notes

CHAPTER ONE: THE IMPLICATIONS OF GRACE

1. C. S. Lewis, *The Last Battle* (New York: HarperCollins, 1956), 207.

2. *Ibid.,* 188–89.

CHAPTER THREE: FINDING FACE—GAINING HEART

1. C. S. Lewis, *Till We Have Faces* (New York: Harcourt Brace, 1980), 180.

2. *Ibid.,* 294.

3. Frederick Buechner, *Telling Secrets* (New York: HarperCollins, 1991), 3.

CHAPTER FOUR: SHALOMED BY GRACE—THE GOAL OF HEALING

1. Cornelius Plantinga Jr., *Not the Way It's Supposed to Be* (Grand Rapids: Eerdmans, 1995), 10, 14, 16.

2. *Ibid.,* 47.

CHAPTER FIVE: THE KING TAKES A BRIDE

1. Raymond C. Ortlund Jr., *Whoredom: God's Unfaithful Wife in Biblical Theology* (Grand Rapids: Eerdmans, 1996), 172.

2. *Ibid.,* 173.

CHAPTER SIX: THE GRACE OF GOD'S DISCIPLINE

1. D. A. Carson, *The Difficult Doctrine of the Love of God* (Wheaton, Ill.: Crossway Books, 2000), 24.

CHAPTER SIX: FURTHER UP AND FURTHER IN: THE GIFT OF DESERT THIRST: HOSEA

1. Ortlund, *Whoredom,* 68.

2. Peter J. Kreeft, *Everything You Wanted to Know About Heaven* (Fort Collins, Colo.: Ignatius Press, 1997).

CHAPTER SEVEN: FREEDOM FOR IDOLATERS AND ADDICTS—LIKE ME

1. *The Book of Confessions* (New York: Office of the General Assembly of the United Presbyterian Church in the U.S.A., 1970), 4.001–.004.

2. Edward T. Welch, *Addictions: A Banquet in the Grave: Finding Hope in the Power of the Gospel* (Phillipsburg, N.J.: P&R Publishing Company, 2001), 35.

3. Plantinga, *Not the Way,* 148.

4. Welch, *Addictions,* 48–50.

CHAPTER SEVEN: FURTHER UP AND FURTHER IN: ONE-OF-A-KIND LOVE AFFAIR: EZEKIEL 16

1. Brent Curtis and John Eldredge, *Sacred Romance* (Nashville: Thomas Nelson, 1997), 19.

2. Ian Duguid, quoted in the NIV Application Commentary *Ezekiel* (Grand Rapids: Zondervan, 1999), 211.

3. Christopher J. H. Wright, *The Message of Ezekiel* (Downers Grove, Ill.: InterVarsity Press, 2001), 137.

4. Welch, *Addictions,* 53.

CHAPTER SEVEN: FURTHER UP AND FURTHER IN: THE GOSPEL WAY OF DISMANTLING OUR IDOLS: GALATIANS

1. Welch, *Addictions,* 248–49.

CHAPTER EIGHT: GRACE-FULL WORSHIP

1. D. A. Carson, *Worship: Adoration and Action* (Grand Rapids: Baker Book House, 1993), 13.

2. *Ibid.,* 15.

3. William Temple, *Readings in St. John's Gospel* (London: Macmillan, 1939), 68.

CHAPTER NINE: GRACED SEXUALITY

1. Michelle Burford, "Girls and Sex," *O* magazine, November 2002, 213.

2. *Ibid.,* 214.

3. Harry W. Schaumburg, *False Intimacy* (Colorado Springs: NavPress, 1992), 149.

4. Richard Winter, *Still Bored in a Culture of Entertainment* (Downers Grove, Ill.: InterVarsity Press, 2002), 104–105.

5. Frank Rich, "Naked Capitalists," *New York Times Magazine,* May 20, 2001, 51.

6. John Eldredge, *The Journey of Desire* (Nashville: Thomas Nelson, 2000), 134.

CHAPTER NINE: FURTHER UP AND FURTHER IN: SEX AND THE CITY: 1 THESSALONIANS

1. John Stott, *The Gospel and the End of Time* (Downers Grove: Ill.: InterVarsity Press, 1991), 81.

2. *Ibid.,* 81.

3. Leland Ryken, James C. Wilhoit, Tremper Longman III, eds., *Dictionary of Biblical Imagery,* (Downers Grove, Ill.: InterVarsity Press, 1998), 778.

4. Tommy Nelson, *The Book of Romance* (Nashville: Thomas Nelson, 1998), 94–96.

CHAPTER TEN: THE WITNESS OF RELATIONSHIPS

1. Walter Kirn, *GQ,* September 2002.

2. David Watson, *I Believe in the Church* (Grand Rapids: Eerdmans, 1982), 364–65.

3. Tim Keller, *Ministries of Mercy: The Call of the Jericho Road* (Phillipsburg: N.J.: 2d ed, P&R Publishing, 1997), 157.

4. Richard Mouw, *When the Kings Come Marching In* (Grand Rapids: Eerdmans, 1983), 63–65.

5. Mike Mason, *The Mystery of Marriage* (Portland, Oreg.: Multnomah, 1985), 34–35, 45.

6. *Ibid.,* 32–33, 35.

CHAPTER TEN: FURTHER UP AND FURTHER IN: THE CHURCH AS MAGNETIC MATRIMONY: MORE ON EPHESIANS 5:25–33

1. David Watson, *Discipleship* (London: Hodder and Stoughton, 1981), 51.

2. C. S. Lewis, *The Weight of Glory* (New York: Simon & Schuster, 1975), 39–40.

3. Dietrich Bonhoeffer, *Life Together* (New York: Harper & Row, 1954), 26–27.

CHAPTER ELEVEN: ROMANTIC GENEROSITY

1. Johann Franck, "Jesus, Priceless Treasure," in the handbook to *The Lutheran Hymnal* (St. Louis: Concordia Publishing House, 1942), 248–49.

2. Ancient Irish hymn, "Be Thou My Vision," trans. by Mary E. Byrne.

CHAPTER TWELVE: FINDING YOUR PLACE IN THE REIGN OF GRACE

1. Pat Conroy, *My Losing Season* (New York: Doubleday, 2002), 3.